D0915966

WITHDRAWN
UTSA LIBRARIES

NEW ESSAYS ON UMBERTO ECO

There is a wealth of critical commentary on Umberto Eco in scholarly books and articles; this collection provides up-to-date and thought-provoking insights into topics that have attracted a great deal of attention in the past without repeating many of the arguments found in earlier publications on Eco.

Representing the most active scholars writing on Eco from a variety of disciplinary perspectives, the international panel of authors provides sophisticated engagement with Eco's contributions to a wide range of academic disciplines (semiotics, popular culture, linguistics, aesthetics, philosophy, medieval studies), as well as his literary production of five important novels. From the impact of the detective genre on Eco's literary work to his place as a major medievalist, *New Essays on Umberto Eco* covers a variety of subjects that will appeal not only to a wide audience interested in Eco's fiction, but also to the serious student delving into Eco's more esoteric writings.

PETER BONDANELLA is Distinguished Professor Emeritus of Comparative Literature, Film Studies, and Italian at Indiana University. He has written or edited many books on Italian literature and film, including *The Cambridge Companion to the Italian Novel* (co-edited with Andrea Ciccarelli, Cambridge, 2003) and *Umberto Eco and the Open Text* (Cambridge, 1997). He is a past President of the American Association for Italian Studies and a member of the European Academy of Sciences and Arts.

NEW ESSAYS ON UMBERTO ECO

EDITED BY
PETER BONDANELLA

CAMBRIDGE
UNIVERSITY PRESS

CAMBRIDGE UNIVERSITY PRESS
Cambridge, New York, Melbourne, Madrid, Cape Town, Singapore, São Paulo, Delhi

Cambridge University Press
The Edinburgh Building, Cambridge CB2 8RU, UK

Published in the United States of America by Cambridge University Press, New York

www.cambridge.org
Information on this title: www.cambridge.org/9780521852098

© Cambridge University Press 2009

This publication is in copyright. Subject to statutory exception
and to the provisions of relevant collective licensing agreements,
no reproduction of any part may take place without
the written permission of Cambridge University Press.

First published 2009

Printed in the United Kingdom at the University Press, Cambridge

A catalog record for this publication is available from the British Library

Library of Congress Cataloging in Publication data
Bondanella, Peter E., 1943–
New essays on Umberto Eco / Peter Bondanella.
p.   cm.
Includes bibliographical references and index.
ISBN 978-0-521-85209-8
1. Eco, Umberto–Criticism and interpretation.   2. Semiotics and literature.   I. Title.
PQ4865.C6Z57 2009
853'.914–dc22   2009011447

ISBN 978-0-521-85209-8 hardback

Cambridge University Press has no responsibility for the persistence or
accuracy of URLs for external or third-party internet websites referred to
in this publication, and does not guarantee that any content on such
websites is, or will remain, accurate or appropriate.

Library
University of Texas
at San Antonio

Contents

Contents

Notes on contributors

EDITOR

PETER BONDANELLA is Distinguished Professor Emeritus of Comparative Literature, Film Studies, and Italian at Indiana University. He is the author, translator, or editor of numerous books on Italian cinema and Italian literary classics (Boccaccio, Cellini, Dante, Machiavelli, Vasari). Besides a book on Eco, *Umberto Eco and the Open Text: Semiotics, Fiction, Popular Culture* (1997), he is the co-editor of *The Cambridge Companion to the Italian Novel* (2003). His recent publications include a new translation of and commentary on Machiavelli's *The Prince* (2004); a three-volume edition, with Julia Conaway Bondanella, of Longfellow's translation of Dante's *Divine Comedy* with a substantial commentary (2003–6); and *A History of Italian Cinema* (2009). He is a past President of the American Association for Italian Studies and a member of the European Academy of Sciences and Arts.

CONTRIBUTORS

CINZIA BIANCHI has a doctorate in Semiotics and is a researcher at the IULM University in Milan. She has published several books on semiotics, including *Su Ferruccio Rossi-Landi* (1995) and *Spot. Semiotica della comunicazione pubblicitaria* (2005).

NORMA BOUCHARD is Associate Professor of Comparative Literature and Italian at the University of Connecticut. She is the author of *Celine, Gadda, Beckett: Experimental Writers of the 1930s* (2000); editor of *Risorgimento in Modern Italian Culture: Revisiting the Nineteenth-Century Past in History, Narrative, and Cinema* (2005); and co-editor of *Umberto Eco's Alternative: The Politics of Culture and the Ambiguities of Interpretation* (1998).

MICHAEL CAESAR is Serena Professor of Italian at the University of Birmingham (UK) and author of *Umberto Eco: Philosophy, Semiotics and the Work of Fiction* (1999); co-author of *Modern Italian Culture* (2007); editor of *Dante: The Critical Heritage* (1996); and co-editor of *Writers and Society in Contemporary Italy: A Collection of Essays* (1993); *The Quality of Light: Modern Italian Short Stories* (1994); and *Orality and Literacy in Modern Italian Culture* (2006).

ROCCO CAPOZZI is Professor of Italian at the University of Toronto and Associate Editor of *Modern Language Studies*. Besides many articles on Eco and contemporary Italian literature, he is the editor of *Hommage to Moravia* (1993) and *Reading Eco: An Anthology* (1997). He has also contributed to the *Cambridge Companion to the Italian Novel* (2003).

THERESA COLETTI is Professor of English and Comparative Literature at the University of Maryland. She is the author of numerous publications on medieval literature and on Eco, including: *Naming the Rose: Eco, Medieval Signs, and Modern Theory* (1988); and *Mary Magdalene and the Drama of Saints: Theater, Gender, and Religion in Late Medieval England* (2004).

CRISTINA FARRONATO is the author of *Eco's Chaosmos. From the Middle Ages to Postmodernity* (2003). She teaches at the University of Southern California in Los Angeles.

MANUELA GIERI is Director of the Program in Semiotics and Professor of Italian at the University of Toronto. She is the co-editor of *"La Strada": Federico Fellini, Director* (1987) and *Luigi Pirandello: Contemporary Perspectives* (1999), as well as the author of *Contemporary Italian Filmmaking: Strategies of Subversion: Pirandello, Fellini, Scola, and the Directors of the New Generation* (1995).

TORUNN HAALAND is Instructor of Italian at the Pennsylvania State University and is the author of articles on Fellini, Nanni Moretti, Pasolini, and Mussolini. She is currently working on studies of Italian neorealism and cityscapes in Italian cinema.

GUY RAFFA is Associate Professor of Italian at the University of Texas at Austin. He teaches and writes on modern Italian fiction and theory, literature and science, and medieval literature and thought. He is the author of *Divine Dialectic: Dante's Incarnational Poetry* (2000) and *The Complete Danteworlds: A Reader's Guide to the "Divine Comedy"* (2009), in addition to essays an Carlo Levi, Calvino, and Eco.

PATRIZIA VIOLI is Associate Professor of Semiotics in the Department of Communication Science at the University of Bologna. Among her many publications, she has written *Significato ed esperienza* (1997) and *Meaning and Experience* (2001); with Umberto Eco she has co-edited *Meaning and Mental Representations* (1990); and she has co-edited an important collection of essays on Eco's works: *Semiotica: storia, teoria, interpretazione: saggi intorno a Umberto Eco* (1992).

Preface

The ten essays in this anthology aim to introduce the reader to the wide range of critical problems associated with Umberto Eco's literary, philosophical, and cultural writings. Only one other Italian thinker has exerted such an enormous influence over Italian culture in the twentieth century – Benedetto Croce – and Croce never turned his hand to fiction. The breadth and scope of Eco's writings qualify him as what the Italians call a *tuttologo* – someone who knows something important about virtually everything. For any student of Eco, it seems that he has read practically everything in print in a variety of original languages and disciplines and, even more amazing, he has remembered it all! His effortless combination of matchless erudition and a wonderful sense of humor sets him apart from equally cerebral Italian writers such as Italo Calvino or Primo Levi, whose postmodern novels lack Eco's wit and sense of irony.

Norma Bouchard's contribution provides a survey of Eco's very early interest in popular culture (comic books, popular song, film, cartoons), a field that was more often identified with Anglo-American scholarship than with Italian writing when Eco began to publish on the subject. It is fair to say that with Eco's treatment of such iconic popular culture figures as Superman, James Bond, and Peanuts, Italian culture began to examine its own popular culture roots. But Eco's interest in cultural theory also produced literary results: his fifth novel (*The Mysterious Flame of Queen Loana: An Illustrated Novel*) provides an encyclopedic perspective upon the popular culture of Eco's adolescence during the Fascist period. Eco moved from popular culture to an interest in semiotic theory (the focus of the chapter by Cinzia Bianchi and Manuela Gieri), hoping that the emerging discipline of semiotics would provide a means of analyzing both high and low culture. He became famous for his semiotic writings long before his turn to fiction, yet his five novels are never far removed from his philosophical musings derived from linguistics and semiotics. Like many other contemporary novelists, Eco has assimilated a great deal of scientific knowledge into his fiction and philosophy, a topic treated by Guy Raffa.

Of course, thanks in part to the international success of his first novel, *The Name of the Rose*, most readers of Eco identify him as a brilliant medievalist. The fact that Eco always gives his interest in the Middle Ages a postmodern twist is the subject of essays by Cristina Farronato and Theresa Coletti. Literary critics, in fact, define Eco's fiction as the essence of the postmodern approach to literature, a subject treated in detail by Rocco Capozzi. Patrizia Violi's discussion of Eco's most recent semiotic thought outlines ideas that find fictional development in *The Mysterious Flame of Queen Loana*. While it is important to note the links between Eco's fiction and his philosophical, linguistic, or scientific interests, it remains important to analyze his debts to literary tradition. Here different chapters treat two fundamental elements of Eco's thought. Michael Caesar discusses Eco's important debt to James Joyce, who became something of an intellectual and fictional template for Eco's entire career. And Peter Bondanella traces the impact of detective fiction upon both Eco's novels and his epistemology in studying how a literary genre from popular or "lowbrow" fiction plays a crucial role in the creation of Eco's postmodern novels. Finally to round out the collection, Torunn Haaland surveys Eco's writings on the movies (the quintessential pop-culture product of the past century) and discusses how his analysis of the cinema contains crucial concepts related to Eco's semiotic theory and his discussion of human communication.

There is a wealth of critical commentary on Umberto Eco in scholarly books and articles. This anthology attempts to provide new and thought-provoking insights into topics that have attracted a great deal of attention in the past without repeating many of the arguments found in earlier publications. The target audience of this companion volume includes not only students but also scholars and the general reading public who find Eco fascinating as a writer and interesting as an original thinker on historical, cultural, and philosophical questions of a timeless nature.

Before reading the chapters in this volume, it would prove useful to read the introduction to the bibliography on Eco's works contained at the end of this book. Every effort has been made to render our treatment of Eco's literary, scholarly, and philosophical career easily accessible, but the complicated history of the appearance of his works in translation should be kept in mind. In most cases, authors have cited available English translations, but in other cases when the available translations seem flawed or incomplete, contributors to this volume have provided their own, more accurate, renderings from the original Italian editions. At any rate, the bibliography provides an important guide through the maze of editions, translations, and revisions of Eco's published work.

Peter Bondanella
St. George, Utah

Acknowledgments

The editor and publishers would like to thank the following for permission to reproduce copyright material:

Figure 4.3 from Marvin Minsky (ed), *Semantic Information Processing* (Cambridge, MA: MIT Press, 1968). Reproduced by permission.

CHAPTER I

Eco and popular culture

Norma Bouchard

Since the beginning of his long and most distinguished career, Umberto Eco has demonstrated an equal devotion to the high canon of Western literature and to popular, mass-produced and mass-consumed, artifacts. Within Eco's large corpus of published works, however, it is possible to chart different as well as evolving evaluations of the aesthetic merit of both popular and high cultural artifacts. Because such evaluations belong to a corpus that spans from the 1950s to the present, they necessarily reflect the larger epistemological changes that ensued when the resistance to commercialized mass culture on the part of an elitist, aristocratic strand of modern art theory gave way to a postmodernist blurring of the divide between different types of discourses. Yet, it is also crucial to remember that, from his earlier publications onwards, Eco has approached the cultural field as a vast domain of symbolic production where high- and lowbrow arts not only coexist, but also are both complementary and sometimes interchangeable. This holistic understanding of the cultural field explains Eco's earlier praise of selected popular works amidst a plethora of negative evaluations, as well as his later fictional practice of citations and replays that shapes his work as best-selling novelist of *The Name of the Rose* (1980), followed by *Foucault's Pendulum* (1988), *The Island of the Day Before* (1994), *Baudolino* (2000), and *The Mysterious Flame of Queen Loana* (2004). Nevertheless, even in a type of writing that might appear as a capitulation to Kitsch art, Eco does not relinquish a desire to innovate upon the already said. By so doing, Eco's fictional works testify to the relative nature of aesthetic merits, standards of taste, cultural levels, and especially the critical categories of modernism and postmodernism that derive from them.

Among the many impressive traits of Eco's extensive bibliography are an almost equal number of publications on lofty subjects when compared to his works on mass-culture forms of communication. Among Eco's works from the late 1950s to the 1970s, one finds scholarly examinations of medieval and contemporary aesthetics – *The Aesthetics of Thomas Aquinas* (1956), *The Open Work* (1962), and *The Aesthetics of Chaosmos: The Middle Ages of James Joyce* (1965) – alongside a significant corpus of studies on various forms of popular culture either authored, edited, or co-edited by Eco: *Apocalyptic and Integrated Intellectuals: Mass Communications and Theories of Mass Culture* (1964); *The Bond Affair* (1965); *The Absent Structure* (1968); *The Culture Industry* (1969); *The Forms of Content* (1971); *Home Customs: Evidences and Mysteries of Italian Ideology* (1973); *The Superman of the Masses: Rhetoric and Ideology in the Popular Novel* (1976); *From the Periphery of the Empire: Chronicles from a New Middle Ages* (1977); *The Reader in the Story: Interpretative Cooperation in Narrative Texts* (1979); and *Invernizio, Serao, Liala* (1979), to mention just the most important ones. Among Eco's monographs, *Apocalyptic and Integrated Intellectuals* – partially translated as *Apocalypse Postponed* – is especially significant. Tracking Eco's many publications on cultural studies is difficult in English, since so many of the translations are incomplete or combine works from many Italian originals.[1]

Published just two years after *The Open Work*, a work widely acknowledged as a most comprehensive treatment of modernist and avant-garde aesthetics, *Apocalyptic and Integrated Intellectuals* could be considered an archive of Eco's various discussions of mass-produced and popular art forms. His essays range from comic strips, music, radio and television programs to popular literary genres, such as science fiction, film noir, and gothic. With *The Superman of the Masses*, Eco turns his attention to popular novels authored by best-selling writers from the eighteenth to the mid-twentieth centuries: William Beckford, Eugène Sue, Alexandre Dumas, Pierre-Alexis Ponson du Terrail, Emilio Salgari, Luigi Natoli, Dino Segre (a.k.a. "Pitigrilli"), and Ian Fleming, among others. As in the case of his monographs, Eco's edited volumes also bear witness to his commitment to the serious study of popular forms of communication. In the introduction to the volume *The Culture Industry*, he explains that while the Italian reading public was familiar with Marshall McLuhan and Herbert Marcuse's discussions of the mass media of the 1950s, much of the theoretical work produced in the United States remained little known. To fill this gap, his volume assembles a cast of cultural theorists, ranging from Daniel Bell and Dwight MacDonald to Clement Greenberg, Edward Shils, Leo Lowenthal, Paul F. Lazarsfeld, and Robert K. Merton. Yet, Eco also hastens to add that in Italy, theoretical pronouncements about popular culture and mass communications have tended to prevail over the studies of the concrete and specific structures, forms, and contents of popular forms of communication. According to Eco, this has had a series of negative ramifications, producing a wealth of abstract theory resting upon an inadequate base of empirical research. The volume on James Bond novels, *The Bond Affair*, even though published in Italian five years before *The Culture Industry*, is a valiant attempt to correct such empirical weakness. It anthologizes essays that examine the genesis and structure of the Bond novels, the social and ideological models that they promote, and their impact on the reading and, in the case of cinematic adaptations, viewing public. Eco's own essay on James Bond, now available in English in *The Role of the Reader: Explorations in the Semiotics of Texts* (1979), was his most widely read work until the publication of his best-selling novel.

Eco's works from the late 1970s onwards continue to prove his commitment to examining all forms of cultural production, to devoting attention to the many symbolic expressions of our collective lives. Once again in Eco's intellectual development, treatments of high-culture subjects, ranging from reception theory or the philosophy of language (*The Reader in the Story*, 1979; *Semiotics and the Philosophy of Language*, 1984) to past and present forms of hermeneutics (*The Limits of Interpretation*, 1990; *Interpretation and Overinterpretation*, 1992), coexist with the analyses of mass and lowbrow forms of communications contained in a number of anthologies in Italy and subsequently translated under such titles as *Travels in Hyperreality* (1986), *Misreadings* (1993), and *How to Travel with a Salmon* (1994). Non-Italian critics have rightly praised Eco's comprehensive approach to the field of cultural production as a pioneering contribution to introducing cultural studies methodologies into Italian scholarly and cultural debate.[2] Thanks both to Eco's own publications and to his pivotal role as an editor for major Italian publishers (thereby helping to select those works that deserved Italian translation), in the 1960s and 1970s, Eco's contributions to this field justly rank him among the key figures of contemporary thought (e.g., Roland Barthes, Raymond Williams, and E. P. Thompson) who have produced what is now an intellectual discipline.

Eco is neither an apocalyptic intellectual who rejects all forms of contemporary culture and despises everything that is not highbrow in nature, nor is he an integrated intellectual who uncritically praises all forms of mass culture and equates comic strips to Shakespeare in terms of importance. Eco's approach to human culture is therefore holistic. Nevertheless, his extensive works encourage the establishment of critical criteria to define cultural artifacts from either high- or lowbrow culture so that the contemporary critic may distinguish between popular and high art with some precision. In short, Eco's bibliography straddles what Andreas Huyssen calls the "Great Divide"[3] and therefore documents the different positions on popular culture taken by two very different twentieth-century views on the subject: modern art theory, on the one hand, with its emphasis on originality, novelty, and innovation; and postmodern aesthetics, on the other hand, that champions repetition, iteration, intertextual citation, and replay.

Eco's publications between *Apocalyptic and Integrated Intellectuals* (1964) and *Invernizio, Serao, Liala* (1979) reflect a predominantly modernist approach to culture. They offer what might be termed a very "apocalyptic" view of popular art forms, defining them as products of a bourgeois, capitalist-driven culture that seeks to provide the public with imaginary resolutions to real, social contradictions. The works examined by Eco fall broadly within two categories: popular nineteenth- and twentieth-century novels; and various forms of mass communication widespread in twentieth-century culture, such as cartoons, songs, television, and films. The first group of works is discussed in great detail in *The Superman of the Masses* and in *Invernizio, Serao, Liala*. Both studies approach their subject from the framework of the sociology of culture and seek to unveil the ideologies that inform popular fiction. Eco's assumption is generally that these ideologies are conservative and support the status quo. *The Superman of the Masses* focuses on the genre of the *feuilleton* and its developments. Eco believes that the *feuilleton*, first produced in the 1830s when Emile de Girardin added an appendix containing serialized novels to a magazine, initially embodied a democratic vision of life. This democratic ideology reveals itself in the many representations of various forms of injustice perpetrated against the poor and the oppressed that one finds in such popular novels as Alexandre Dumas' *The Count of Montecristo* or Eugène Sue's *Les mystères de Paris*. However, the representation of social injustice in popular literature – for Eco a commendable ideological stance – often unfortunately goes hand in hand with the resolution of injustice by the figure of a superman. Variously embodied in characters such as Balzac's Vautrin, Dumas' Montecristo, or Sue's Rodolphe, the superman intervenes on behalf of the poor and the oppressed by being an enlightened reformer and a generous benefactor. However, according to Eco, the superman is an essentially consolatory figure whose sphere of action remains highly localized and circumscribed. More importantly, the reformism of the superman serves as an antidote for revolution. As a result, this kind of pseudorevolutionary literature actually ultimately preserves and reaffirms the social injustice that it pretends to attack, leaving the larger social fabric and its conditions of exploitation unchanged. In Eco's words, "The basis of Sue's ideology is this: to try to discover what we can do for the humble (by means of brotherly collaboration between classes) while leaving the present structure of society unchanged."[4]

Eco believes that in the second half of the nineteenth century, the popular democratic novel undergoes an additional process of degradation. Novelists such as Ponson du Terrail, Montepin, Richepin, and Richebourg – extremely popular then but infrequently read today – might represent the evils and problems of society, but they do so only to add a touch of color to their fiction. Such novels focus primarily no longer on the larger socio-historical fabric of society but now concentrate their narrative energies upon the private sphere where bourgeois dramas take place. The earlier figure of the superman endures, but its intervention is now limited to the resolution of domestic affairs. This last phase of the popular novel, located by Eco between the last years of the nineteenth century and the beginning of the twentieth century, reflects an even more conservative ideology. In such popular works as Pierre Souvestre's *Fantomas* series or Maurice Leblanc's cycle of stories featuring the gentleman criminal Arsène Lupin, the narratives look beyond the bourgeois sphere, but their ampler social outlook strives towards the promotion of imperialistic, racial, and even anti-Semitic ideologies, as Eco argues in *The Superman of the Masses*. The examinations of popular art forms contained in *Invernizio, Serao, Liala* lead Eco to analogous conclusions, even though his focus is on popular novels written by Italian women. The best-known and most successful of these writers, Carolina Invernizio, transforms the superman figure into a society of females whose role is that of guaranteeing the order of the bourgeois family and the sanctuary of a middle-class domesticity that is being threatened and/or violated. The result, however, is a further strengthening of the status quo and of a social order that, as it has been amply documented by sociologists and historians, was confining women to the domestic and private spheres of life.

Eco believes that in the course of the twentieth century, the novel's popular appeal as a genre diminishes. Narrative migrates into the newer media of films, television, songs, and cartoons. The analysis of these new forms is at the center of *Apocalyptic and Integrated Intellectuals*. Once again, however, Eco's analysis reveals that the conservative ideology bolstering the status quo of the nineteenth-century popular novel has an impact upon new media of the subsequent century. Thus, popular comic strips such as *Steve Canyon* and *Dennis the Menace* exemplify a resurgence of the Manichean logic of late bourgeois society: discipline and order are associated with friendship; war is linked with just conflict; the metropolis becomes associated with prestigious achievement; and the desirable women are linked to a lack of sensuality. Eco examines other examples of cartoons – mostly American – that he faults: *Little Orphan Annie* for its support of the nationalistic ideology of the McCarthy era; *Terry and the Pirates* for its association with the rhetoric of militarism; and *Joe Palooka* for its promotion of the political and moral conservatism of American society. Even Al Capp's *Li'l Abner* does not escape Eco's criticism, since he believes its satire of American culture is only superficial. In reality, the strip betrays a deep faith in the system that is even more damaging since it is concealed in a structure of deception. Of course, Eco rarely admits that his critique of popular American culture reflects his own leftist ideology, one colored (if not dominated) by Marxist values and a common disrespect for American popular culture often found among European intellectuals. Eco's corrosive critique also analyzes Italian popular music, and his evaluation of some of it reaches the same negative conclusions. The lyrics of Rita Pavone, a popular Italian singer, voice social discontent and express the outrage and anarchy of the young, but ultimately Eco believes her songs focus on sentimental matters that neutralize the potential for change in superficial, non-dangerous forms of protest. As for mainstream cinema and television, Eco cites the medieval debate between Suger and St. Bernard over the translation of the Biblical doctrine into visual images as an early expression of the perennial conflict between integrated and apocalyptic thinkers. Suger approved of art as an illustration of doctrine (a medieval form of an "integrated" intellectual praising popular culture), while St. Bernard (an apocalyptic figure who rejected all visual pandering to the masses) wanted no such lowering of standards. Eco argues that cinema and television, as iconic mediums, impair the viewer's analytical ability and are therefore more permeable to ideological coding than traditional fictional narrative. Eco believes that the culture industry exploits such ideologically loaded coding to foster the subjection of consumers into a critical acceptance of the values and beliefs of the hegemonic culture these consumers inhabit.

While Eco's discussions strive towards the unveiling of the ideology behind forms of cultural production, his approach to the field of mass media and popular forms of communication proceeds from the assumption that political categories cannot be divorced from aesthetic ones. As he often comments in *The Open Work,* strict homologies exist between the formal structures of the text and the world from which these structures have sprung forth:

In every century, the way that artistic forms are structured reflects the way in which…contemporary culture views reality. The closed, single conception in a world by a medieval artist reflected the conception of the cosmos as a hierarchy of fixed, pre-ordained orders. The work as a pedagogical vehicle, as a monocentric and necessary apparatus (incorporating a rigid internal pattern of meter and rhymes) simply reflects the syllogistic system, a logic of necessity, a deductive consciousness by means of which reality could be made manifest step by step without unforeseen interruptions. (Umberto Eco, *The Open Work*. Trans. Anna Cancogni. Cambridge, MA: Harvard University Press, 1989, p. 13)

It comes as no surprise, then, that the acritical acceptance of the socio-political structures that Eco traces in various popular art forms is expressed not only at the level of content, but also of style, where the lack of social innovation translates itself in a repetition of formulae, schemes, and conventional expressions. In other words, the redundancy of content in support of dominant ideologies repeats itself in a redundancy of form. This idea constitutes the core of Eco's definition of Kitsch that he treats at length in a long chapter, "The Structure of Bad Taste," that was originally published in the Italian version of *Apocalyptic and Integrated Intellectuals* but which appears in English as a chapter in *The Open Work*. In this essay, Eco describes Kitsch as a typical phenomenon of popular culture, unabashedly poaching the innovating procedures developed by high art in order to sell them as authentic expressions: "We could say that the term Kitsch can be applied to any object that (a) appears already consumed; (b) reaches the masses, or the average customer, because it is already consumed; and (c) will quickly be reconsumed, because the use to which it has already been put by a large number of consumers has hastened its erosion" (Eco, *The Open Work*, p. 197). The 1965 essay "Narrative Structures in Fleming" – a work that appeared first in *The Bond Affair* and was then widely distributed in English by its appearance in *The Role of the Reader* – illustrates perfectly the strict nexus that Eco establishes between conventional stylistic and semantic effects, on the one hand, and a conservative political ideology encoded in such conventional effects, on the other. Basing his argument on Fleming's first novel, *Casino Royale* (1953), and not really extending his analysis beyond that single novel to the entire collection of novels featuring Bond or to the many films adapted from Fleming's works, Eco argues that Ian Fleming's 007 series contains a set of binary oppositions of characters and value systems corresponding to the schemata of an hegemonic social and political order. The series' style epitomizes the practice of a *bricoleur:* an author who creates texts as collages by way of the repetition of previously existing literary stylemes in a "clever montage of déjà vu"(Eco, *The Role of the Reader*, p. 163). It is an interesting reflection of Eco's intellectual integrity that years later, after having written a number of best-selling novels himself, Eco retracts much of his negative opinion of Fleming's prose style in the prestigious Norton Lectures delivered at Harvard University in 1992 to 1993, comparing Fleming to Manzoni and seeing stylistic traits in the first Bond novel that were praised by the Russian Formalists (Umberto Eco, *Six Walks in the Fictional Woods*, Cambridge, MA: Harvard University Press, 1994, pp. 70, 84). His change of heart probably also contains an admission that his own cultural theory from this period was colored by political ideologies even though he did not acknowledge this to be the case.

Some scholarly evaluations of Eco's discussions of popular culture have argued that Eco himself was not immune to the theory of the "culture industry" developed by the theoreticians of the Frankfurt School.[5] Obeying the reifying logic of a capitalist economy, the culture industry, according to this line of thinking, reproduces dominant ideological beliefs in fictions whose formulaic and conciliatory structures offer the public imaginary resolutions to the contradictions of their daily lives. The only works that supposedly escape the grips of the culture industry are the artifacts of modernity and avant-gardism, such as Samuel Beckett's *Endgame*, according to a famous essay by Theodor Adorno who argues that the work's formal open-endedness and fragmentation also embodies a negative critique (or "negative dialectics") of industrial capitalism and its suffocating institutions.[6] In spite of this criticism of Eco's position, originality and innovation are precisely the chief traits that Eco locates in the "high" works of modernism and the avant-garde. He cites with approval the poetry of Verlaine, Mallarmé, and Montale; the novels of Proust, Kafka, and Joyce; and the music composed by Pousseur, Stockhausen, Berio, and Boulez. In all of these works, originality and innovation question the already known and therefore are values that Eco sees as coterminous with social change. In Eco's words, "So the avant-garde musician rejects the tonal system not only because it alienates him to a conventional system of musical laws, but also because it alienates him to a social ethics and to a given version of the world. . .By rejecting a musical model, the avant-garde musician actually rejects (more or less consciously) a social model."[7]

Given Eco's promotion of originality, novelty, and invention as anti-Kitsch in nature, it comes as no surprise that in an early elaboration of his semiotic theory contained in the last chapter of *The Absent Structure* (1968), he endorses politically empowering acts of "misreading," the deciphering of messages on the basis of other, oppositional codes that might occur during the moment of reception. As Eco puts it, to force closed semiotic systems into an open-ended process means to open the symbolic field to an understanding of culture not just as a space of passive consumption and silent acceptance but also as a pragmatic arena of resistance and conflict:

This is a "revolutionary" aspect of the semiological consciousness... where it appears impossible to alter the modality of emission or the form of the message, it remains possible (as in an ideal semiological guerrilla warfare) to change the circumstances according to which the readers will select their own interpretative codes...Against a technology of communication that seeks to promote redundant messages in order to ensure a pre-established reception, the possibility of a tactics of decoding capable of creating different circumstances for different types of decoding begins to take shape.[8]

Besides laying bare Eco's intent to integrate semiotics within a Marxist philosophical system, this quotation also sets the foundations upon which distinctions between high and low art rest. Indeed, a work allegedly created to foster the passivity of the consumer can be interpreted, in the moment of reception, in a way that might potentially alter its original effects and, with them, rigid taxonomic divisions between different forms of communication. Challenges to these taxonomies are not limited to *The Absent Structure* since often, amidst Eco's negative judgments, there remain areas where his understanding of popular versus high art forms tests clear boundaries and definitions. For example, in the preface to *The Culture Industry*, Eco ironically notes that many of the writers that he has anthologized are "enlightened intellectuals" who examine popular culture from the premise of high art and therefore view it as a degenerate form of expression. From this group, Eco singles out Robert K. Merton and Paul F. Lazarsfeld precisely because their works have demythologized the notion that the culture industry is an omnipotent force, subjecting people to its control. While many passages of *Apocalyptic and Integrated Intellectuals* seem hostile to popular culture, other key parts of the book – sections devoted to the myth of Superman, to a discussion of Joseph Heller's novel *Catch 22*, and to Charles Schultz's famous cartoon *Peanuts,* as well as another often-cited 1975 essay first collected in *From the Periphery of the Empire* entitled "Casablanca: Cult Movies and Intertextual Collage" – show Eco's attitude to be more positive.

In his reading of the Superman myth, Eco takes a different stance vis-à-vis the consoling structures that popular artworks give the reader. After a modernist condemnation of redundancies and iterations of form and content on the grounds that such techniques promote an a-critical view of the world, Eco then praises them for their promotion of an a-critical view of existence in the context of Rex Stout's Nero Wolfe stories:

The attraction of the book, the sense of repose, of psychological extension...lies in the fact that plopped in an easy chair or in the seat of a train compartment, the reader continuously recovers, point by point, what he already knows, what he wants to know again: that is why he has purchased the book. He derives pleasure from the non-story (if indeed a story is a development of events which should bring us from the point of departure to a point of arrival where we would never have dreamed of arriving); the distraction consists in the refutation of a development of events, in a withdrawal from the tensions of past-present-future to the focus on an *instant*, which is loved because it is recurrent.[9]

Likewise, in the essay on Michael Curtiz's *Casablanca,* Eco offers unexpected words of praise for a work that some critics would say might exemplify Kitsch. He repeatedly describes the film as a "textual syllabus" produced by the recycling of endless other works, but in spite of this, Eco does not find the redundancy of the "déja vu" and the collage of a reifying *bricoleur* criticized elsewhere but, rather, something akin to a sublime experience: "When all the archetypes burst out shamelessly, we plumb Homeric profundity. Two clichés make us laugh but a hundred clichés move us because we sense dimly that the clichés are talking among themselves, celebrating a reunion."[10] In other words, Eco indicates here that the pleasure that we can derive from consolatory structure is not only a positive feeling, but also one that now seems to be divested of ideological implications. Eco's reading of Heller's *Catch 22* represents an even more drastic shift. Despite admitting that the novel, as a work of Kitsch, makes an unabashed use of pre-existing conventions, Eco writes that it corrosively critiques the systems of social control and relationships of property and, by so doing, indicts the state of anarchism and absurdity of contemporary life. In short, Eco is pointing to the fact that conventional, formulaic, and redundant works of Kitsch can have the same aesthetic, and – by implication – the same social effects as those produced by the avant-garde. In Eco's discussion of *Peanuts*, he advances the claim that even though the strip borrows from high art, it is not a product of Kitsch, but rather, something close to a "work of art," since it provides a novel perspective on the human condition of isolation and alienation brought about by capitalist, bourgeois society. Here again, the popular comes to occupy the privileged position of the avant-garde. Eco also believes that the avant-garde can borrow the reifying effects of Kitsch:

Given the spread of mass culture, it would be impossible to say that this sequence of mediations and loans is a one-way street: Kitsch is not the only borrower. Today it is often avant-garde culture which, reacting against the density and the scope of mass culture, borrows its own stylemes from Kitsch.[11]

In light of these remarks, the full implications of a statement from Eco's preface to *Apocalyptic and Integrated Intellectuals* emerge: "the system of conditioning called the culture industry does not conveniently present us with the possibility of distinguishing two independent spheres, with mass communication over here and aristocratic creation over there…From this point onwards, the notion of 'culture' itself has to be re-elaborated and reformulated."[12]

Such re-elaboration and reformulation stands at the center of Eco's works from the 1980s onwards, where he revisits many of the premises of the earlier decades, including his understanding of the mass media, the role of the intellectual, the political possibility of modernism and the avant-garde, and so forth. In the 1983 essay "The Multiplication of the Media," which first appeared in the collection *Seven Years of Desire*, Eco rethinks the notion of Kitsch in all its rhetorical, semantic, and especially ideological implications. After having assessed how the institution of the museum has become permeable to pop art and vice versa, he argues that the relationship between artistic innovation and mechanical reproduction, mass-produced goods and high art, is much more complex than he had previously supposed. As a correlative, the political valorization of avant-garde work, or, conversely, the demotion of the formulaic expressions of mass-produced goods that was at the center of modern aesthetics and theories of art, no longer hold:

Once upon a time there were the mass media, and they were wicked, of course, and there was a guilty party. Then, there were the virtuous voices that accused the criminals. And Art (ah, what luck!) offered alternatives, for those who were not prisoners of the mass media. Well, it's all over. We have to start again from the beginning, asking one another what's going on.[13]

Eco concludes that everything that was believed in the 1960s and 1970s by leftist scholars of traditional, modern critical theory – scholars precisely like himself – is in dire need of re-examination:

Power is elusive and there is no longer any telling where the "plan" comes from. Because there is, of course, a "plan" but it is no longer intentional, and therefore it cannot be criticized with the traditional criticism of intentions. All Professors of theory of communications, trained by the texts of twenty years ago (this includes me) should be pensioned off. (Eco, *Travels in Hyperreality*, p. 149)

In a group of five untranslated essays from the section "Between Experimentation and Consumption" in *On Mirrors and Other Essays* (1985), Eco elaborates on the limits of a modern theory of art and aesthetics and argues that any formulation of artistic value is, by necessity, provisional because it remains always relative to history and pragmatic context: "I believe that, at this point, it is necessary to acknowledge the fundamental relativity of these notions and manipulate them for what they are: notions relative to the patrimony of knowledge, to the encyclopedia of a given public, rather than take them as 'objective' aspects of a text."[14] Eco reminds his readers that classical art enshrined the copy, the use of a previous model as the standard for good art, and that artistic values embody historical relativity. He playfully suggests that in an imagined cultural landscape in the year AD 3000 after an envisioned apocalyptic destruction of all our art – both lowbrow and highbrow – the sole surviving example of a serialized television episode will appear to us as a masterpiece of originality and innovation!

With the publication in 1980 of Eco's best-selling novel *The Name of the Rose*, as well as the important *Postscript* appended to it after its international success, Eco's definition of culture acquired greater sophistication. As the book jacket suggested to the millions of readers who bought it, *The Name of the Rose* represents an intricate weaving of texts, a book made of other books. Its core is a historical novel set in the fourteenth century. It is replete with allusions to a number of real historical figures (Ubertino di Casale, Bernard Gui, William of Ockham, Bernard de Cluny, and Roger Bacon) as well as real historical events (the Babylonian Captivity of the Church, the Black Death, the Hundred Years' War, ecclesiastical disputes over the meaning of property). The narrative voice (Adso of Melk, who seeks to recover the experiences of his youth, when he was a young monk at the service of the Franciscan William of Baskerville) follows the pattern of the European *Bildungsroman*, or novel of initiation. Its models are none other than the high canonical authors of European modernism: Marcel Proust's *In Search of Lost Time* (1913 – 27) and Thomas Mann's *Doctor Faustus* (1947). However, on the trunk of these lofty models of the historical novel and the *Bildungsroman*, Eco grafts well-recognizable popular artifacts. The story of William of Baskerville's conjectures, for example, owes much to two popular detective novels: Conan Doyle's *The Hound of the Baskervilles* and Dorothy L. Sayers' *Gaudy Night*.

Eco discusses at length the collapse of distinctions between high and low verbal artifacts that his first novel exemplifies in the para-textual apparatus that appeared in print shortly after the publication of the novel: *Postscript to "The Name of the Rose"*.[15] In this important work of postmodernist literary theory, Eco contends that one of the correlatives of modernity's fragmentation of a unified culture is the loss of aesthetic norms, the wane of shared standards of aesthetic judgment. In contemporary culture, modern and avant-garde arguments that indict popularity as a lack of merit, or, conversely, infuse unpopularity of the message with value, are no longer valid assumptions. Likewise, artistic worth is no longer necessarily identified with difficult experimentation and daring originality, but can also be located in a poetics of citations and replays:

> Between 1965 and today, two ideas have been definitively clarified; that plot could be found also in the form of the quotation of other plots, and that the quotation could be less escapist than the plot quoted…The real problem at stake then was, could there be a novel that was not escapist and, nevertheless, still enjoyable? This link, and the rediscovery not only of plot but also of enjoyability, was to be realized by the American theorists of postmodernism. (Umberto Eco, *The Name of the Rose*. Trans. William Weaver. New York: Harcourt Brace Jovanovich, 1980, p. 529)

Thus, for Eco, in the changed configuration of the contemporary world the postmodern artist has become a *bricoleur*. Originality and invention have receded into the background, while quotation and citation have become predominant. In his *Postscript*, this consideration unfolds into his famous, most humorous definition of a postmodern poetics of citation:

> But the moment comes when the avant-garde (the modern) can go no further… The postmodern reply to the modern consists in recognizing that the past, since it cannot really be destroyed…must be revisited: but with irony, not innocently. I think of a postmodern attitude as that of a man who loves a very cultivated woman and knows he cannot say to her, "I love you madly," because he knows that she knows (and that she knows that he knows) that these words have already been written by Barbara Cartland. Still, there is a solution. He can say, "As Barbara Cartland would put it, I love you madly." (Eco, *The Name of the Rose*, pp. 530 – 1)

Do statements such as these mean that for Eco, the cultural field has truly become an undifferentiated domain where qualifications of low versus high, exceptional versus marginal have lost all legitimacy? Are we to infer that all measures of distinction between forms of cultural expressions have ceased to have any meaning whatsoever? Should we decide that the novels of James Joyce, Marcel Proust, and Franz Kafka stand on the same plane as the writings of Pierre-Alexis Ponson du Terrail, Emilio Salgari, and Carolina Invernizio?

One of Eco's latest publications, *On Literature* (2002) would seem to point in this direction. In a book designed to define the nature of literature, Eco includes essays on such diverse figures as the universally acclaimed epic poet Dante, the less than famous novelist Piero Camporesi, and the lowbrow Italian novelist "Pitigrilli" whom Eco earlier treated disparagingly in *The Superman of the Masses*. Moreover, in a handful of essays where Eco touches on the topic of what constitutes "literariness," his arguments bog down in excessively broad, sweeping generalizations. For example, in his opening essay "On Some Functions of Literature," Eco explores the relationship between life and literature and makes only three vague points: that literature provides the reader with an image of the ambiguities of life and language; that it is a universe that tests the soundness of our sense of reality; and that it gives us a knowledge of the inexorable laws of death and destiny that govern our existence. Eco concludes his essay with the admission that there might very well be other functions of literature but then he merrily admits that he simply cannot recall them!

Despite Eco's hybrid incorporation of high- and lowbrow culture in *The Name of the Rose* and subsequent novels, their author is still far from relinquishing a desire for originality of vision in both the semantic and formal structures of his work. His departure from the structures of the popular novel of reassurance and consolation and the representation of the limits of modern rationalism in *The Name of the Rose* also includes the belief that endless quotations from the already-said can still involve artistic creativity, even if such creativity is necessarily situated and relocated into an ironic, palimpsestic rewriting of the many codes – both high and low – preserved in our cultural archive. Indeed, *The Name of the Rose* represents the rewriting of the genres of the detective novel, the *Bildungsroman*, and the historical novel. The story of William's detection is, in the end, the narrative of a failure. William arrives at Jorge by following the apocalyptic scenario of the prophecy of the seven angels with the seven trumpets from the *Book of Revelation*, but he finally discovers that such connections are a meaningless coincidence. The stable sense of identity – the *telos* sought by the traditional *Bildungsroman* – is never achieved. Adso's attempt to set to paper the events of his past life in order to recover a unified experience of himself remains highly problematic, producing at best a very precarious sense of identity. With regards to the historical novel, *The Name of the Rose* represents the philosophical inversion of the genre since, unlike its classical models, Eco's work heightens the tensions between reality and fiction. Such overt carnivalization of genres and conventions finally leads to the creation of other forms, capable of being described only by what they are not: the anti-detective novel, the non-mystery novel, the failed *Bildungsroman*, or the historiographic metafiction.

The Name of the Rose might easily be accused of being the quintessential work of Kitsch. Nevertheless, in it Eco does manage to innovate upon the novel's semantic and formal structures. The status quo is not reaffirmed, as it was in the popular novel, but neither are the forces that lead to its change. Likewise, extensive practices of parody and replay provocatively question modern aesthetics and modern theories of originality, but, in their creation of innovative anti-forms, they do not fully abandon them. Eco's four subsequent novels continue, by and large, the cultural practices that were inaugurated with *The Name of the Rose*. Ultimately Eco's fictional works, combined with the many essays and books he has dedicated to the definition of culture (both popular and lofty), demonstrate that his understandimg of culture, in its evolution from the modern specter of Kitsch to the postmodern celebration of intertextuality, suggests an intellectual development growing out of his initial intuitions about the arbitrary and relative nature of various kinds of culture. Eco's collected works emerge as a major contribution to the definition of postmodern culture because they bear eloquent witness to the interconnectivity of lowbrow and highbrow forms of expression in the contemporary world.

NOTES

1 Eco's essays on popular culture appear in a number of different translations and few of the original Italian works are translated in full. For example, *Apocalyptic and Integrated Intellectuals* is only partially translated as *Apocalypse Postponed*, and the partial translation contains essays from other sources. *The Bond Affair* (1966) is a hard-to-find version of the Italian original, *Il caso Bond*. Eco's famous essay on Ian Fleming's super spy is best read in *The Role of the Reader* (1979), which also contains essays from *The Open Work*, *The Absent Structure*, *The Forms of Content*, *The Superman of the Masses*, and *The Reader in the Story*. The English version of *The Open Work*, appearing in 1989, also contains important essays from *Apocalyptic and Integrated Intellectuals* and *The Absent Structure*. The original Italian edition of *Opera aperta: forma e indeterminazione nelle poetiche contemporanee* (1962) contained material on James Joyce that, in English, appears separately as *The Aesthetics of Chaosmos: The Middle Ages of James Joyce*. *The Culture Industry*, *The Forms of Content*, *From the Periphery of the Empire*, and *Invernizio, Serao, Liala* have no complete English translations, although portions of *From the Periphery* appear in *Travels in Hyperreality*, which also contains essays from other Italian anthologies, such as *Home Customs* and *Seven Years of Desire*. Peter Bondanella, *Umberto Eco and the Open Text: Semiotics, Fiction, Popular Culture* (Cambridge University Press, 1997), pp. 41–92, outlines the various forms these writings take in Italian and English editions.

2 Robert Lumley, "Introduction" in Umberto Eco, *Apocalypse Postponed* (Bloomington: Indiana University Press, 1994), pp. 1–14; David Robey, "Umberto Eco and the Analysis of the Media," in Zygmunt G. Baranski and Robert Lumley (eds.), *Culture and Conflict in Postwar Italy: Essays on Mass and Popular Culture* (New York: St. Martin's Press, 1990), pp. 160–77; David Forgacs and Robert Lumley, "Introduction: Approaches to Culture in Italy" in David Forgacs and Robert Lumley (eds.), *Italian Cultural Studies: An Introduction* (Oxford: Oxford University Press, 1996), pp. 1–11.

3 I borrow the term "Great Divide" from Andreas Huyssen, *After the Great Divide: Modernism, Mass Culture, Postmodernism* (Bloomington: Indiana University Press, 1986).

4 "Rhetoric and Ideology in Sue's *Les Mystères de Paris*," in Umberto Eco, *The Role of the Reader: Explorations in the Semiotics of Texts* (Bloomington: Indiana University Press, 1979), p. 138.

5 See Christine Ann Evans, "Eco's Fifth Column: The Critic of Culture Within the Precinct of the Popular," in Norma Bouchard and Veronica Pravadelli (eds.), *Umberto Eco's Alternative: The Politics of Culture and the Ambiguities of Interpretation* (New York: Lang, 1998), pp. 241–56.

6 Theodor Adorno, "Trying to Understand *Endgame*," *New German Critique* 26 (1982): 119–50.

7 Eco, *The Open Work*, p. 140.

8 Umberto Eco, *The Absent Structure* (Milan: Bompiani, 1968), pp. 417–18 (author's translation). A similar argument in English translation may be found in "Towards a Semiological Guerrilla Warfare" in Umberto Eco, *Travels in Hyperreality*, trans. William Weaver (New York: Harcourt Brace Jovanovich, 1989), pp. 135–44, a work that originally appeared in *Home Customs*.

9 "The Myth of Superman," in Eco, *The Role of the Reader*, pp. 119–20.

10 "Casablanca: Cult Movies and Intertextual Collage," in Eco, *Travels in Hyperreality*, p. 209.

11 "The Structure of Bad Taste," in Eco, *The Open Work*, p. 215 (this essay originally appeared in *Apocalyptic and Integrated Intellectuals* as was previously noted).

12 "Apocalyptic and Integrated Intellectuals: Mass Communications and Theories of Mass Culture," in Umberto Eco, *Apocalypse Postponed,* ed. Robert Lumley (Bloomington: Indiana University Press, 1994), p. 22.

13 "The Multiplication of the Media," in Eco, *Travels in Hyperreality*, ed. Robert Lumley (Bloomington: Indiana University Press, 1994) p. 150.

14 "Between Experimentation and Consumption," in Eco, *On Mirrors and Other Essays* (Milan: Bompiani, 1985), p. 108 (author's translation). The five sections of this study may be found on pp. 91–158 of the Italian edition and are not translated into English.

15 This was first published as a separate volume in Italian as *Postille a "Il nome della rosa"* (Milan: Bompiani, 1983) and as a separate volume in English in 1984 as *Postscript to "The Name of the Rose"* before being included with the text of the novel itself in all editions of it published after 1994.

CHAPTER 2

Eco's semiotic theory

Cinzia Bianchi and Manuela Gieri

The last pronouncement in Umberto Eco's fifty-year-long period of reflection on the processes of cognition and interpretation comes in the form of a novel, *The Mysterious Flame of Queen Loana: An Illustrated Novel*. Some readers of Eco see continuity between his first two novels (*The Name of the Rose* and *Foucault's Pendulum*) and the semiotic theory he produced up to that period in his career, while others argue that there is a discontinuity of sorts between his last three novels and his semiotic theory, or at least an expressive independence. It might be more useful in an attempt to understand the development of Eco's semiotic theory if we assume that after the publication of his third novel, *The Island of the Day Before*, in 1994, Eco entered a new phase of his reflection on semiotics that did not destroy the organic nature of the development of his work on this subject that had begun in 1975 with the publication of *A Theory of Semiotics* (Italian edition).

A number of reasons led Eco to write this general treatise. One of his preoccupations was the urgency to define the field, the methods, and most importantly the disciplinary boundaries of semiotic inquiry. Up to 1975, in books such as *The Open Work*, the frame of reference that Eco either accepted or criticized was structuralism and the theory of codes as it developed, beginning with the linguistic theory of Ferdinand de Saussure and Louis Hjelmslev, and later modified in new ways by Roland Barthes.

Beginning with *A Theory of Semiotics*, which represents a most original attempt to spark an intellectual dialogue between structuralism and American pragmatism, Eco slowly but surely translates a theory of codes associated with structuralism into a theory of interpretation dominated by the ideas of Charles S. Peirce, a reading of semiosis in which the construction of meaning is a dynamic process. In subsequent works after *A Theory of Semiotics* – *The Role of the Reader*, *The Limits of Interpretation*, *Interpretation and Overinterpretation*, and *Six*

Walks in the Fictional Woods – interpretation explicitly stands at the center of Eco's reflections. A concern for interpretation runs through his entire work, beginning with *The Open Work* where, even though in a "pre-semiotic" way, the analysis of such diverse topics as aleatory music, Joyce's poetics, informal painting, and Antonioni's films helped Eco define what he meant by the "opening" of a text and thereby began his reflection on the collaborative relationship between text and interpreter:

A work of art is a complete and closed form in its uniqueness as a balanced organic whole, while at the same time constituting an open product on account of its susceptibility to countless different interpretations which do not impinge on its unadulterable specificity. Hence, every reception of a work of art is both an interpretation and a performance of it, because in every reception the work takes on a fresh perspective for itself. (Eco, *The Open Work*, p. 4).

In these works, and others – such as *Semiotics and the Philosophy of Language* (1984) – there is also an investigation of such fundamental semiotic concepts as "sign," "dictionary vs. encyclopedia," "metaphor," "symbol," and "code," all topics that could easily be developed in other essays. Here we wish to suggest a specific itinerary within Eco's semiotic theory, one that moves from *A Theory of Semiotics* – specifically, from the notion of encyclopedia – and eventually becomes a connecting concept between a theory of knowledge and a theory of interpretation.[1] On the one hand, this concept allows Eco to overcome a code-based semiotic theory, and, on the other, it provides him with a necessary framework for the regulation of interpretation.

In *A Theory of Semiotics* Eco still foresees semantic expansions connected to a dictionary-like conception of each term. Yet, he then proposes a semantic model in which he moves from a fairly static dictionary-like model to the dynamic one that stands at the heart of the encyclopedia. Beyond a quantitative expansion of the structuralist idea of code, the most significant difference is a qualitative one. Indeed, the notion of encyclopedia allows one to go from a fundamentally static idea of decoding to a dynamic notion of abduction. According to Peirce, abduction (or hypothesis) is one of the three types of logical inference that regulate our reasoning. Deduction allows one to comprehend that what we perceive can be brought back to a given general rule. Induction allows one to come to a general rule even though moving from particular and individual cases. The reasoning Peirce defines as abduction is slightly more complex, since it proceeds by tentative and hazardous acts of inference. Abduction is, in fact, a case of inference "where we find some very curious circum-stances, which would be explained by the supposition that it was a case of a certain general rule, and thereupon adopt that supposition" (Charles S. Peirce, *Collected Papers*, 8 vols., Cambridge, MA: Harvard University Press, 1931–58, 2:624).[2] The example par excellence of abduction is the act of criminal detection. Facing the scene of a murder, the detective forms an hypothesis starting from the traces left by the murderer; such an hypothesis must then be verified by comparison with other data (such as the relationships between the victim and the murderer, the alibi of the suspect, the motive, and so on) before the correct solution, the identity of the criminal, can be discovered.

With the wider range of vision that the concept of encyclopedia entails, Eco's thought also moves from a fairly limited correlation between expression and content to a vast system of possible inferences. By joining semantics and pragmatism, the notion of encyclopedia avoids the impasse provoked by the clash between the rigor of a dictionary that dismisses situational meaning, and the supposedly unlimited wealth of mean-ings generated by the plethora of possible uses one can identify for each term. Eco further develops the notion of encyclopedia in *Semiotics and the Philosophy of Language* where he argues that "the encyclopedia is…the ensemble of all registered interpretations, conceivable in objective terms as the library of all libraries, where a library is also an archive of the non-verbal information that has been somehow recorded, from rock paintings to film libraries."[3] Therefore, the encyclopedia is like a net, a labyrinth conceived as an infinite aggregation of units of meaning, or a rhizome conceived "as a tangle of bulbs and tubers appearing like rats squirming one on top of the other" (Umberto Eco, *Semiotics and the Philosophy of Language*, Bloomington: Indiana University Press, 1984, p. 81). Eco bor-rows this "vegetable metaphor" from Gilles Deleuze and Felix Guattari,[4] and particularly he draws the suggestion that "every point of the rhizome can and must be connected with every other point"; furthermore, "a rhi-zome is not a calque but an open chart which can be connected with something else in all of its dimensions; it is dismountable, reversible, and susceptible to continual modifications," and "no one can provide a glo-bal description of the whole rhizome; not only because the rhizome is multidimentionally complicated, but also because its structure changes through time; moreover, in a structure in which every node can be con-nected with every other node, there is also the possibility of contradictory inferences" (Eco, *Semiotics and the Philosophy of Language*, pp. 81 – 2).

Even though the rhizome is the only model that can reasonably explain the connection of semantic units into the encyclopedia, from Eco's perspective on general semiotics, it is still impossible to provide a global representation in which contradictory interpretations coexist with conflicting perceptions of the world. In such a way, the encyclopedia cannot be apprehended in its entirety nor can it be represented except by the model of the rhizome – a net of connections where every point can and must be linked to all the others.

On the contrary, if we consider the encyclopedia not from the perspective of general semiotics but from a socio-semiotic perspective, for instance, it becomes a sort of reservoir for all the possible interpretations amongst which the receiver of the sign can then select the most appropriate. This is the process through which one can detect and emphasize one's own various levels of command of the encyclopedia itself. In every interpretative activity, the interpreter is asked to know that segment of the encyclopedia that is necessary to comprehend a given text. Thus, every interpreter, either an individual or a group, has a partial or limited competence that depends upon various conditionings, but most importantly from those coming upon the culture of belonging.

Because of this connection to culture and its internal structures, encyclopedia is based on a semantics of the "interpretants," where every sign constantly refers back to another sign in a process of unlimited semiosis. The principle of unlimited semiosis is vital to Eco's semiotic theory and is derived from Peirce. According to this principle, the meaning of every sign, both verbal and non-verbal, can be understood only through another sign, its "interpretant," as Peirce calls the second sign. But the meaning of this second sign, in turn, can only be seen again through another sign, and so on ad infinitum. As Peirce himself states, a sign is "anything which determines something else (its *interpretant*) to refer to an object to which itself refers (its *object*) in the same way, the interpretant becoming in turn a sign, and so on *ad infinitum*" (Peirce, *Collected Papers,* 2:303). The encyclopedia thus explains partial semiotic competence and elucidates the complexity of semiosis. At the same time, Eco maintains that by bringing the semiotic process back to the object, the encyclopedia becomes a kind of regulating hypothesis for interpretative activity. This notion of encyclopedia is complex insofar as it implies both a collective and an individual competence. Yet, in Eco's vision, even though individual encyclopedias belong either to a group (ethnic or otherwise), or to a social class, they must be considered as segments of a global encyclopedia. This means that they become interesting to semiotic inquiry only to the extent that they form part of a shared background – a repertoire of socially and culturally defined knowledge in a precise historical moment and belonging to a specific group.

In his major treatise on semiotics, Eco identifies two thresholds – an upper and a lower one – within which semiotic research ought to take place (Umberto Eco, *A Theory of Semiotics*. Bloomington: Indiana University Press, 1976, pp. 19–28). If semiotics bypassed the "lower threshold," the one that involves the analysis of humans' non-intentional reactions to the stimuli coming from the natural environment, it would find itself immersed within the territory of other disciplines, such as psychology. The upper threshold pertains to cultural phenomena and elucidates the fact that "objects, behavior and relationships of production and value function as such socially precisely because they obey semiotic laws." To identify an "upper threshold" of semiotics means to believe that it is possible to analyze objects in their materiality (p. 27). This is why, according to Eco, it is possible to study the whole culture as *sub specie semiotica*. From a semiotic perspective, a study of culture becomes possible only if and when a certain object or value is communicated with verbal or non-verbal signs and circulates within a given community. Thus, "to reduce the whole of culture to semiotics does not mean that one has to reduce the whole of material life to pure mental events" (p. 27). As we shall discover, the notion and role of cultural and social community is a crucial part of Eco's thinking.

Eco has repeatedly stressed the fact that semiotics must identify the limit of its own investigation in the emergence of a communal dimension of experience in what he comes to recognize as an enrichment, a transformation, and a historical crystallization of the encyclopedia. Semiotics is not interested in how an individual perceives the world, what she or he thinks or desires; nor is semiotics engaged in investigating one's psychological motivations or personal interpretative processes as such. Since an individual is defined by specific competences that characterize one's own knowledge, she or he can be considered only as having been formed by a number of competences negotiated and avowed through intersubjective communication. This communal dimension of experience constitutes the field of semiotic investigation, and this way of delineating the limits of the discipline has theoretical consequences for Eco's subsequent theory of interpretation as well.

Eco presents an organic theory of textual interpretation for the first time in *The Reader in the Story*, suggesting that a semantic model in the

form of encyclopedia implies the possibility of accounting for the multiplicity of interpretations in each given text. According to Peirce, semiosis
occurs through the interaction of three elements – the object, the sign, and
the interpretant – a process that may generate "infinite interpretations"
thanks to the ability of the interpretant to engender yet another interpretant ad infinitum. Indeed, Eco comes to explain the process of how a text
is received by further investigation of the notion of unlimited semiosis
where a reader is called upon to perform an abductive activity. Thus, he
provides a pragmatic definition of interpretation, coherent with Peirce's
theory, in which reading comes to be defined as a process of cooperation
between reader and text. In *The Reader in the Story*, Eco's analysis con-
centrates on what occurs when one activates the semiotic activity that
each text demands from its readers in order to be actualized. Eco does not
consider this pragmatic activity of the reader as central simply because it
fosters the comprehension of the text, but because it is a constitutive part
of the text – only because of this process does a text acquire meaning.
Thus, for Eco, the act of reading is already envisaged and regulated by the
text.[5] In this case, as well, we no longer have an "empirical reader" but a
true "textual strategy" – that is, a series of operations inscribed in a text
and conceived to actualize it.

Eco discusses this notion frequently in his work, but perhaps nowhere
as clearly as in *Interpretation and Overinterpretation*:

A text is a device conceived in order to produce his Model Reader. I repeat that
this reader is not the one who makes the "only right" conjecture. A text can foresee a Model Reader entitled to try infinite conjectures. The empirical reader is
only an actor who makes conjectures about the kind of Model Reader postulated
by the text. Since the intention of the text is basically to produce a Model Reader
able to make conjectures about it, the initiative of the Model Reader consists
in figuring out a Model Author that is not the empirical one and that, in the
end, coincides with the intention of the text (Umberto Eco with Richard Rorty,
Jonathan Culler, and Christine Brook-Rose. Ed. Stefan Collini. *Interpretation
and Overinterpretation*. Cambridge: Cambridge University Press, 1992, p. 64).

It is the Model Reader which constitutes, together with the Model Author,
a communicative scheme that explains both the production and the interpretation of a text without considering the empirical author and the various empirical readers. The Model Reader is thus inscribed in the text,
and somehow coincides with the wealth of knowledge the text demands –
that is, the ability to recognize codes and subcodes, to actualize the
narrative structures of fabula, topic and frames, and finally the capacity to
recognize ideological structures. The text manifesting itself in the surface

is indeed a structure made of unspoken matter, of premises that must be comprehended and integrated by the reader thanks to a more or less complex net of encyclopedic competences demanded by the text itself.

Within this net of competences required by the text, aberrant processes of decoding can take place. With a cooperative attitude and following a non-linear strategy, the reader may decide where to expand and where to block the process of unlimited interpretability. Eco further clarifies his views by stating:

> frames and sememic representations are both based on processes of unlimited semiosis, and as such they call for the responsibility of the addressee. Since the semantic encyclopedia is in itself potentially infinite, semiosis is unlimited, and, from the extreme periphery of a given sememe, the center of any other could be reached, and vice versa (Eco, *The Role of the Reader*, p. 24).

The notion of encyclopedia implies a fair amount of freedom, since transformations are certainly possible in a system open to change and subject to constant metamorphosis. On the other hand, such a notion also offers a regulating principle for the interpretative act, it provides criteria to evaluate different types of decoding or, as Eco stated a few years later, it provides the parameters to distinguish the interpretations from other possible uses, no matter how legitimate, of the same text. In *The Reader in the Story*, such a regulating principle is enacted by the Model Reader who not only comes to limit the freedom of the empirical reader, but also reduces the field of cooperation as well as the possibility of "free readings."

Later, in *The Limits of Interpretation*, Eco takes a further step in the individuation of criteria to limit the possible interpretations of a text and maintains that the most radical results obtained by deconstruction make it necessary for us to emphasize the power implicit in the encyclopedia to limit the possibility of infinite interpretations:

> To say that interpretation (as the basic feature of semiosis) is potentially unlimited does not mean that interpretation has no object and that it "riverruns" for the mere sake of itself. To say that a text potentially has no end does not mean that *every* act of interpretation can have a happy ending. (Eco, *The Limits of Interpretation*, p. 6)

Reacting against exaggerated deconstructionist interpretations, Eco opens up the field of the discussion, and connects his reflection to a larger, classical debate that discusses the nature of interpretation as the search of what he calls the *intentio auctoris* (the intention of the author), the *intentio operis* (the intention of the work), and the *intentio lectoris* (the intention of the reader). While analyzing a text, classical literary interpretation paid attention to the search for

(a) what its author intended to say or (b) what the text says independently of the intentions of its author. Only after accepting the second horn of the dilemma can one ask "whether what is found is (i) what the text says by virtue of its textual coherence and of an original underlying signification system or (ii) what the addressees found in it by virtue of their own system of expectations." (pp. 50–1)

While hardly ever taking the side of the author, and yet giving centrality to the classical debate on this topic, Eco restates the necessity of a kind of regulation of interpretative hermeneutics. Indeed, he also intended to emphasize the necessity of a constant dialectic between the initiative of the reader and the fidelity to the text at a time when most scholars seemed to privilege the role of the reader or the *intentio lectoris*. Most importantly, Eco deemed problematic and even questionable the tendency shown by most deconstructionist thought that considered the text solely as generated by the initiative of the reader and in so doing exasperated and multiplied the possible reading paths in order to underscore the inconsistency of more traditional approaches to literary criticism.

While referring to the American school of deconstruction, Eco certainly has in mind Jacques Derrida and the two essays – *Of Grammatology* and *Writing and Difference*[6] – in which, as he maintains, "Derrida wants to establish a practice (which is philosophical more than critical) for challenging those texts that look as though dominated by the idea of a definite, final, and authorized meaning" (Eco, *The Limits of Interpretation*, p. 33). What challenges is an interpretative practice rather than a text, and what is at stake is the refusal to acknowledge the existence of a critical metalanguage different from the language that is analyzed. According to Eco, the core of Derrida's theory is the notion of the impossibility of a one-to-one relationship between signifier and signified, and the necessity to acknowledge the infinite possibility for both the signifier and the signified to be submitted to a never-ending process aimed at the creation of signification. In short, as Eco concludes, Derrida "wants to show the *power* of language and its ability to say more than it literally pretends to say" (Eco, *The Limits of Interpretation*, p. 33).

It is along this path that Derrida encounters Peirce as the French philosopher acknowledges the fact that Peirce went a long way in the direction of what has been called "deconstruction" with his idea of an infinite semiosis. Such indefiniteness is the criterion that allows one to recognize the very presence of a segnic system. As Peirce states in his classic definition of a sign, when "the series of successive interpretants comes to an end, the sign is thereby rendered imperfect, at least" (Peirce, *Collected Papers,* vol. II, p. 303). The sign thus functions merely because it generates an interpretant that becomes itself a sign. In this way, meaning moves incessantly without having the ability to interrupt the process. Upon explaining the triadic relationship between sign, object, and interpretant, Peirce concludes by saying: "The interpretant is nothing but another representation to which the torch of truth is handed along: and as representation, it has its interpretant again" (p. 339).

Umberto Eco's critique of Derrida's reading of Peirce departs from a different understanding of the infinite possibility of interpretation. Furthermore, Eco does not believe that the infinite drift of deconstruction is a form of unlimited semiosis, as Derrida does. In fact, if it is true that a notion of literal meaning is highly problematic, one cannot deny that in order to explore all possibilities of a text, even those that its author did not conceive, the interpreter must first of all take for granted a zero-degree meaning that can be found in dictionaries, texts that allow one to discover different meanings for a single word in a given historical moment. But Peirce's concept of infinite semiosis does not also imply that interpretation has no object, as Derrida maintains.

Peirce recognized the fact that in the semiotic process we can never know the Dynamical Object as such but can only know it through the Immediate Object. Yet, the Dynamical Object – even though not present in the moment of interpretation – is still the motor of the semiotic process, a process that, by moving from interpretant to interpretant, leads us inevitably to the conclusion, no matter how transitory, of a final logic interpretant, the Habit.[7] The formation of this Habit as a disposition to action stops – or rather, momentarily appeases – the never-ending process of interpretation. In fact "multiple reiterated behavior of the same kind, under similar combinations of percepts and fancies, produces a tendency – the *habit* – actually to behave in a similar way under similar circumstances in the future" (p. 487).

To maintain that a text potentially has no conclusion does not mean that every act of interpretation can reach a happy ending. In essence, the principle of unlimited semiosis requires that each and every time, a sign tells us something *more*, but can never tell us something *else*. The difference between something more and something else is, in substance, the difference between the "interpretation" and the "use" of a text, and in this distinction one finds the limits that every interpretative act must respect. Contrary to what Derrida suggested, Eco agrees with a pragmatic rule by which the meaning of any proposition is only made of the possible practical effects implicated within it. Eco also maintains that the decision to stop or continue the process of interpretation cannot be taken by one interpreter arbitrarily, but must be taken by an entire interpretative community: "from the moment in which the community is pulled to agree with a given interpretation, there is, if not an objective, at least an *intersubjective* meaning which acquires a privilege over any other possible interpretation spelled out without the agreement of the community" (Eco, *The Limits of Interpretation*, p. 40).

Consequently, Eco makes a distinction between interpretations that are acceptable to a vast segment of the community and others that are agreeable to an individual only. Such interpretative agreement becomes the primary aim of the encyclopedia, and it is this very distinction that Derrida disregards completely. Eco believes that as soon as a text is inserted in a historical, social, and cultural context, the local encyclopedia allows one to comprehend the text and establishes the very limits of our conjectures – that is, the limits of the inferential walks or interpretative abductions one can sustain.

According to Umberto Eco, then, in principle, our interpretations can be infinite, as Peirce maintained, and yet, they can be truly considered "interpretations" only if they respect the *intentio operis*. Otherwise, they are simply subjective and unjustified, and thus true and simple "uses" of the text. The limits of interpretation thus coincide with the rights of the text; there are some privileged interpretations and not every interpretation has the same value as another. This idea runs through Eco's speculation throughout the 1990s, and he investigates this further in *Interpretation and Overinterpretation*. This volume is of particular interest for two reasons: it collects the proceedings of a series of lectures Umberto Eco gave as Tanner lecturer at Clare Hall in Cambridge in 1990; and it also records the debate between Eco and a community of scholars who advance different views. Near the conclusion of his lecture on overinterpretation, Eco argues:

It is clear that I am trying to keep a dialectical link between *intentio operis* and *intentio lectoris*. The problem is that, if one perhaps knows what is meant by "intention of the reader," it seems more difficult to define abstractly what is meant by "intention of the text." The text's intention is not displayed by the textual surface. Or, if it is displayed, it is so in the sense of the purloined letter. One has to decide to "see" it. Thus it is possible to speak of the text's intention only as a result of a conjecture on the part of the reader. The initiative of the reader basically consists in making a conjecture about the text's intention. A text is a device conceived in order to produce its model reader...A text can foresee a model reader entitled to try infinite conjectures. (Eco, *Interpretation and Overinterpretation*, p. 64)

He then concludes his lecture by asking himself and his audience "can we still be concerned with the empirical author of a text?" (p. 67). This query is immediately connected to a statement Eco makes in his conclusive remarks in response to his critique of Richard Rorty's reading of *Foucault's Pendulum*, and in answer to Christine Brooke-Rose who defended over-interpretation: "I accept the statement that a text can have many senses. I refuse the statement that a text can have every sense" (p. 141). While Eco seems to agree with Jonathan Culler when he supports the notion that even overinterpretation can be fruitful, he argues that while it is "difficult to say whether an interpretation is a good one, or not," one must "recognize that *it is not true that everything goes*" (p. 144; Eco's emphasis).

If we willfully make what Eco believes to be an arbitrary interpretation, we would merely "use" rather than "interpret" a text. That is, if we were somehow to superimpose on the text our own personal knowledge, our own personal encyclopedia, we would look in the woods for what is, instead, a part of our own private memory, as Eco points out in *Six Walks in the Fictional Woods* (Umberto Eco, *Six Walks in the Fictional Woods*. Cambridge, MA: Harvard University Press, 1994, p. 9). While it is legitimate to take a stroll in these woods to understand one's life, one's present, past, and future, and while it is also legitimate to "use" a text to wander and fantasize about one's own life, Eco notes, one ought to remember that this constitutes a private, not a public activity. "It is not at all forbidden to use a text for daydreaming, and we do this frequently, but daydreaming is not a public affair; it leads us to move within the narrative wood as if it were our own private garden" (p. 10). Eco employs the image of the woods as a metaphor for the narrative text, an image he borrows from Jorge Louis Borges insofar as he takes it to be a garden in which all paths split, and the wanderer or the reader must make a choice at all times (p. 6).

Eco's subject matter is only apparently different in *Kant and the Platypus: Essays on Language and Cognition* (2000). Here, Eco discusses a number of semiotic issues related to cognitive processes, and he consolidates the notion that meaning can be attained and defined through continuous negotiations. All the themes discussed in this text pertain to what Eco had previously defined in *A Theory of Semiotics* as "the lower threshold" (Eco, *A Theory of Semiotics*, pp. 19–21). By the end of the 1990s, the sphere of individuality and personal experience had indeed become increasingly interesting to all those disciplines concerning themselves with the complex notion of semiosis, such as cognitive science, and in this book Eco scrutinizes in detail the notion of a lower threshold in continuity with his previous work. In fact, Eco's main inspiration continues to be Peirce and, in particular, the idea that perception is the primary stage of semiosis, an initial cognitive act from which the whole interpretative process begins. One must, however, underscore the fact that the need to address this threshold of semiotic inquiry is a logical consequence of Eco's earlier work on the limits of interpretation.

To clarify this proposition of ours, one must return to Peirce's distinction between Dynamical Object and Immediate Object. In *A Theory of Semiotics*, Eco almost exclusively focuses upon the Immediate Object. He defines meaning as a "cultural unit," and therefore he must necessarily consider its social and historical character as well. As he states: "if, in a Peircean sense, there is such a thing as a Dynamical Object, we know it only through an Immediate Object. By manipulating signs, we refer to the Dynamical Object as a *terminus ad quem* of semiosis" (Umberto Eco, *Kant and the Platypus: Essays on Language and Cognition*. Trans. Alastair McEwen. New York: Harcourt Brace, 2000, p. 3). This is why in *A Theory of Semiotics* "the lower threshold of semiotics" – the place in which the Dynamical Object acquires centrality – is placed in a secondary position. Subsequently, particularly in *The Limits of Interpretation* where Eco focuses on the interpretational limits that the text poses to its reader and interpreter and develops his critique of Jacques Derrida and deconstruction, his work moves towards the investigation and definition of the Dynamical Object – an analysis of what takes place before the interpretative process conceived in Peircean terms as a "chain of interpretants" begins.

This is the main subject of *Kant and the Platypus*, a work in which Eco studies what happens when a subject – in general terms, whether it be the reader, the interpreter, and so on – comes into contact with the world – that is, with the Dynamical Object. As Eco states:

When we presume a subject that tries to understand what it experiences (and the object – that is to say, the Thing-in-Itself – becomes the *terminus a quo*), then, even before the formation of the chain of interpretants, there comes into play a process of interpreting the world that, especially in the case of novel or unknown objects (such as the platypus at the end of the eighteenth century), assumes an "auroral" form, made up through trial and error; but this is already semiosis in progress, which calls pre-established cultural systems into question. (p. 4)

In this citation, one finds virtually all the subjects Eco investigates in detail in the book: his focus is the perception of the objects of the world moving from a knowledge generated either from our own previous experiences or from a consolidated encyclopedic knowledge. Such knowledge of ours can be undermined by unknown phenomena and, in this case, one may proceed by approximation; that is, one may, for instance, bring the new evidence back to what we already know, and it is philosophically and semiotically interesting to unveil the procedures that we follow to accomplish such recognition. Unquestionably, Umberto Eco proposes a cognitive semiotics that still claims our knowledge is formed through the mediation of cultural schema but does not ignore the fact that something in the world – the Dynamical Object – determines our interpretation:

Yet the Dynamical Object is what drives us to produce semiosis. We produce signs because there is something that demands to be said. To use an expression that is efficacious albeit not very philosophical, the Dynamical Object is Something-that-sets-to-kicking-us and says "Talk!" to us – or "Talk about me!" or again, "Take me into consideration!" (p. 14)

In order to become cultural facts, cognitive processes must develop from the object that is to be interpreted – the Dynamical Object – and then they must meet its "lines of resistance." As a *datum* of the world, the object can come to our perception in an unpredictable way, and at times even impose itself through revisions of segments, no matter how large, of our knowledge.

Thus, if our way of experiencing the world is always tentative, there are cases in which this general principle becomes particularly interesting, as occurs when we encounter an object never seen before or hardly traceable within an already given cultural category. This was the celebrated case of the platypus: it was discovered in Australia at the end of the eighteenth century and its nature was an object of discussion for almost an additional hundred years. Named at first *watermole, duck-mole,* or *duckbilled platypus*, it shares the characteristics of all mammals, but it lays eggs, has no nipples, and nurses its babies. Its history is similar to that of a beaver, for it has a fur coat, the beak of a duck, and webbed "feet." All these odd characteristics make the platypus an animal that foils all scientific or popular classifications. At times, observation of the animal emphasized contradictory aspects of it. Some scientists, for instance, maintained that the platypus was a mammal (and would negate the fact that it laid eggs), while others claimed it to be oviparous (and would dismiss the presence of mammae). For several decades, observers of the platypus could not conceive of what we now accept to be an accurate scientific description of this unusual Australian animal: the platypus is a mammal and an oviparous contemporarily, and it belongs to the Monotremes. As Umberto Eco maintains, it is almost as if the story of the platypus was "a splendid example of how observation sentences can be made only in the light of a conceptual framework or of a theory that gives them a sense, in other words, that the first attempt to understand what is seen is to consider the experience in relation to a previous categorial system"(pp. 248 – 9).

At the same time, though, the observational data have undermined the pre-existent categorial framework, moving from some limitations posed by the object itself. Scientists agreed on the fact that the platypus was a strange animal that resembled, at the same time, the beaver, the duck, and the mole, and yet they also agreed that the platypus was certainly dissimilar to a horse, a cat, or even a plant. It was impossible to negate some characteristics, while on others the scientific community debated for a long time. This striking example of difficult classification led Eco to conclude that knowledge is continuously negotiated; categories can be redefined constantly, and new phenomena can be recognized by moving from the new category. Yet, we can only negotiate by moving from an object that inevitably defines its own lines of resistance: "There were eighty-odd years of negotiation, but the negotiations always revolved around resistances and the grain of the *continuum*. Given these resistances, the decision, certainly contractual in nature, to acknowledge that certain features were undeniable, was obligatory" (p. 250).

To negotiate meanings is an activity that permeates various aspects of our cultural existence. In three different volumes, two in English and one in Italian – *Experiences in Translation; Mouse or Rat? Translation as Negotiation*; and *Saying Almost the Same Thing: Experiences in Translation*[8] – Eco demonstrates how negotiation is of utmost relevance even in the act of translation. Translation may entail moving from one language to another (what Eco calls "translation proper"); or it may involve what he calls "intersemiotic translation," such as the adaptation of a novel by a film, a musical score that becomes a dance, and so forth. Eco prefers to term the second type of translation "transmutations" or "adaptations" to distinguish them from "translations proper" – the main object of his inquiries.

To translate means to start from a text that belongs to a specific linguistic system and to build another one, its "double," in yet another linguistic system. If the translation is adequate, this latter text should produce effects that are analogous to those produced by the source text from the syntactical, semantic, stylistic, metric, and even emphatic point of view. Translation is, however, a fairly complex activity and Eco maintains that every translation presents inevitable margins of infidelity that depend on the translator and her or his continuous activity of *negotiation*:

Numerous are the elements that come into play in the process of negotiation; on one side, there is the original text, with its own rights, sometimes an author who claims rights over the whole process, along with the cultural framework in which the original text is born; on the other side, there is the destination text, the cultural milieu in which it is expected to be read, and even the publishing industry, which can recommend different translation criteria, according to whether the translated text is to be put in an academic context or in a popular one (Umberto Eco, *Saying Almost the Same Thing: Experiences in Translation*. Milan: Bompiani, 2003, p. 18).[9]

In every process of translation, one negotiates losses of meaning, one violates and adjusts the various semantic implications, and so on. Yet, in any case, this can occur only bearing in mind that to translate means to respect the principle of equivalence, no matter how imperfect, between a source text and a target text, between the text to be translated and the one that is the result of such translation. It is indeed the very principle of equivalence that undergoes a constant process of negotiation, and not merely the process of translation itself, whether it be from one natural language to another or from a linguistic system to another, or else from a segnic system to another. As Umberto Eco remarks in the opening of the introduction to the Italian volume of his essays on translation:

What does it mean to translate? The first and reassuring answer should be: to say the same thing in another language. If it did not mean that, in the first place we would experience numerous problems in establishing what "to say the same thing" truly means, and we would not know this because of all those operations that we call paraphrasis, definition, explanation, or rephrasing, not to mention the so-called sinonimic substitutions. In the second place, we would experience numerous problems because we do not know what the "thing" is when we are faced with a text requiring translation. Finally, in some circumstances, one wonders even what "to say" means. (p. 9; authors' translation)

It is apparent, then, that what constantly undergoes negotiation is the very notion of equivalence. This leads Eco to declare that "even though knowing that one never says the same thing, one may say *almost* the same thing" and to equivocate even on the meaning and flexibility of the word "almost" itself (p. 10).

Once again, negotiation rests at the very heart of any process of translation. In Eco's conclusion, he emphatically connects his reflections on translation to his long-standing speculation on the processes of interpretation when he states that:

faithfulness is not a method which results in an acceptable translation. It is the decision to believe that translation is possible, it is our engagement in isolating what is for us the deep sense of a text, and it is the goodwill that prods us to negotiate the best solution for every line. Among the synonyms of *faithfulness* the word *exactitude* does not exist. Instead there is loyalty, devotion, allegiance, piety. (Umberto Eco, *Mouse or Rat? Translation as Negotiation.* London: Weidenfeld & Nicolson, 2003, p. 192)

Back to the dictionary, back to the encyclopedia, back to interpretation, back to negotiation of the limits of any cognitive process: this is the trajectory of our journey through the Echian woods. We began our walk by identifying in *A Theory of Semiotics* the means by which Eco aimed at defining the field of semiotic inquiry, its methods, and its theoretical foundations – in short, its thresholds. In discussing the limits of the discipline, we have reviewed Eco's famous distinction between the static dictionary-like model, and the encyclopedia – that is, a fairly dynamical cognitive model. Through the notion of encyclopedia, a connecting concept between the theory of knowledge and the theory of interpretation, we managed to disentangle a number of other issues investigated by Eco in several different works. Ultimately, we have focused our attention on the issue of interpretation because of its inherent theoretical relevance, as well as its importance in critical and theoretical debates up to the 1990s. We have also underscored the centrality of interpretation to Umberto Eco's reflections on translation in his more recent theoretical works. As Eco relentlessly repeats in his writings, the problem of interpretation rests at the very heart of his entire work, a theoretical obsession of his. The theory of interpretation also remains an important focus in Eco's latest novel, *The Mysterious Flame of Queen Loana.* As the main character of the novel traumatically and suddenly loses memory of his personal past, he can still recollect events and even details of a collective past – the past of a collectivity, of his generation. Indeed, this fifth novel Eco has produced may be the most striking metaphor for Eco's beloved notion of encyclopedia and may offer fruitful and heuristic suggestions to the reader about the impact of semiotics upon his entire intellectual career.

NOTES

1 For an important discussion of the role that the concept of encylopedia plays in the shaping of Eco's semiotic theory, see Patrizia Violi, "Individual and Communal Encyclopedias," in Norma Bouchard and Veronica Pravadelli (eds.), *Umberto Eco's Alternative: The Politics of Culture and the Ambiguities of Interpretation* (New York: Peter Lang, 1998), pp. 25–38.

2 All references to Charles S. Peirce's *Collected Papers* come from this standard edition as per international convention.

3 This particular sentence, translated into English by the authors from p. 109 of the original Italian edition of this work, is not included in the English edition, *Semiotics and the Philosophy of Language* (Bloomington: Indiana University Press, 1984).

4 See Gilles Deleuze and Felix Guattari, *Rhizome* (Paris: Minuit, 1976).

5 Violi's "Individual and Communal Encyclopedias," in Bouchard and Pravadelli (eds.), *Umberto Eco's Alternative*, underlines how, when formulating his notion of encyclopedia, Eco does not intentionally consider that subjective sphere constituting an individual perspective on the world and states that the "individual competence" is "a type of knowledge necessary for an individual to become an active participant in a given language and culture" (p. 32).

6 Jacques Derrida, *Of Grammatology*, trans. Gayatri Chakrovorty Spivak (Baltimore, MD: The Johns Hopkins University Press, corrected edn., 1998); and *Writing and Difference*, trans. Alan Bass (Chicago: University of Chicago Press, 1980). It should be noted that in his discussion of deconstruction, Eco only makes direct reference to *Of Grammatology*.

7 The difference between Dynamical Object and Immediate Object is a fairly complex aspect of Peirce's theory to which Eco repeatedly returns. Peirce believes that "it is necessary to distinguish the *Immediate Object*, or the object as the sign represents it, from the *Dynamical Object*, or really efficient but not immediately present object" (Peirce, *Collected Papers*, vol. VIII, p. 343).

8 The Italian volume on translation, *Dire quasi la stessa cosa: esperienza di traduzione* (*Saying Almost the Same Thing: Experiences in Translation*) appeared after the English volume *Experiences in Translation* and before *Mouse or Rat? Translation as Negotiation*.

9 This passage and others subsequently cited in this chapter are translated by the authors from the Italian edition of *Saying Almost the Same Thing*; page references refer to this edition and to neither of the English volumes in translation.

CHAPTER 3

Eco's scientific imagination

Guy Raffa

As Umberto Eco has declared, "there is something artistic in a scientific discovery and there is something scientific in that which the naive call 'brilliant intuitions of the artist.' What they share is the felicity of Abduction" (Eco, *The Limits of Interpretation*, p. 159). No Italian novelist and thinker in recent years has contributed more to the crossing and redrawing of disciplinary boundaries than Eco, whose work strategically engages with transformative moments in the history and philosophy of science. Examples from Eco's writings – journalistic, literary, and academic – amply demonstrate his observation. Science, as both object of study and method of inquiry, plays an important role in his fiction, particularly in his first three novels – *The Name of the Rose*; *Foucault's Pendulum*; and *The Island of the Day Before*. While not as engaged with science as Eco's previous novels, *Baudolino* and *The Mysterious Flame of Queen Loana* nonetheless touch on scientific themes. In *Baudolino* a series of machines – a pump (to create a vacuum), mirrors of Archimedes (to set fire to attacking forces), a Dionysius ear (to overhear conversations) – are implicated in the mystery of the Grasal and the death of the emperor Frederick; in *The Mysterious Flame of Queen Loana*, Yambo (a.k.a. Giambattista Bodoni), the novel's protagonist, suffers from a scientifically challenging event – a stroke that has left him without autobiographical memory. Thus, science serves as a focal point for all of Eco's fiction, just as his theoretical works take account of the state of scientific work on a number of topics.

William of Baskerville, the erudite and inquisitive medieval investigator in *The Name of the Rose*, attempts to solve a series of mysterious deaths by using his scientific acumen to penetrate the abbey's labyrinthine library, an architectural embodiment of mathematical symbolism. In *Foucault's Pendulum* three editors at a modern Italian publishing house exploit the combinatory prowess of computer technology, in conjunction with all manner of esoteric doctrine, to rewrite history by inventing an entertaining "Plan" that, in the hands of true believers, turns deadly serious. A similarly creative yet unsettling contamination of science with pseudoscience and Hermetic doctrine animates the quest of Roberto della Griva and other seventeenth-century adventurers in *The Island of the Day Before* to solve the problem of longitudes. Taken together, these novels not only celebrate an investigative procedure – the "felicity of Abduction" – common to scientific discovery and artistic creation, they also show how the line between beneficial and detrimental interpretive practices can be a very fine one indeed.

CREATIVE ABDUCTION

Eco defines abduction, in semiotic terms, as "the tentative and hazardous tracing of a system of signification rules which will allow the sign to acquire its meaning" (Eco, *Semiotics and the Philosophy of Language*, p. 40). *Hazardous* is an apt word in Eco's definition, for abduction involves taking a gamble (*hazard* derives from a game of chance played with dice), and sometimes, if the gamble does not pay off, the danger of adopting this hazardous method is fully realized. A concept formulated by Charles S. Peirce in relation to (but distinct from) deductive and inductive reasoning, abduction is an inferential process followed when some strange event cannot be explained satisfactorily by a ready-made rule (deduction) or by experience in the form of sufficient empirical evidence (induction). The investigator in such cases may be tempted to "think outside the box," to put forth a working hypothesis based less on sound reason than on a gut feeling (intuition) or on the aesthetic appeal of a particular solution. Errors and even pure luck may play a fruitful role in the abductive process. Subsequent events naturally determine the wisdom or folly of the investigator's abduction, but Eco reminds us that a good abduction, even if it is technically wrong, may "endure for long periods, until a more suitable, more economical, and more powerful abduction comes onto the scene" (Eco, *Kant and the Platypus*, pp. 96–7).

For Eco, abduction serves an important function in many if not all semiotic phenomena, from criminal investigations and medical diagnoses to literary interpretations and scientific discoveries (Eco, *The Limits of Interpretation*, p. 159). The astronomers Nicholas Copernicus (1473 – 1543) and Johann Kepler (1571–1630) provide two revolutionary examples of abduction used to advance science. When Kepler, in "an act of imaginative courage" (Eco, *Semiotics and the Philosophy of Language*, p. 40), posits an elliptical orbit for Mars, he proceeds according to what Eco calls undercoded abduction: "when the rule must be selected among a series of equiprobable alternatives" (p. 42). Faced with an even greater challenge, Copernicus must resort to "creative abduction," a method employed when "one is not sure that the explanation one has selected is a 'reasonable' one" (p. 43). Perceiving the Ptolemaic system as "inelegant, without harmony," Copernicus decides, after an "intuition of heliocentrism," the sun *ought to be* at the center of the universe because only in this way the created world would have displayed an admirable symmetry" (p. 42). Creative abduction, frequently used for interpreting poetry and "solving criminal cases" (p. 43), plays a special role in Eco's literary works insofar as his characters (and readers) are faced with some mysterious event, at times even a crime. Abduction, Eco reminds us, can also refer to kidnapping, suggesting that the investigator (reader and character) "must go and 'abduct,' or 'borrow,' a Rule from elsewhere" (Eco, *The Limits of Interpretation*, p. 158): in certain cases, a theory must be taken hostage to discover how or why a victim has been abducted (or worse) and by whom.

THE LABYRINTH

William of Baskerville, a disciple of Roger Bacon (*c.* 1220–*c.* 1292) and contemporary of William of Ockham (*c.* 1285–*c.* 1347), two illustrious Franciscans who taught at Oxford University, presents himself as a bona fide man of science (natural philosophy) as it was understood and practiced in the Middle Ages. Adso, the Benedictine novice in William's charge, is amazed by the "wondrous machines" his master carries in a bag and occasionally tinkers with during their time together at the abbey. In conversations with Adso, William not only extols the virtues of such instruments as the clock, astrolabe, and magnet, but he also endorses Bacon's faith in the "science of machines" eventually to include several inventions that would in fact come to mark the modern era: swift ships powered by some source other than sails or oars, "self-propelled wagons," flying machines with artificial wings, small devices capable of lifting heavy objects, and vehicles capable of traveling on the bottom of the sea (Eco, *The Name of the Rose*, p. 17). William himself raises more than a few eyebrows when he dons a pair of thick reading glasses in the library. This technological aid, William explains to the abbey's master glazier, is but one of the beneficent outcomes of "holy magic," the scientific impulse "not only to discover new things but also to rediscover many secrets of nature…" (p. 87). William's scientific world view, which distinguishes him from the other residents and guests of the abbey, provides him with the tools for discovering how and why monks begin to die from unnatural causes.

The novel meticulously establishes the abbey's Aedificium as an architectural embodiment of medieval mathematical symbolism even before William is called upon to apply his erudition and wits to investigate the murders that all seem somehow related to the secrets of this imposing building. Housing the scriptorium and library on the upper two floors (with the kitchen and refectory on the ground floor), the Aedificium makes a visual impression consistent with its reputation as one of the greatest centers of learning in all Christendom. Adso describes it as an octagonal structure that from a distance looks like a tetragon (cube) due to its quadrangular base, while three rows of windows give it a "triangular" spiritual quality. On closer inspection, he realizes that from each of the four corners rises a heptagonal tower (seven-sided), but only five of the seven sides show on the outside, thus making the towers appear as pentagons. Good medieval schoolboy that he is, Adso sees in these shapes and numbers the sort of moral and theological values that Eco documents in his earlier work on medieval aesthetics, *Art and Beauty in the Middle Ages*: the tetragon is "a perfect form, which expresses the sturdiness and impregnability of the City of God," whereas four is "the number of the Gospels," five corresponds to "the number of the zones of the world," and seven to "the number of the gifts of the Holy Ghost" (pp. 21, 22). In sum, every part of the structure reflects the harmonious mapping of the divine order onto the natural world according to the idea that "number is the principle of the universe" (Umberto Eco, *Art and Beauty in the Middle Ages*. Trans. Hugh Bredin. New Haven, CT: Yale University Press, 1986, p. 35).

Designed as a labyrinth, the renowned library on the top floor of the Aedificium shows that mathematics serves more than just a symbolic purpose in the building. Informing Adso that "without mathematics you cannot build labyrinths," William likewise employs the "mathematical sciences" to map the arrangement of rooms and passages in the library (Eco, *The Name of the Rose*, p. 215). Although his initial approach – to use a magnet (with cork floating in a basin of water) – proves impractical, he soon realizes that they can imagine the inside of the building through knowledge of its external architecture: taking into account the geometry of the Aedificium and the placement of windows, William and Adso are thus able to construct a diagram showing all fifty-six rooms of the labyrinthine library. However, possessing a mathematically accurate map, while necessary, will not suffice for successfully negotiating the library. Because the library, as a labyrinth, poses multiple challenges, "you might enter," the Abbot warns William, "and you might not emerge" (p. 38). Alinardo, the oldest monk in the abbey, who provides tantalizing clues about its history, reiterates this warning when he cites a Latin inscription (found in the church of St. Sabinus in Piacenza, Italy) claiming the labyrinth as a symbol of the world: *intranti largus, redeunti sed nimis artus* (wide for one who is entering it, but too narrow for one who would leave it) (p. 158).

This combination of mathematical precision in its structure with the bewildering effects it can have on visitors is what makes the labyrinth such a compelling sign of the inextricability of order and chaos. Even young Adso quickly grasps that their familiarity with the Aedificium from the outside hardly prevents them from becoming disoriented once they are inside the library. Labyrinths, after all, possess a dual nature: "they simultaneously incorporate order and disorder, clarity and confusion, unity and multiplicity, artistry and chaos."[1] This duality, as William and Adso learn, is perspective-dependent, according to whether they are inside the library trying to reach a particular location or outside the building with a privileged view of the labyrinth's grand design. Now armed with a map identifying the library's fifty-six rooms, William and Adso still find the labyrinth a difficult place to traverse, particularly at night, due to the asymmetrical arrangement of openings between rooms as well as the presence of a mirror and vision-inducing substances. The library, William announces with a mixture of chagrin and admiration, represents "the maximum of confusion achieved with the maximum of order: it seems a sublime calculation" (p. 217).

In addition to the mathematical sciences, then, it takes the felicity of Abduction – along with a strong measure of serendipity – for William and Adso to succeed in unraveling the secrets of the labyrinthine library. This comes as no surprise, for Eco writes in the *Postscript to "The Name of the Rose"* that the labyrinth is itself "an abstract model of conjecturality" (p. 525), a place requiring interpretive prowess to find the center (and at times the way out, as well) or to overcome the danger lurking within. One of their first breaks occurs as a result of Adso's fortunate clumsiness. Holding a lamp to enable William to read the Greek text on a sheet of parchment, Adso accidentally burns the back of the page, thus revealing a series of strange signs. To decipher this secret message, coded in a zodiacal alphabet, William summons the full powers of his abductive reasoning. Faced with the overwhelming task of testing numerous cryptographic systems, he informs Adso that "the first rule in deciphering a message is to guess what it means" (p. 166). When Adso objects that the rule's logic appears circular, William responds with a brief lesson on abduction: "Not exactly. Some hypotheses can be formed on the possible first words of the message, and then you see whether the rule you infer from them can apply to the rest of the text" (p. 166). He goes on to explain that they must invent a "rule of correspondence" in their heads and then see if it bears fruitful results (p. 166). Applying this abductive method, William decodes the instructions for discovering the "secret of the end of Africa," the Latin words *manus supra idolum age primum et septimum de quatuor*, translated by Adso as "The hand over the idol works on the first and seventh of the four" (p. 209). They later learn that the plan of the library corresponds to a map of the world, with rooms arranged according to the geographic origin of books contained therein and regions spelled out with letters from verses of the Apocalypse placed over entrances to the rooms (pp. 313–14). This knowledge enables them to identify the *finis Africae* (end of Africa) as a room marked with the phrase *Super thronos viginti quatuor*, the letter *S* of *Super* (colored red) standing as the last letter of the word *leones* (lions) – used to indicate Africa (pp. 318 – 19). Of course, without knowing what the writer means by the phrase "the first and the seventh of the four," the riddle remains unsolved.

William and Adso eventually unravel this mystery through a combination of abduction, bad grammar, and chance. After the first two deaths, one monk (Adelmo) falling to his death during a snowstorm and the other monk (Venantius) drowned in a vat of pig's blood, Alinardo ascribes these events to the punishments of the Apocalypse (announced by seven trumpets), unleashed because someone "has broken the seals of the labyrinth…" (p. 159). When Alinardo later repeats his theory, William conjectures that the killer, perhaps inspired by the manner of the first death (Adelmo's suicide), indeed arranged for his succeeding crimes to follow the apocalyptic pattern; this is indeed born out when they find Berengar's body in the baths (death by water). After two more murders consistent with trumpets four and five (stars in the form of a head-splitting armillary sphere, and poison with the power of a thousand scorpions), William and Adso follow their abductive hypothesis to the stables, since trumpet six announces horses. Here Adso, as if by chance, recalls an earlier visit, during which Salvatore, whose Latin is poor, referred to the third horse as "tertius equi," or "third of horse" (p. 457). William now realizes that the message – in true metalinguistic fashion – tells them to push the "first" and "seventh" letters of *quatuor*, the Latin word for "four" (p. 458).

Therefore it is an error (Salvatore's ungrammatical Latin), serendipitously recalled because of a useful abduction (the apocalyptic conjecture brings Adso and William to the stables), that leads to truth. Yet even this truth is tainted with falsehood and failure. When William and Adso have a showdown with Jorge, the blind guardian of the abbey's secrets whom they now know to be the killer, they learn that the deaths only followed the apocalyptic pattern by coincidence – all, that is, except the last. Malachi spoke of "the power of a thousand scorpions" because Jorge, once he knew William found Alinardo's apocalyptic explanation plausible, became convinced that there was in fact a divine plan directing the deaths and therefore threatened Malachi that he would die according to the plan if he tried to read the forbidden manuscript containing the only copy of the second book of Aristotle's *Poetics* (on comedy). William grasps the cruel irony: "So, then…I conceived a false pattern to interpret the moves of the guilty man, and the guilty man fell in with it. And it was this same false pattern that put me on your trail" (p. 470). Far worse, William and Adso not only fail to recover the book (partially ingested by Jorge before he throws it into the flames), but the entire library is destroyed as the Aedificium, despite its tetragonous appearance (suggesting the "sturdiness and impregnability of the City of God" [p. 21]), burns to the ground. In this battle at least, the building's divine geometry and William's enlightened scientific mind are no match for the ruthless determination of a blind reactionary.

For all William of Baskerville's erudition and curiosity, the setting of *The Name of the Rose* (a Benedictine abbey in 1327) restricts its overt scientific content. Treating intellectual and cultural developments in later periods, Eco's next two novels, *Foucault's Pendulum* and *The Island of the Day Before*, engage with science in a more direct and sustained manner. At the same time, these novels hold nothing back in depicting the mayhem unleashed when the felicity of Abduction crosses the line separating creative yet valid conjectures from the sort of interpretive excesses Eco variously labels "use," "Hermetic semiosis," or "overinterpretation."[2]

COMPUTER AND CABALA

The pendulum of Eco's second novel is named for Jean Bernard Léon Foucault, a French physicist who in 1851 demonstrated the rotation of the earth by charting the oscillations of a pendulum suspended from the Panthéon in Paris. Within the modern setting of *Foucault's Pendulum* (most of the story unfolds in the 1970s and early 1980s), the pendulum is suspended from a ceiling of the Conservatoire des Arts et Métiers in Paris, a museum of technology containing a vast and varied collection of machines, devices, and instruments, primarily from the age of the Enlightenment through the early twentieth century. Since 1855 the pendulum has been housed in a part of the museum that was once the medieval church of

Saint-Martin-des-Champs. The opening scene takes place in this museum as Casaubon (the first-person narrator) awaits the start of a climactic ritual – recounted towards the end of the novel – in which the pendulum serves a decidedly sinister function. Through the eyes of Casaubon, who tries to behave like both a detective (Sam Spade) and a scientist, we see in these framing episodes how the irrational and mystical forces behind the events that have led him to the pendulum exert their influence even, and especially, on the history of science and technology as it is presented in the museum, from the periscope (in which he hides when the museum closes for the night) to such objects as automobiles, planes, engines, mirrors, laboratory equipment, counting machines, electrical devices, glassworks, and even a sewing machine.

Casaubon first learns of this museum (and the pendulum) during the course of his work on the history of metals. He is hired by a Milanese publishing house to search libraries and archives for illustrations to accompany a book that Signor Garamond, the eccentric owner of the press who wants the book's scientific content to "grab the reader by the throat," rechristens *The Wonderful Adventure of Metals* (Umberto Eco, *Foucault's Pendulum*. Trans. William Weaver. New York: Harcourt Brace Jovanovich, 1988, p. 241). Although Casaubon's work on the project occasions research in Germany and France (including a short stay in Paris), he fails to see the pendulum during this trip because he carelessly plans to visit the museum on a day (Monday) when it is closed. He does, however, return with historical illustrations that show "science and magic going arm in arm," an idea particularly attractive to Garamond insofar as the book "must be, most of all, the story of science's mistakes" (p. 255). Casaubon takes notice of this unholy alliance of science and magic in the present when he examines the display window and inventory of a Parisian bookshop: "on one side, books on computers and the electronics of the future; on the other, occult sciences. And it was the same inside: Apple and cabala" (p. 255). Not coincidentally, computers and cabala join forces in enabling Casaubon and his fellow editors at the publishing house (Belbo and Diotallevi) to create the "Plan," a reinterpretation of history in terms of esoteric and Hermetic doctrine in accordance with a presumed secret plot by spiritual descendants of the Templars, the medieval order of crusading knights, to rule the world.

This reciprocity of computer and cabala is established in the novel even before the three editors invent the Plan. Diotallevi, an ardent believer in Jewish mysticism, initially objects to the computer on the grounds that it can rapidly (and soullessly) change the order of letters. To arrive one day at the "original Torah," he insists, letters of the book must be rearranged only by learned believers working with traditional methods over long periods of time, by someone, that is, along the lines of Abraham Abulafia, whose "*Hokhmath ha-Zeruf* was at once the science of the combination of letters and the science of the purification of the heart" (pp. 33–4). Belbo promptly names the computer after this medieval cabalist (a contemporary of Thomas Aquinas) who authored widely read books dealing with "Sacred Names and the letters of the alphabet and their combinations, both comprehensible and incomprehensible."[3]

This is not the only time Eco has addressed the metaphysical ramifications of computer technology. In his work on medieval aesthetics, he compares Scholastic theology – Aquinas' system in particular – to computers: "when all the data have been fed in, every question necessarily receives a complete answer," concluding that "a medieval Summa is, so to speak, a medieval computer" (Eco, *Art and Beauty in the Middle Ages*, p. 26). And with the rapid increase in e-mail and internet use since the mid-1990s, he gained notoriety for "MAC vs. DOS," a humorous description of computer operating systems in terms of religious doctrine that first appeared in his back-page column for *L'Espresso* (September 30, 1994) and is now included in an anthology of these columns entitled *Minerva's Matchbook* (1999). Here Eco argues that Macintosh, with its user-friendly icons and step-by-step instructions allowing salvation for all, is decidedly Catholic (counter-reformist, to be precise), whereas DOS, which requires painful personal decisions under the assumption that not all are within reach of salvation, is Protestant (Calvinist). The advent of Windows, he allows, represents a sort of Anglican schism that brings DOS closer to the more tolerant Macintosh Catholicism, with subsequent releases of Windows (95 and 98) bringing both systems closer still. Eco concludes the essay by playfully associating computer machine language (the underlying code) with Jewish thought, one aspect of which – cabala – leads Belbo from *Foucault's Pendulum*, as we have seen, to name his computer Abulafia.

The reinforcing influences of computer and cabala are embedded in the novel's textual arrangement and presentation of information. Major chapters are titled with the ten Sefirot, the cabalistic spirits which, combined with the twenty-two "elemental" letters of the Hebrew alphabet, constitute "the foundations of all creation" (Scholem, *Kabbalah*, p. 23). An illustration of the Sefirot appropriately appears before the title page of the novel in both the original Italian edition and in the English translation. Computerwise, Casaubon learns much of what he narrates from Belbo's word-processed files, twelve of which appear on the novel's pages just as they would on a computer screen or a print-out. Also appearing as print-outs in the novel are the steps of a computer program (fourteen lines of basic programming code) that discovers and prints all possible combinations of four letters, and the output (720 combinations) of a program to find anagrams of the six letters in the Italian transcription of the Hebrew name for God (IAHVEH).

Most important, Belbo, Casaubon, and Diotallevi celebrate "the nuptials of Tradition and the Electronic Machine" (Eco, *Foucault's Pendulum*, p. 369) by spawning the Plan, a product of abductive reasoning that is hardly felicitous but certainly creative. Colonel Ardenti, a reactionary occultist possessing a copy of a parchment believed to date from the fourteenth century, sets into motion this lethal Plan when, appearing almost as a negative double to William from *The Name of the Rose*, he decodes and interprets the document according to a wild and far-reaching abduction: history can be reduced to a vast conspiracy of the medieval Templars (and their later followers) to transmit over the centuries a secret that will enable them to avenge the execution of their leader, Jacques de Molay, and attain world dominion. Accordingly, Ardenti decodes one text written in a parody of a Semitic language and fills in missing letters and words from a second text (written in fourteenth-century French) to arrive at a message indicating the dispersal of the Templars into six groups, with meetings at one of six special sites every 120 years (from 1344 to 1944). With the help of the computer and an abundance of ideas from occultist authors and their own research, the three editors adopt Ardenti's interpretation and elaborate on it (playfully at first) by feeding Hermetic data into Abulafia (along with an occasional neutral line, such as "Minnie Mouse is Mickey's fiancée" [p. 375]) and having the computer randomize the information. They then use these random results to "refine" their rewriting of history in agreement with the perverse logic of the Plan. Imagining that the goal of the Plan is to harness the energy of currents beneath the earth's surface, the editors decide that "the entire history of science had to be reread. Even the space race became comprehensible, with those crazy satellites that did nothing but photograph the crust of the globe to localize invisible tensions, submarine tides, currents of warmer air. And speak among themselves, speak to the Tower, to Stonehenge..." (p. 466). Now that Casaubon is "addicted," Diotallevi physically "corrupted," and Belbo "converted" as a result of this unhealthy interpretive game (p. 468), the boundary between science and magic quickly dissolves.

However, not every use of the computer and not every interpretive act has negative consequences in the novel. When Casaubon needs a password to access Belbo's computer files, he benignly employs abductive reasoning by trying to enter the mind of his colleague. Knowing Belbo is threatened because of the Plan, Casaubon imagines his friend would choose a password somehow connected with their story. He therefore tries (with no luck) the ten Sefirot, symbolic numbers (including 666, number of the Beast), and the name of God (the Tetragrammaton), which he recalls was the subject of office conversation when the computer was first installed. It is to test this conjecture that Casaubon writes the computer program to print all 720 combinations of the name in its Italian transcription (IAHVEH), from which he then chooses significant results (the 36th and 120th anagrams, counting from both left and right) for the password. Still unsuccessful, he consoles himself with the thought that his stubborn attachment to "an elegant but false hypothesis" is something that happens to everyone, even "to the best scientists" (p. 40). After Casaubon tries a simpler entry and fails, serendipity trumps clever abduction when, frustrated and drunk (he has been drinking whiskey), he at last prevails by angrily answering the computer's prompt – "Do you have the password?" – with the brutal truth: "NO" (p. 42).

Abduction itself bears better results when Lia, Casaubon's companion, sees the message of Provins (which formed the basis of the Plan) for what it is: a note by an ordinary merchant with the amount of money he is to receive from a list of deliveries. By relying on local history (a tourist guide) and a manual of abbreviations used at the time (rather than on a web of conspiracy theories), Lia shows that places named in the message refer not to foreign locations (where the Templars supposedly took refuge) but to buildings and streets in the town of Provins itself; she further shows that certain abbreviations, which the Colonel (and the three Plan writers) took to stand for numbers of years, refer instead to amounts of money for the merchant's goods: hay, cloth, and six bunches of the red roses for which Provins was famous. Yet, by this time in the story, Lia's very healthy investigative work, like that of William in *The Name of the Rose*, is too little too late. Belbo, literally abducted by Diabolicals who believe the Plan to be true, is hanged so that his dead body becomes the new fixed point of Léon Foucault's pendulum. Diotallevi dies the very same night from cancer, which he considers divine justice for his role in the Plan (as he manipulated combinations of letters of the Book, so the cells in his body undergo changes in shape and order). And the fate of Casaubon, as he awaits the arrival of the murderous Diabolicals, hangs in the balance. The Plan that was born of the "nuptials of Tradition and the Electronic Machine" thus wreaks havoc on its human creators.

LONGITUDES AND LOVE

In *The Limits of Interpretation* Eco discusses two models of interpretation, each of which risks degenerating into a type of fundamentalism: at one extreme "every text speaks of the rational and univocal discourse of God," while in the other direction "every text speaks of the irrational and ambiguous discourse of Hermes" (p. 20). Both forms of interpretive excess are dramatized in Eco's fiction but their relative weights vary with the novel. Forces obsessed with the "rational and univocal discourse of God" – namely, Jorge and the Inquisition – inflict the most damage and pose the greatest threat to social and scientific progress in *The Name of the Rose*. Conversely, the Diabolicals and (through their complicity) the three Plan writers in *Foucault's Pendulum* bring about ruin by worshipping the irrational, Hermetic side of Eco's fundamentalist coin. These two fundamentalisms combine to contaminate the scientific quest that is at the heart of *The Island of the Day Before*: to solve "the mystery of longitude" (Umberto Eco, *The Island of the Day before*. Trans. William Weaver. New York: Harcourt Brace Jovanovich, 1995, p. 188), the chief navigational problem of the seventeenth century.

While it was easy, as one character explains, to determine latitudes by using astronomical instruments that measure the altitude of a star above the horizon and its distance from the zenith, "every means conceived to establish longitude has always proved faulty" (p. 190). And this was no small matter insofar as whoever discovered a way to calculate longitudes would become "master of the oceans" (p. 219), a powerful advantage in this age of exploration and colonization. Knowledge of longitudes would also enable a navigator to find a place visited on an earlier voyage, such as the Solomon Islands, which were renowned for riches but still unsuccessfully revisited nearly a century after their discovery (p. 190). The history of the longitude problem, finally solved when John Harrison invented the marine chronometer in the eighteenth century, has been entertainingly told by Dava Sobel.[4] Her book provides historical corroboration for several methods – some quite bizarre – described or attempted by characters in Eco's novel. Two characters in particular, Dr. Byrd and Father Caspar, put their formidable scientific expertise to the test by attempting to solve this mystery of longitude. However, their efforts are harmed by one or another of the interpretive fundamentalisms described by Eco. Each holds a set of beliefs – the "irrational and ambiguous discourse of Hermes" in Byrd's case, the "rational and univocal discourse of God" in Caspar's case – that gives rise to creative yet flawed interpretations of the natural world and therefore severely compromises their science.

Roberto della Griva, the Italian nobleman whose papers form the basis of the narrative, comes to know Dr. Byrd aboard the *Amaryllis*, a Dutch vessel sailing west from Europe with the (secret) aim of testing the doctor's "new and prodigious means to determine the meridian, based on the use of the Powder of Sympathy" (p. 193). Roberto, having been caught in a web of French political intrigue, is sent to spy on the English physician (and thereby evade capital punishment) because he, too, is a presumed expert on this Sympathy Powder, so named because it "is based on the principles of universal analogy and sympathy" that Eco elsewhere identifies as distinguishing features of Renaissance Hermeticism (Eco, *The Limits of Interpretation*, p. 24). The substance is also known as "weapon salve" because, applied to a sword that has caused a wound, it is believed to heal the patient by drawing the iron particles in the wound back to the blade. Roberto himself witnesses the successful application of this "weapon salve" in his youth, and again later as a young man in Paris, this time when a cloth stained with the injured man's blood is dipped in a basin containing the dissolved powder. Here the practitioner is Monsieur d'Igby, an Englishman "rich in medical and naturalist knowledge" (Eco, *The Island of the Day Before,* p. 163) who espouses theories of the Void in the Parisian salons frequented by Roberto and traces the Sympathy Powder back to authoritative figures in the Hermetic tradition (Paracelsus and Agrippa).[5] Taking the theory of universal sympathy as "an allegory of falling in love" (p. 171), Roberto makes an impassioned speech on the Powder of Sympathy and the Sympathy of Love that earns him attention not only from the object of his affections (Lilia) but also from the French authorities, who coerce him to monitor Dr. Byrd's attempt to use the Sympathy Powder to determine longitudes at sea.

To accomplish this goal, Dr. Byrd uses the Sympathy Powder not to provide relief from pain but to inflict it – in a timely fashion – on a wounded dog, a "daft idea" actually put into practice.[6] The poor creature yelps when the doctor's colleagues back in London do something to an item stained with the dog's blood (a rag or the knife that cut him) at an agreed upon hour each day. For instance, they could aggravate the dog's wound by removing a bloodied rag from a solution of the Sympathy Powder and placing it near a flame. By comparing the time on the ship with the time back in London, Dr. Byrd can calculate the longitude. Roberto is skeptical enough to posit other reasons for the dog's behavior, but, despite the doctor's crackpot method, the *Amaryllis* has in fact arrived close to the antimeridian of London as predicted.

Sailing on the *Daphne* from west to east, Father Caspar has also arrived at the 180th degree of longitude from London but believes the ship is at the antimeridian of the Isla de Hierro, the prime meridian in that period (18 degrees west of today's prime meridian at Greenwich). He is therefore not at the Solomon Islands, as he thinks, but in the vicinity of Fiji, close to today's international date line, a temporal convention (we add a day crossing from the west and subtract a day from the east) that he and Roberto take literally: they believe they can go backwards in time (to the day before) if they reach the island on the other side of the line. Caspar's indisputable scientific ability is compromised by similarly suspect reasoning. He is thoroughly familiar with traditional methods for finding longitudes – keeping track of time at a known location, observing eclipses, measuring the ship's velocity (with the loch or navicella) – and with the problems preventing accurate calculations. Yet he assumes the errors caused by each method balance out, thus producing a reliable result: "And this est mathematica!" he triumphantly exclaims (p. 281). His experiment with the Instrumentum Arcetricum, a device that neutralizes a boat's rocking motion to enable precise observations of the eclipses of Jupiter's moons, is marred by circular logic: certain he is at the 180th meridian (what he seeks to prove), he therefore already knows the time at the Isla de Hierro. Father Caspar's science, in the end, is based less on sound reason than on faithful adherence to his theological beliefs. Thus, when he decides to walk underwater to the island (neither he nor Roberto can swim) to retrieve the Specula Melitensis ("that treasure of all methods" for finding longitudes [p. 285]), he is supremely confident in the safety of his Aquatic Bell, a cone-shaped contraption covered in hide: he "believed in his Bell as he believed in his Specula, and he believed he had to use the Bell to reach the Specula, and he believed that everything he was doing was for the greater glory of God" (p. 331).

After a full day has passed and Caspar fails to resurface, Roberto realizes "with mathematical, indeed cosmographical and astronomical certitude, his poor friend was lost" (p. 339). Yet as "the only man in human memory to have been shipwrecked and cast up upon a deserted ship" (p. 1), he inevitably succumbs to the flawed if seductive worldviews of Dr. Byrd and Father Caspar and seeks refuge "not in unbridgeable Space but in Time" (p. 340). Roberto lowers himself into the water and pushes off the boat, convinced he will either arrive at the island "the day before" to prevent Lilia's death or float forever along the magical longitude, thus stopping time and achieving a mystical union with his beloved in an eternal present.

"Historiography has shown us," Eco observes, "that it is impossible to separate the Hermetic thread from the scientific one or Paracelsus from Galileo" (Eco, *Interpretation and Overinterpretation*, p. 34). He breathes creative life into this entwining of science and Hermeticism in each of his first three novels. Taking place in the early 1600s, *The Island of the Day Before* dramatizes the influence of various theological and esoteric traditions on the mathematically oriented sciences that mark the period. Casaubon, as he becomes ever more deeply involved in the Hermetic world of the Diabolicals who inhabit *Foucault's Pendulum*, likewise realizes how even the most illustrious "bearers of mathematical and physical enlightenment...had worked with one foot in cabala and the other in the laboratory" (Eco, *Foucault's Pendulum*, p. 360). Indeed, one such person is Roger Bacon, William of Baskerville's trailblazing mentor from *The Name of the Rose* who considers science a "new natural magic" (Eco, *The Name of the Rose*, p. 206) and includes astrology and alchemy within its purview. It is precisely this amalgam of science and Hermeticism that Eco transmutes into gold within the crucible of his fictional universes.

The separation of the sciences and the humanities into "two cultures," as C. P. Snow famously posited in his 1959 lecture,[7] no doubt still rings true today. Eco acknowledges the continuing force of this "negative myth of two cultures," but he also observes how Snow's paradigm "ignored the many interdisciplinary ties that give life to contemporary culture" (Umberto Eco, "In Memory of Giorgio Prodi: A Challenge to the Myth of Two Cultures." Trans. Marina Johnston. In Leda Giannuzzi Jaworski (ed.), *Lo studio bolognese: campi di studio, di insegnamento, di ricerca, di divulgazione*. Stony Brook, NY: Forum Italicum, 1994, p. 75). Indeed, Eco's own longstanding engagement with science in all major areas of his writing admirably serves to generate and strengthen such interdisciplinary ties. Perhaps it is fitting that Eco most convincingly bridges this cultural divide in the imaginative space of his novels, where he not only treats scientific and technological material but also dramatizes the investigative mode of abduction common to both scientific discovery and artistic creation.

NOTES

1 Penelope Reed Doob, *The Idea of the Labyrinth from Classical Antiquity through the Middle Ages* (Ithaca, NY: Cornell University Press, 1990), p. 1.
2 For these three definitions, see: Eco, *The Limits of Interpretation*, pp. 57–8; Eco, *Interpretation and Overinterpretation*, pp. 45–66; and Eco, *Six Walks in the Fictional Woods*, pp. 9–10.

3 Gershom Scholem, *Kabbalah* (New York: Meridian, 1978), p. 54.

4 Dava Sobel, *Longitude: The True Story of a Lone Genius Who Solved the Greatest Scientific Problem of His Time* (New York: Walker, 1995).

5 Sir Kenelm Digby is in fact credited with discovering this "miraculous powder" in southern France (Sobel, *Longitude*, pp. 41–2).

6 Sobel, *Longitude*, p. 42.

7 C. P. Snow, *The Two Cultures* (original edn. 1959; Cambridge: Cambridge University Press, 1998).

CHAPTER 4

From the Rose to the Flame: Eco's theory and fiction between the Middle Ages and postmodernity

Cristina Farronato

Umberto Eco's fifth novel, *The Mysterious Flame of Queen Loana,* is by far the most autobiographical of his books, clearly referring to episodes and experiences of his Piedmontese childhood. It not only deals with personal memories of a profoundly sorrowful period in Italian history – the Fascist era and the Second World War – but also with the literature and culture of that same period. And if Yambo, the protagonist of the book, is not exactly Eco, he is definitely a man to whom Eco has loaned some of his deepest memories and a man who has experienced the childhood, the education, the Italy of the thirties and forties, Fascism, the war, the Resistance movement – in summary, all the main events of Eco's generation. Like Eco, the young Yambo has read *The Phantom, Mandrake the Magician, Flash Gordon*, and *Mickey Mouse*; he remembers the rhythms of Italian popular songs of the 1930s, he recognizes the soundtrack of *Casablanca*, he has smelled Vichy cologne, and has tasted Idrolitina selzer water.

When Yambo wakes up from a coma in the very beginning of the book, he has forgotten his identity: he has lost his autobiographic or episodic memory, while he still retains his implicit memory (which registers automatisms, like brushing one's teeth) and his explicit memory (which can be both semantic – the ability to remember historical data, for example – and public – which comprises common knowledge, such as the fact that birds fly). He has become a walking encyclopedia, made of bits and pieces, but no bit or piece brings him back to recognition; only a sudden, thorough recollection towards the middle of the book gives him a newly found awareness and gives him back his soul, if only for a short period, before dying.

At a first, superficial reading, through which one can enjoy the plot and admire the fantastic pictures that are included in the book, this novel/memoir would seem to depart from Eco's most recurrent themes and semiotic preoccupations. One might think that Eco has finally decided to depart from a basic characteristic of his previous four novels

50

that implied infusing his fictional narratives with his semiotic theories. In many instances, talking to journalists or to audiences during his world-wide book tour, Eco has said that in fact his mind was set on recording an extraordinary time in Italy, which meant so much to the development of the nation, to his own intellectual and personal growth, and to the forming of his generation. What has happened then, one might ask, to the philosophical ideas that Eco so forcefully developed in the previous decades, and how has he evolved as a fiction writer whose strength was in imbedding his theoretical background so well in his fiction? In *The Name of the Rose*, Eco wrote about medieval semiotics and the Peircean theory of abduction; in *Foucault's Pendulum*, he dealt with the issues of interpre-tation and overinterpretation; in *The Island of the Day Before*, he discussed the Baroque theory of signs and how human beings perceive reality; and in *Baudolino*, he reflected on the issue of truth and lying.

Some of these themes reappear in *The Mysterious Flame of Queen Loana*, and, once again, Eco has given us a novel that perfectly combines his theoretical interests with his narrative, giving his writing sophisticated depth. In this last fictional work, he returns to the questions of unlimited semiosis and encyclopedia, and ponders the semiotic self. Because Eco has chosen to offer further insight on the concept of encyclopedia – a notion and an intellectual choice fundamental for his semiotic theory and his philosophical thought because it connects his theory of knowledge and his theory of interpretation – a summary of these concepts in Eco's semi-otics illuminates the original contribution made in *The Mysterious Flame of Queen Loana*.

ECO'S THEORY OF THE SIGN AND THE CONCEPT OF ENCYCLOPEDIA

Eco outlines his early theories on the sign in a small treatise entitled *The Sign* (1973) that summarizes the conclusions of a large number of studies on the subject, including the works of Hjelmslev, Jakobson, Kristeva, Chomsky, Greimas, Lévi-Strauss, and also Hobbes, Locke, Leibniz, and Peirce. First, Eco acknowledges the treatment of the three levels of a linguistic sign, mainly referring to the Saussurian model (see Figure 4.1).

He recognizes the persistence of a problem for the grammarians and linguists of antiquity, from Aristotle to the Stoics, and for medieval schol-ars. The central question was: "Do words signify things directly or do they firstly signify concepts and only reach the level of *res* through the intermediary link of concepts?"[1] The answer for thinkers such as Boethius

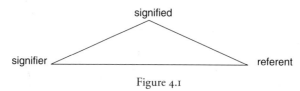

Figure 4.1

leaned towards the second solution, and this view prevailed in medieval logic through the time of Thomas Aquinas. But the Oxford philosophers Roger Bacon and Duns Scotus argued in favor of the first solution. In Aquinas' view, the linguistic sign produces a concept both in the mind of the speaker and in the mind of the listener. Aquinas went so far as to say that a concept is not a linguistic sign unless the speaker has the will to manifest it to others. For other philosophers, things were signs and the universe a symbolic system through which God speaks to us.

Eco compares this medieval view of the world as God's way of communicating to us with a whole tradition of aesthetics that stretches from the Romantics to Heidegger. Although secularized, Baudelaire's view of nature as a symbolic forest is not dissimilar, for example, to Alain de Lille's. For Heidegger, the path is the same: "It is not humans who create language to dominate things, but things, nature, or Being manifest themselves through language; language is the voice of Being; Truth is nothing but the unveiling of Being through language" (Umberto Eco, *The Sign*, Milan: Istituto Editoriale Internazionale, p. 97; author's translation). If we accept this view, Eco believes, there is no semiotics – only hermeneutics.

With the help of the American philosopher Charles S. Peirce, Eco avoids this hermeneutic impasse by reshaping the triadic structure of the sign. He leaves at the base of the triangle the *representamen* and the *object*, but he gives the position of the *signified* or *reference* to the *interpretant*. This has important consequences for the whole of Eco's semiotics and theory of interpretation. The concept of interpretant still alludes to the earlier concept of the signified, because it is what the sign represents in the interpreter, what the sign signifies for the interpreter, but it has a different ontological status. This is because the interpretant is not a mode of expression of the object, but it is in itself a sign, one of those signs that clarify another sign. As Eco explains:

The most fruitful hypothesis would seem to be that of conceiving the *interpretant as another representation which is referred to the same "object."* In other words, in order to establish what the interpreter of a sign is, it is necessary to name it by means of another sign which in turn has another interpretant to be named by another sign and so on. At this point there begins a process of *unlimited semiosis*, which, paradoxical as it may be, is the only guarantee for the foundation of a semiotic system capable of checking itself entirely by its own means. Language would then be an auto-clarificatory system, or rather one which is clarified by successive systems of conventions that explain each other. (Eco, *A Theory of Semiotics*, pp. 68–9)

The *signifier* is therefore replaced with a process of cultural substitution, a series of synonyms and paraphrases that can substitute for the sign. Consequently, signs are cultural units, and "every attempt to establish what the referent of a sign is forces us to define the referent in terms of an abstract entity which moreover is only a cultural convention." (p. 66)

This idea liberates semiotics from the metaphysics of the referent and makes of it a science of cultural phenomena, because communication is shown as a system of continuous permutations, and the sign as cultural unit is posed as its object. Similar is the position of the German philosopher Wittgenstein, whose writings on language much inspired Eco – for example, this passage in the *Philosophical Investigations*: "The meaning of a word is what explains the explanation of meaning. That is: if you want to understand the use of the word 'meaning', consider what is named 'explanation of the meaning'."[2] Wittgenstein's argument is here also anti-ontological: there is no meaning in an ontological sense, but only points of reference through which we can get to the meaning.[3] Meaning is not an entity existing between the word and the object, but the continuous substitution of signs.

Although this explanation seems to lead to a circularity without hope, it defines the normal functioning of communication, and for that reason it needs to be studied and analyzed. Attempts to schematize the laws of communication go back to the Middle Ages. The Porphyrian tree, for example, took into consideration the five "predicabili" (gender, mode, difference, property, and accident), but this model was criticized by Boethius and Abelard for being constructed on difference. For Eco a bi-dimensional tree cannot represent the complex semantics of a culture. He takes for example the model created by Katz and Fodor (see Figure 4.2).

This model cannot reflect a process of unlimited semiosis, and it needs to be made more complex. Eco arrives at the so-called Model Q, which he takes from the American linguist M. Ross Quillian, a version of which is illustrated in Figure 4.3.

This brings us to the concept of encyclopedia, according to which multiple connections are possible, but in which, in a singular situation,

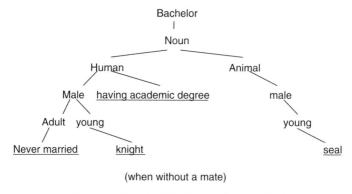

Figure 4.2 Katz Fodor's diagram for bachelor (1963).

certain properties of the sign are narcotized while others are emphasized. Paraphrasing Eco, a natural language is a system of signification that was thought up for the production of texts, and texts serve to emphasize or narcotize parts of the encyclopedic information. Patrizia Violi has made an intelligent study of Eco's model of encyclopedia in her essay "Individual and Communal Encyclopedias."[4] According to Violi, this concept occupies a pivotal role in Eco's semiotic reflection. On the one hand, it makes possible a departure from the semiotic model that depends on the code and so moves towards "a more dynamic and open vision of semiotics as an inferential process" (p. 25). And on the other hand, it opens up a static vision of interpretation towards a more dynamic concept of abduction, which is fundamental for the growing of knowledge. Violi identifies four types of encyclopedias: the global encyclopedia, the encyclopedia as situated knowledge, the encyclopedic competence, and the semantic competence. She is conscious that this division may appear problematic, but she suggests that her perspective is compatible with Eco's approach. But what is most relevant for our analysis is that Violi sees in Eco's theory a problematic notion of subjectivity, since the individual assumes an apparently passive role. This role results from the subject's coming to be "constructed and defined by and within cultural semiosis" (p. 35): the implication is that individual experiences are inscribed in the complexity of the inventories making up the common encyclopedia. The subject does not create ex nihilo, but restructures and reinterprets what is already present in the encyclopedic universe.

What Violi's discussion achieves is an interesting positioning of the subject in terms of the distinction between the empirical and the abstract

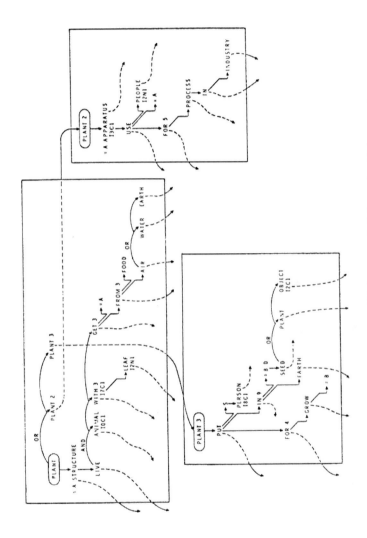

PLANT: 1. Living structure which is not an animal, frequently with leaves, getting
its food from air, water, earth.
2. Apparatus used for any process in industry.
3. Put (seed, plant, etc.) in earth for growth.

Figure 4.3 Model Q, which Eco reproduces in *A Theory of Semiotics*, p. 123.

subject, a central concept in Eco's theory, particularly in connection to the role of the reader and the concept of interpretation. It could be argued that Eco in part has already solved the dilemma of global versus local encyclopedia through the concept of narcotization explained above. Nevertheless, Violi's study once again brings to light the gray area, the mysterious zone that exists in Eco's theory between the individual and the global encyclopedia. If this area is not critically discussed in Eco's scholarly texts, it appears more indefinitely in his novels.[5]

UNLIMITED SEMIOSIS AND THE NOTION OF ENCYCLOPEDIA IN ECO'S NOVELS

All five of Eco's novels deal with unlimited semiosis and with the notion of encyclopedia, as they are all based on his theory of knowledge and interpretation. *The Name of the Rose*, which takes place in the Middle Ages but follows the postmodern format of the detective novel, best exemplifies our vision of a universal encyclopedia in the famous library that is at the center of the story. According to the description in the book, the abbey's is the largest library of the time and contains a universe of knowledge. But what is most relevant is that this Borgesian labyrinth of knowledge becomes also a spiritual labyrinth that might conceal the answers to the most pressing existential interrogatives. The protagonist of the book, William of Baskerville (whose name is a blending of William of Ockham and the Sherlock Holmes' story *The Hound of the Baskervilles*), proceeds in his attempts to discover the "truth" through abductions, which he uses for interpreting simple facts (as in the case of the horse Brunellus[6]) and for solving mysterious deaths, like the chain of murders that cast a shadow on the abbey. Abduction is, in simple terms, an inference, "a 'hunch' as to what something entails or presupposes,"[7] like the one made by the English physicist Ernest Rutherford, who "guessed" that the structure of the atom imitates the structure of the solar system. Rutherford's abduction was later verified to be correct, but not every abduction proves so successful. In fact, all abductions are subject to *fallibility*, which Peirce defines as "the doctrine that our knowledge is never absolute but always swims, as it were, in a continuum of uncertainty and of indeterminacy."[8]

Towards the end of the novel, William concludes that the murders that have been plaguing the abbey are the work of a single person and that they are committed following a specific scheme. This abduction reveals itself to be wrong, as not all the murders are committed by the same person and some of them are of an accidental nature. Therefore, in the end, William's

endeavor to give coherence to the encyclopedia fails, because he has over-
interpreted the connections between the signs. Still, the conclusion of *The
Name of the Rose* is that there are only signs and that the study of signs is
the only way for humans to understand the directions of the world.

I have never doubted the truth of signs, Adso; they are the only things man
has to orient himself in the world. What I did not understand was the relation
among signs. I arrived at Jorge through an apocalyptic pattern that seemed to
underlie all the crimes, and yet it was accidental. I arrived at Jorge seeking one
criminal for all the crimes and we discovered that each crime was committed by
a different person, or by no one. I arrived at Jorge pursuing the plan of a perverse
and rational mind, and there was no plan, or, rather, Jorge himself was overcome
by his own initial design and there began a sequence of causes…Where is all my
wisdom, then? I behaved stubbornly, pursuing the semblance of order, when I
should have known well that there is no order in the universe. (Eco, *The Name
of the Rose*, p. 492)

Although William realizes he has gone too far in his coherent explanation of events, Eco defends the personal attempt at acting on our human
impulse to create order out of chaos, and this is reflected in Adso's words:
"But in imagining an erroneous order you still found something…" to which
William replies: "What you say is very fine, Adso, I thank you. The order
that our mind imagines is like a net, or like a ladder, built to attain something. But afterward you must throw the ladder away, because you discover
that, even if it was useful, it was meaningless" (p. 142). Here Eco is following
his contemporary, Wittgenstein, whom he quotes immediately afterwards
("Er muoz gelîchesame die Leiter abewerfen, sô Er an ir ufgestigen…"
p. 142).[9] William's reflection goes beyond the medieval sense of universal
order and it represents well the mixture of medieval and contemporary philosophy that constitutes the postmodernism of *The Name of the Rose*.

William's extreme attempt to save the library, the closest materialization of the medieval encyclopedia, fails as well, as our hero emerges
from the flames of the Aedificium with only a few remnants of manuscripts, which reminds us of how ambitious and how precarious our effort
actually is to collect an ensemble of all the world's knowledge. Even when
Adso, years later, revisits the abbey and, going through the ruins of the
library, finds pieces of parchment, he cannot but attempt to reconfigure
an order, to reconstitute a minor library, although he is conscious that it
can only be composed of "fragments, quotations, unfinished sentences,
amputated stumps of books" (p. 500).

The same struggle to reconstitute an encyclopedic order, in which *tout
se tient* –each piece of the puzzle fits – occurs in *Foucault's Pendulum*. Eco

structures his second novel like the *Sepher Yezirah*, the Jewish book on metaphysics that is supposed to synthesize the story of the universe. Each chapter of *Foucault's Pendulum* takes its title from one of the Sephirots, the points of manifestation and outpouring of the divine in the world. Eco toys with the idea that a single articulated text could hide the most profound mysteries and that, by properly deciphering the book, one could get to the ultimate truth. But *Foucault's Pendulum* warns against the risks of pursuing such an ideal and in fact orchestrates the demise of its protagonist, Casaubon, who, even after he realizes that the text he was investigating is nothing but a laundry list, perseveres in his search for meaning. Like William of Baskerville, Casaubon represents the semiotician in general, who follows the links of the chain that connect one sign to the other and is often carried away by the semiotic machine of his unstoppable, but fallible intellect. Driven by a wistful longing for some center of meaning, both William and Casaubon break their own rules and transgress in their search, escorting the reader into an ambiguous realm in which everything is decentralized.

When Casaubon opens his cultural information agency, he becomes an investigator of knowledge, "the Sam Spade of culture," as his friend Belbo calls him. The most telling aspect of his profession is his collection of information and the way the different pieces are catalogued. He uses reference cards that link subject with subject by way of association, like the process of unlimited semiosis. With his files, he is trying to reconstitute the encyclopedia and, at the same time, by exploring the connections between files, he is trying to unveil a hidden message. Only in the end, as he awaits his death, does he have a realization: he understands that there is nothing to understand. Nevertheless, the final message of the book is that we must pursue our desire for interpretation and our search for meaning, because if we do not, somebody else will take possession of and manipulate knowledge to our detriment.

A realization similar to that of Casaubon overtakes Roberto, the protagonist of *The Island of the Day Before*. After he starts the fire that will burn the *Daphne*, the ship in which he has sailed and has shipwrecked, and as he disappears in the ocean, Roberto understands that our voyage in the waters of unlimited semiosis never stops, or stops only for each of us at the moment of death. As the sign refers to an object only through an unlimited chain of interpretants, unlimited semiosis represents "a circle that closes every second and never closes at all" (Umberto Eco, *The Reader in the Story: Interpretative Cooperation in Narrative Texts*. Milan: Bompiani, 1979, p. 46, author's translation). The interpretant increases our understanding of the sign, but never explains it completely; this is why the orange dove can continue its eternal fugue.

Similar to all the heroes of Eco's other novels, Roberto tries to expand the encyclopedia of his time with the new phenomena he observes at the antipodes: new plants and new animals generate new perceptions and new feelings. "An embarrassed Adam," as Eco calls him, Roberto does not have names for all these new creatures, and the appellations he contrives seem ridiculous: "It was like calling a goose a swan" (Eco, *The Island of the Day Before*, p. 41). Thus, Eco underscores the idea of the inadequacy of language, the notion that nature always seems to supersede our capacity to define. Father Emanuele hopes to construct an artificial machine whose rollers and moving drawers will permit the combinations of letters that can potentially encompass all the world's knowledge and bring us closer to God's message. His project is presented as one of the eccentricities of "that bizarre century" (p. 66).

Baudolino, the protagonist of Eco's fourth novel of the same name, plays a similar role as he tries to rewrite the history of the world through his own tales, which are a mixture of truth and lies. But even his lies and fakes become a part of the universal library and of the common encyclopedia, once the community accepts them. "So in the library there are also books containing falsehoods...", William asks the abbot in *The Name of the Rose*, and the abbot replies: "Monsters exist because they are part of the divine plan, and in the horrible features of those same monsters the power of the Creator is revealed. And by divine plan, too, there exist also books by wizards, the cabalas of the Jews, the fables of pagan poets, the lies of the infidels"(Eco, *The Name of the Rose*, p. 37). Everything known is contained in this improbable Aedificium, even the monsters that Baudolino's lively imagination encounters in the Orient.

The library that Eco envisions in *The Name of the Rose* is similar to Borges' Library of Babel, a never-ending structure that reproduces the infinity of the cosmos or, more precisely, of the chaosmos, for according to both Borges and Eco, the appearance of order is just a human illusion or a wishful longing, an elegant hope to see a method in the madness, or at least in the eternal return of the same disorder. The insurmountable epistemological problem is that each single individual can only enter so many hexagonal rooms of this interminable library, can only know limited bits and pieces of so much assembled knowledge, and can never possibly read all the books it contains.

Eco goes back again and even more specifically to this idea of knowledge as fragments and pieces of the encyclopedia in his latest novel, *The Mysterious*

Flame of Queen Loana, which takes place in the 1990s. Its protagonist, Yambo, both resembles and differs from William of Baskerville. William is a learned medieval monk with a passion for books who gets involved in the search for a murderer; he is the rational mind, despite his philosophical doubts and the final failure – at least in part – of his reasoning, which opposes religious intolerance. Yambo is a contemporary man who is both learned and a bibliophile, but when the novel opens, he has lost his personal memory. Even more of a postmodern figure than William, he searches not for murderers but for his lost self, guided by a mysterious flame he hopes can explain the enigma of life and death and the significance of our own subjectivity in an eerily befogged world.

In writing *The Mysterious Flame of Queen Loana*, Eco seems to respond to Violi's critique of his notion of encyclopedia, for he creates a protagonist with a vast encyclopedia but without personal memories, and therefore without personal identity. In fact, Yambo tries to reconstruct his identity through a common encyclopedia made of quotations. But how much of Yambo's personality can be inscribed in the general encyclopedia? With a complete loss of his personal experiences, how can he reconstruct his own self through bits and pieces of encyclopedia? How many books constitute Yambo's paper memory? There seems to be an almost perfect correspondence between books and brain: memory is like a file of citations. Borges' library becomes the labyrinth of the mind. If Swann, Proust's protagonist, recalls memories by virtue of flavors and smells, for Yambo words constitute memory.

Therefore, meditating on Violi's criticism, Eco experiments and decides to play out the interrelations between the collective and the personal encyclopedia, between the *langue* and the *parole*. "My life as an encyclopedia continues… – says Yambo – My memories have the depth of a few weeks. Other people's stretch for centuries" (Umberto Eco, *The Mysterious Flame of Queen Loana: An Illustrated Novel*. Trans. Geoffrey Brock. New York: Harcourt, 2005, p. 40). When Violi criticizes the aspect of the encyclopedia that relates to the subject,[10] she declares that the individual remains at the margins of the theory of encyclopedia and of semiosis as a non-theorizable residue derived from an old tradition of epistemology. What can be saved through memory is what we have in common, not what makes us unique and different. Violi quotes Eco as saying: "As subjects, we are what the form of the world produced by signs makes us be" (Patrizia Violi, "Individual and Communal Encyclopedias." In Bouchard and Pravadelli (eds.), *Eco's Alternative*, p. 27). In other words, our subjectivity is founded in the network of relations with our fellow human beings that our culture defines. If this is the case, the most individual and subjective aspects of experience are certainly sacrificed. Violi praises Eco's ethically admirable position, as it implies an underlining of the common aspects of experience and knowledge, against any mystique of the individual. This, she believes, is an enlightened and equalitarian ideal of culture. Yet, what becomes of the individual in the stratified system of repertoires that Eco has envisioned?

Eco discusses the subjective versus the intersubjective in *A Theory of Semiotics* while analyzing the symbol, and, in his conclusion, he declares: "Maybe, in this integration of the individual experience in the collective encyclopedia, something is lost and remains unexpressed, an area of mystery and unknown that resists any translation, a noumenon that does not emerge in the clear universe of the encyclopedic order" (Eco, *A Theory of Semiotics*, p. 109). Could that be *the mysterious flame*? Perhaps Yambo needs a mysterious stimulus to recollect his own self. Or is the flame only a destructive mechanism, since in fact it will eventually blaze his brain into an orgasmic explosion?:

I do not know whether it is the mysterious flame of Queen Loana that is burning in my crumpled-parchment lobes, whether some elixir is attempting to wash the browned pages of my paper memory, still marred by the many stains that render illegible that part of the text that still eludes me, or whether it is I who am trying to drive my nerves to the point of unbearable exertion…But I also feel on the verge of orgasm, as my brain's corpora cavernosa swell with blood, as something gets ready to explode – or blossom…Why is the sun turning black? (Eco, *The Mysterious Flame of Queen Loana*, pp. 448–9).

If Violi's critique was not on Eco's mind when writing his fifth novel, Eco was certainly thinking of recent studies about the semiotics of the self, maybe in tribute to his late friend, Thomas A. Sebeok, who wrote several articles on the subject. For Sebeok, the strongest natural and cultural link that belongs to the self is with memory: "Each individual requires information and needs the representation of events previously incorporated in a code."[11] These are necessary because they allow individuals to orient themselves with the reasonable certainty of surviving in their specific Umwelt, a concept that reminds us of Eco's notion of encyclopedic competence, intended as the average competence that an individual must possess in order to "belong" to a certain culture. In Sebeok's view, memory constitutes "a private multi-sensorial document archive, composed of non-verbal signs with a verbal cover. It is the *articulatio secunda*, or the syntax aspect of language, to supply the mechanism with which memory organizes, continuously remodels like a child playing with his building blocks, and finally imposes on each of us a cohesive and personal narrative scheme" (Sebeok, "L'io semiotico," p. 19, author's translation).

The subject in Peircean terms is a very complex sign, made of both verbal and non-verbal language, and it expands as a semiotic process with infinite possibilities. There are at least three aspects characteristic of the self that were identified originally by Peirce and have since been explored further by scholars such as Sebeok, Susan Petrilli, and Augusto Ponzio. The first aspect is the dialogic nature of the self, meaning that the self is in continuous conversation with itself and with others, which is why the boundaries of the self are difficult to define. As Peirce writes: "…one man's experience is nothing, if it stands alone. If he sees what others cannot, we call it hallucination. It is not 'my' experience, but 'our' experience that has to be thought of; and this 'us' has indefinite possibilities" (Peirce, *Collected Papers*, 5:402, n. 2).

The second important aspect, as Petrilli underlines, is that the self is anchored to the body:

That the subject is inevitably an incarnate subject, thus intercorporeal being, that is to say, a body connected to other bodies from the very outset, an expression of the condition of intercorporeity on both the synchronic and diachronic levels for the whole of its subsequent life, that the subject is not incarnated in a body isolated from other bodies is not indifferent to our conception of the person…The body plays a fundamental role in the development of awareness or consciousness: consciousness is incarnate consciousness. The body is a condition for the full development of consciousness, of the human being as a semiotic animal.[12]

Eco also emphasizes the same physical qualities of the self often throughout his novel.

The third important aspect of the self given prominent place in *The Mysterious Flame of Queen Loana* is creative love or, in Peircean terms, *agapasm*. According to Peirce, agapastic development is in its nature abductive and iconic; it is not tied to chance, but to "immediate attraction for the idea itself, the nature of which is guessed even before it is possessed by the mind, because of the power of sympathy, that is to say because of the continuity of the mind" (Peirce, *Collected Papers*, 6:307, 1893a). This is the mind of the genius, who discovers the idea because of the force of its attraction "in the context of the relational continuity of the interpretants in the great network of the semiotic universe…"[13] For Peirce, love is at the basis of the development of knowledge and of reason because of the power of creative rationality. Kissed by Agape, reason becomes rationality and what is hateful becomes lovable. Peirce considers the growth of rationality to be the *summum bonum*, the ultimate value and an extremely important part of the evolutionary process. This explains why Yambo identifies himself in the love of three women: his wife Paola, his assistant Sibilla, and his adolescent love, Lila. "Tre donne intorno al cor mi son venute" (the "three blessed ladies in the court of heaven"); *L'albergo delle tre rose* (*The Hotel of the Three Roses*, a detective novel by Augusto Maria de Angelis); but in fact three is one, and what is at stake is Yambo's erotic desire: *A rose by any other name*.[14]

Let us also not overlook the fact that Yambo graduated from the university with a dissertation on the *Hypnerotomachia Poliphili*, a Renaissance romance and love story traditionally attributed to Francesco Colonna (1433 – 1527) and published in Venice by the famous typographer Aldo Manuzio (1449 – 1515) in 1499. This extraordinary and mysterious work, generally considered the most beautiful book of early modern printing, integrates text and images (woodcuts) much as Eco's fifth novel integrates illustrations from popular culture and text. Poliphilo (his name means lover of many things but also lover of Polia, his beloved) searches for his lost love; Polia has shunned Poliphilo, just as Lila rejects Yambo. Perhaps Yambo is more "poliphilo" than he thinks, because in fact, there is more than one woman in his life. Besides Lila, there is Sibilla, his fascinating young assistant, an example of perfect beauty and grace. Unfortunately, with his loss of memory, Yambo cannot remember whether or not he has had an affair with Sibilla. Even more important, there is Paola, his wife, whose name is most similar to Polia (many things) and who has stood by him, helped him, and protected him for thirty years.[15]

In the dream of his search for Polia, Poliphilo encounters a variety of people and objects, particularly buildings and architecturally significant structures that become love objects. In Manuzio's work as in Eco's, the erotic is indissoluble from the erudite. The strength of this erotic creative impulse is felt by Yambo in the form of the mysterious flame that burns inside him and that makes itself most felt looking at those objects, listening to those sounds, and reading those lines that are connected with important and suggestive memories of his childhood and youth. The erotic and the intellectual appear to be so fused together that Yambo's collapses are attributed either to news concerning his love interest (the death of Lila) or to intellectual finds (the shock discovery in his grandfather's attic of an original complete first folio of 1623 containing all of Shakespeare's works).

Because the *Hypnerotomachia Poliphili* is more than just a romance, perhaps it sheds some light on Eco's idea of his novel. In the Renaissance book, Poliphilo's adventures take place almost entirely within a dream. Very often Yambo thinks about the difference between reality and dreams, and the second part of his novel takes place while he is in a coma. Ultimately, Yambo asks himself what the distinction really is between what he has experienced in real life and what he has experienced only in his mind. His thought process during his second coma goes from memories of childhood events to visions of a heaven full of cartoon characters and real people, and he wonders which of these possible worlds is real and whether his imagination has constructed everything.

But who can say that everything I remembered in the course of this sleep really happened?...I never lost my memory, am some other man...Otherwise why would everything I believed I was remembering until now have been dominated by the fog, which was nothing if not the sign that my life was but a dream. That is a quotation. And what if all the other quotes, those I offered the doctor, Paola, Sibilla, myself, were nothing but the product of this persistent dream?...if anything exists outside of me it is a parallel universe in which who knows what is happening or has happened...But had I conceived an entire universe within my brain...I would have to have drawn on a capacity for invention exceeding that of an individual... (Eco, *The Mysterious Flame of Queen Loana*, p. 418)

On the following page, Yambo goes on to remark: "I cannot let myself go, I want to know who I am. One thing is certain. The memories that surfaced at the beginning of what I believe to be my coma are obscure, foggy, and arranged in patchwork fashion, with breaks, uncertainties, tears, missing pieces (why can I not remember Lila's face?)" (p. 419). Yambo is struggling to fuse together in continuity the pieces of memories that constitute his lacerated encyclopedia, so much so that in the end his own love becomes cosmic love and his personal erotic desire becomes mysticism. Like Dante, who in the last canto of his *Paradiso* prepares himself for the vision of the Virgin Mary and invokes her in prayer, Yambo prepares himself to see Lila and invokes Queen Loana.[16] Yambo's mystical side is apparent also in his own name: does not the name Yambo faintly evoke the name Iamblichus from *Iamblichus de mysteriis Aegyptiorum*, a Renaissance book that Yambo owns and that he has always been strangely unwilling to sell for personal reasons? Iamblichus was a Neoplatonic philosopher, born in Syria in AD 240, who created a synthesis of the pagan world's deepest spiritual insights. He taught that there are two valid answers to the question "Who am I?" The first answer is that the individual is a being with a body and an inner life, or soul. The second answer, from the point of view of cosmic Eros, is that the individual life blends into the life of the daimones, gods, archetypal Numbers, and the One; the individual immersion in the universe is so thorough that the "self" is in some sense the totality. While Yambo may not embrace Iamblichus' philosophy, his last thoughts seem to reflect the notion of theurgy, the idea of living the erotic cosmos.

The interplay of personal and cosmic encyclopedia goes beyond human experience. When Adso reflects on his closeness to death, towards the end of *The Name of the Rose*, he mentions such an inexpressible union:

I shall sink into the divine shadow, in a dumb silence and an ineffable union, and in this sinking all equality and all inequality shall be lost, and in that abyss my spirit will lose itself, and will not know the equal or the unequal, or anything else: and all differences will be forgotten. I shall be in the simple foundation, in the silent desert where diversity is never seen, in the privacy where no one finds himself in his proper place. I shall fall into the silent and uninhabited divinity where there is no work and no image. (Eco, *The Name of the Rose*, p. 501)

Also, in the moment of Adso's initiation, love is compared to light and a flame:

As, half fainting, I fell on the body to which I had joined myself, I understood in a last vital spurt that flame consists of a splendid clarity, an unusual vigor, and an igneous ardor, but it possesses the splendid clarity so that it may illuminate and the igneous ardor so that it may burn. Then I understood the abyss, and the deeper abysses that it conjured up. (p. 247)

Love implies ecstasy and the abyss for young Adso, and also for Yambo, who sees in his beloveds the possibility of inflaming passion. At the same time, these loves appear to bring him closer to death. Does not his first collapse occur after he has heard of the death of his adolescent flame, Lila? Even the name Sibilla encompasses the ideas of hope and death: the Cumanean Sybil shows Aeneas the future, but also the abyss of Tartarus. The young unnamed woman of *The Name of the Rose* and the women of *The Mysterious Flame of Queen Loana* represent the discovery of the eternal feminine, the discovery of desire, of that mysterious flame that guides Yambo in the reconstruction of his memory.

THE DETECTIVE, UNLIMITED SEMIOSIS, AND THE REMAKING OF THE ENCYCLOPEDIA

Despite the fact that Yambo is not exactly a detective trying to solve criminal puzzles, some of the first figures that come to his mind at the beginning of the novel, when he awakens from his first coma, are Maigret and Sherlock Holmes, both lost in the fog, both fumbling in the dark, because the fog seems to hide the most precious of secrets.

*Maigret plunges into a fog so dense that he can't even see where he's stepping...
The fog teems with human shapes, swarms with an intense, mysterious life.
Maigret? Elementary, my dear Watson, there are ten little Indians, and the hound
of the Baskervilles vanishes into the fog.* (Eco, *The Mysterious Flame of Queen
Loana*, p. 4)

This fog, in which a whole secret world is veiled, is a recurring image in
the novel. In fact, Yambo has spent his entire life filling a notebook full of
citations on the fog, and his conscientious assistant Sibilla has diligently
transferred these notes onto his computer. Clusters of these citations constitute very interesting postmodern palimpsests throughout the work, as
in the following passage:

*Le brouillard indolent de l'automne est épars ... Unreal City, / under the brown fog
of a winter dawn, / a crowd flowed over the London Bridge, so many, / I had not
thought death had undone so many ... Spätherbstnebel, kalte Träume, / überfloren
Berg und Tal, / Sturm entblättert schon die Bäume, / und sie schaun gespenstig
kahl ...* (p. 31)

In these multilingual lines, we may recognize a poem by Georges
Rodenbach, T. S. Eliot's *The Waste Land*, and a song by Alban Berg with
a text by Heinrich Heine. When Yambo sees his file and reads these bits
of encyclopedia, he realizes he has collected 135 pages of citations on the
fog, including paragraphs from Abbott's *Flatland* (a book about a country
where people live in two dimensions), from Dante, D'Annunzio, Dickens,
Emily Dickinson, Pascoli, Pirandello, Savinio, Vittorio Sereni, *King Lear*,
Campana, Flaubert, Baudelaire, and so on.

Yambo is thinking, of course, of the fog that has taken possession of
his mind and is hoping that Sibilla, taking him by the hand, can help him
penetrate it. Perhaps when he finally feels the mysterious flame, everything will be clear and understandable: perhaps love really is the answer.
As this thought occurs to him, Yambo fishes once again in his paper
memory and quotes a poem by Vincenzo Cardarelli (1887–1959) entitled
"Adolescente" ("The Adolescent"). What Eco does not quote is this con-
tinuation: "Like a flame that melts in the light, / at the touch of reality
/ the mysteries that you promise / will dissolve into nothing" (author's
translation). While he fumbles in the fog searching for signs that might
give him back his self, Yambo does feel like Sherlock Holmes exploring
the clues that will help him to the truth:

... de te fabula narratur[17] [the story is about you]. At that very moment Sherlock
Holmes was me, intent on retracing and reconstructing remote events of which
he had no prior knowledge, while remaining at home, shut away, perhaps even in

an attic. He too, like me, motionless and isolated from the world, deciphering pure signs. He always succeeded in making the repressed resurface. Would I be able to? At least I had a model. And like him, I had to combat the fog. (p. 152)

But what is Eco's model: Sherlock Holmes or Poliphilo?

Who had been my hero? Holmes, reading a letter by the fire, rendered politely amazed by his seven-percent solution, or Sandokan, tearing his chest madly as he utters the name of his beloved Marianna? (p. 154)

Who is Yambo in the end? Is he the purely rational hero or the passionately absorbed lover? Is he Arthur Gordon Pym, as he reveals in the first page of the book? In fact, Eco also cites the ending of Edgar Allan Poe's novel,[18] and immediately thereafter he quotes Melville: "Call me Ishmael." Both *The Narrative of Arthur Gordon Pym of Nuntucket* and *Moby Dick* are stories centered on the question of what determines the self. How much of the "other" constitutes our self and how much of our self is just our own creation, Eco seems to be asking his reader.

Yambo reconstructs his self by filling it with a schizophrenic list of books, songs, pictures, films, and contemporary historical events, an ensemble of notions that seem to remain nonsensical and often contradictory. He then becomes attached to these bits and pieces of encyclopedia that he finds going in boxes of stored-away things in the attic of his Solara home. He is hoping that one item at least could be for him a sort of Proustian Madeleine and make him remember. Instead nothing happens and he finds himself lost in a labyrinth: "I was in a maze. No matter which way I turned, it was the wrong way. And besides, what did I want to get out of? Who was it who said *Open sesame, I want to get out*? I wanted to go in, like Ali Baba. Into the caverns of memory" (p. 75).

He spends eight days reading in a confused and furious way. Some readings excite in him the mysterious flame and some almost give him a heart attack. He drinks wine and his blood pressure rises more and more, but he does not arrive at any revelation: "That is no way to reconstruct a memory. Memory amalgamates, revises, and reshapes, no doubt, but it rarely confuses chronological distances...So I had to...put things back in their places, and savor them over the course of time" (p. 157). Yambo then starts reading all the books from his adolescence, but even then, he comes up with nothing ("... you came to Solara to rediscover yourself, because you felt oppressed by an encyclopedia full of Homer, Manzoni, and Flaubert, and now you've entered the encyclopedia of pulp literature" (p. 163). At this point, he asks himself, why try to remember? "Memory is a stopgap for humans...I was enjoying the marvel of beginning *ab ovo*"

(p. 225). Suddenly, Yambo discovers something: he finds *The Hotel of the Three Roses* and what interests him in this book is that it seems to narrate his own story, the three roses being the three important women of his life: Lila, his wife Paola, and Sibilla. "Where was the Hotel of the Three Roses? Everywhere, for me. *A rose by any other name*" (p. 297). Immediately afterwards, as already mentioned, he discovers Shakespeare's folio of 1623. His heart starts beating fast: "This is surely the greatest stroke of my life" (p. 298). He finds himself immersed in the fog once again, and then he starts remembering. Is it really the idea of finding a most precious, antique book that makes his heart pound, or is it the realization that his love is his love, no matter what its name, and this realization is provoked by Juliet's words: "That which we call a rose/By any other name would smell as sweet" (*Romeo and Juliet*, II, ii, 1–2)? Does Yambo become a victim of his inquisitive mind, like the Casaubon of *Foucault's Pendulum*?

Yambo's dilemma stems from the desire of giving shape to shapelessness, and it is interesting that in all of Eco's novels, the investigative search concludes with a mixture of failure and success. In part, his protagonists are wrong in their assumptions/abductions that appear to be aiming too far and too high. But they also strongly exert their limited minds in the understanding of something complex, and their rational effort, together with their courage in taking risks, deserves to be rewarded. In this sense, we do admire them for their humanity and for their valiant attempts. As Eco, the literary theorist, has put it:

> In any case we should not stop reading fiction works, because in the best of cases it is in them that we look for a formula which gives meaning to our life. After all, throughout our life, we look for a story of origin that tells us why we were born and why we have lived. Sometimes we look for a cosmic story, the story of the universe, sometimes for our personal story (which we tell the confessor or the psychoanalyst)…Sometimes we hope to make our personal story coincide with that of the universe. (Eco, *Six Walks in the Fictional Woods*, p. 173)

All of Eco's novels appear to offer the reader the possibility of searching for more, whether it is personal or universal. In fact, his five narratives try as much as possible to connect the personal with the universal, revealing the "elegant hope" for a meaning and exemplifying that oftentimes personal thoughts and actions are tied to far greater purposes that go beyond our understanding. Despite this, the characters of Eco's novels ambitiously make the effort to offer explanations, most of them incomplete, but all of them partially illuminating, like every nuance that we can append to the multiple facets of the sign. This is why the encyclopedic model of categorizing knowledge, despite its limitations, is more powerful than the Greimassian dictionary ideal. Although often quite practical, the dictionary model is philosophically inadequate to explain the functioning of our inquisitive, but imperfect minds, while the encyclopedic model leaves open the indefiniteness of a still mysterious universe.

NOTES

1 Andrea Tabarroni, "Mental Signs and the Theory of Representation in Ockham," in Umberto Eco and Costantino Marmo (eds.), *On the Medieval Theory of Signs* (Amsterdam, PA: John Benjamins, 1989), p. 196.

2 Ludwig Wittgenstein, *Philosophical Investigations*, trans. G. E. M. Anscombe, 2nd edn. (Oxford: Blackwell Publishers, 1997), p. 149.

3 Armin Burkhardt, "Die Semiotik des Umberto 'von Baskerville'," in Armin Burkhardt and Eberhard Rohse (eds.), *Umberto Eco zwischen Literatur und Semiotik* (Braunschweig: Verlag Ars & Scientia, 1991), pp. 29–89.

4 The essay is contained in Norma Bouchard and Veronica Pravadelli (eds.), *Eco's Alternative*, pp. 25–38.

5 For a discussion of this topic, see Cristina Farronato, *Eco's Chaosmos. From the Middle Ages to Posmodernity* (Toronto: University of Toronto Press, 2003).

6 When arriving at the abbey, Adso and William spot the footprints of a horse. When he meets the monks who are chasing the horse, William, enacting a medieval Zadig, informs them that Brunellus, the abbot's favorite horse – black, 5 feet tall, with a sumptuous tail and small hooves, a small head, thin ears, and big eyes – has turned to the right: all this without having even seen the horse.

7 Marcel Danesi, *Encyclopedic Dictionary of Semiotics, Media, and Communications* (Toronto: University of Toronto Press, 2000), p. 3.

8 In Charles Hartshorne and Paul Weiss (eds.), *Collected Papers of Charles Sanders Peirce* (Cambridge, Mass.: Harvard University Press, 1931–55), 5:170, 171–5.

9 An English translation is provided by Adele J. Haft, Jane G. White, and Robert J. White, *The Key to "The Name of the Rose"* (Ann Arbor: The University of Michigan Press, 1999), p. 172: "One must cast away, as it were, the ladder, so that he may begin to ascend it."

10 Patrizia Violi, "Le molte enciclopedie," in Patrizia Magli, Giovanni Manetti, and Patrizia Violi (eds.), *Semiotica: storia, teoria, interpretazione – saggi intorno a Umberto Eco (*Milan: Bompiani, 1992), pp. 99–113; English translation as "Individual and Communal Encyclopedias" in Norma Bouchard and Veronica Pravadelli (eds.), *Eco's Alternative*, pp. 25–38. Violi's chapter in this anthology – "'The Subject is in the Adverbs.' The Role of the subject in Eco's Semiotics" – provides further consideration of this key problem in Eco's work on semiotics and its application to his fiction.

11 Thomas A. Sebeok, "L'io semiotico," in Thomas A. Sebeok, Susan Petrilli, and Augusto Ponzio (eds.), *Semiotica dell'io* (Rome: Meltemi, 2001), pp. 18–19 (author's translation).

12 Susan Petrilli, "Modeling, Dialogue, and Globality: Biosemiotics and Semiotics of Self," *Sign Systems Studies*, 31 1 2003): 91–2.

13 Susan Petrilli, "Basi per una semiotica dell'io," in Sebeok, Petrilli, and Ponzio (eds.), *Semiotica dell'io*, p. 100 (author's translation).

14 The Italian poem "Tre donne intorno al cor mi son venute" (rendered by Joseph Tusiani as "Around my heart three ladies have descended") is one of the poems Dante wrote in his later career when he was in exile from Florence. See a copy on the Dante Studies website (www.italianstudies.org/poetry/ex7.htm) that contains all of Dante's poetry translated by Tusiani. This fixation on the number three is typical not only of Dante but of people who are out of their minds (Yambo?). We see in *The Name of the Rose* that number fixation abounds.

15 It is interesting that a best-selling "whodunit" written by two former Princeton University undergraduates based on the *Hypnerotomachia Poliphili* appeared during the same year as *The Mysterious Flame of Queen Loana*: Ian Caldwell and Dustin Thomason, *The Rule of Four* (New York: Dial Press, 2004). For a discussion by the English translator of Francesco Colonna's masterpiece, see Joscelyn Godwin's *The Real Rule of Four* (New York: The Disinformation Company, 2004).

16 The parallel is not gratuitous, as Eco, in the dreamlike quality of his apparition, uses Dante's same simile, even though for Eco the vision appears while for Dante it disperses. See *Paradiso*, Canto XXXIII, 64–7 for Dante's verse.

17 Eco cites this same Latin phrase in *The Name of the Rose*, p. 388.

18 "…we rushed into the embraces of the cataract, where a chasm threw itself open to receive us. But there arose in our pathway a shrouded human figure, very far larger in its proportions than any dweller among men. And the hue of the skin of the figure was of the perfect whiteness of the snow" (Eco, *The Mysterious Flame of Queen Loana*, p. 217).

CHAPTER 5

Eco's Middle Ages and the historical novel

Theresa Coletti

In the past twenty-five years, the ascendancy of Umberto Eco's reputation
as a historical novelist has coincided with increased critical attention to
the historical novel's theoretical possibilities and cultural significance.
The enormous international success of *The Name of the Rose* is itself
responsible for some of this new critical interest in the genre. The late
twentieth-century mass-market appeal of a deeply erudite story set in a
fourteenth-century Benedictine monastery has encouraged analysis of
Eco's decision to render his central concerns as a theorist, journalist, and
cultural critic in that narrative form. Eco's subsequent endeavors as a fiction writer have demonstrated an abiding affinity between those concerns
and opportunities for representation that the historical novel affords. In
different senses of the word, all of Eco's novels engage fundamentally with
the challenges and problems of writing history and thinking historically,
whether these are articulated through carefully constructed, temporally
distant worlds, as in the case of *The Name of the Rose*, *The Island of the Day
Before*, and *Baudolino*, or through more contemporary settings and characters preoccupied with the past and memory, as in *Foucault's Pendulum*
and *The Mysterious Flame of Queen Loana*. Through their extended
meditation on the means by and materials through which we encounter
the past, these novels illustrate central attributes of postmodern historical
fiction identified in recent theoretical analyses of that genre.[1] Eco's novels
bear witness to this fiction's reflexive scrutiny of the human capacity for
historical knowledge and critique the prospects for historical and fictive
discourses to give access to such knowledge.

In *The Name of the Rose* and *Baudolino*, medieval settings and cultural phenomena provide the crucial occasion for these novels' exploration of theoretical and philosophical concerns. The Middle Ages have
long provided compelling subject matter for historical fiction; Georg
Lukács located the modern foundations of the genre in the novels of Sir
Walter Scott, who is best remembered today for medieval fictions such as

Ivanhoe.[2] Contemporary historical novels set in medieval spaces and times speak to a range of cultural impulses at least as diverse as the "ten little Middle Ages" that Eco delineates to account for the perennial fascination with medieval history and culture in a famous essay, "Dreaming of the Middle Ages" (Eco, *Travels in Hyperreality*, pp. 61–72). In this fascinating work, Eco illustrates how the Middle Ages have always been historically misconstrued or interpreted according to contemporary requirements, underscoring just how mobile the category "medieval" or the role it plays in historical thinking really is. Illustrating how "the Middle Ages have always been messed up in order to meet the vital requirements of different periods," such diverse understandings of this historical era should signal for us the mobility of the category "medieval" and of the role it plays in historical thinking. As Eco concludes, "the fact is that everyone has his own idea, usually corrupt, of the Middle Ages" (Eco, *The Name of the Rose*, p. 535). Eco's statement also applies to ideas of the Middle Ages in *The Name of the Rose* and *Baudolino*. Over the two decades that separate the publication of these novels, what persists and what has changed in Eco's version of the Middle Ages? It should be possible to explore common ground between historical study of the period and its fictional incarnations in Eco's various novels.

USES OF THE MIDDLE AGES

In a recent essay on his work as a novelist, Eco suggests that his choice of a medieval setting for *The Name of the Rose* was more a function of circumstance than the result of a plan: "At first I thought that they [the events he imagined] should have taken place in the present day; then I decided that, seeing as I knew and loved the Middle Ages, it was worth using it as the theatre for my story."[3] Eco's description of the casual genesis of what would become his blockbuster novel's most essential feature is typical of his tendency to downplay processes of intention that might bring his novels into deliberate conversation with his other intellectual endeavors. From the writing of his 1954 doctoral thesis on the aesthetics of Thomas Aquinas (*The Aesthetics of Thomas Aquinas*), the Middle Ages have been foundational to Eco's work as a theorist and critic, providing a textual and cultural resource for some of his most important concerns. In academic circles, the success of *The Name of the Rose* even helped to shed new light on the medieval preoccupations of Eco's theoretical writings.[4]

Eco's long study of the Middle Ages prior to writing *The Name of the Rose* may have rendered inevitable his decision to give that novel a medieval setting, yet it is difficult to imagine his having made a more studied and appropriate choice. The Middle Ages offered the novelist a crucial historical purchase on his semiotic interests. Like that of the contemporary world which his novel addressed, intellectual discourse in the Middle Ages was centered on a linguistic paradigm, specifically the idea that language is not only subject matter for intellectual inquiry but also the ground or model for disciplinary practice itself. One major achievement of *The Name of the Rose* is its detailed representation of the congruence between medieval and (post)modern language theory.[5] This lively dialogue between a contemporary semiotic self-consciousness and medieval thinking about the linguistic sign permeates the novel at every level: it informs plot, theme, and character development and governs the novel's symbolic architecture as well as its famous intertextuality. *The Name of the Rose* exquisitely deploys medieval ideological concepts and academic debates precisely because they anticipate modern semiotics and language theory; the medieval in that novel signifies a mode of interpretation, view of language, and attitude towards experience that are both historically specific and transhistorically central to the dialogic relationship between past and present. The representation of the Middle Ages in *The Name of the Rose* thus contributes crucially to the legitimate theoretical work that Eco intends his novel to perform – in this instance, to demonstrate that fictional narrative can communicate complex ideas and cognitive structures as effectively as theoretical discourses of the academy.

The overarching presence of medieval sign theory and modes of interpretation in Eco's highly entertaining yet intellectually complex novel accomplishes still another form of cultural work. By historicizing the semiotic interests of twentieth-century critical theory through an excavation of their medieval counterparts, *The Name of the Rose* makes a case for revising modes of historical understanding that are more likely to construct the medieval and the modern as oppositional rather than complementary, especially through a binary relation that negatively inflects the medieval.[6] More compellingly than his theoretical writings addressing such issues, Eco's novel thus recuperates the medieval not only as a historical category that provides a temporal point of reference for cultural phenomena depicted in his novel, but also as a symbolic category whose meaning is inseparable from its relationship to concepts of modernity and postmodernity. This latter understanding paradoxically renders the "medieval" complicit in the undermining of conventional linear conceptions of history and of historical periodization, a project that *The Name of the Rose* enacts on a grand scale.

Given Eco's acknowledged habit of revisiting and reworking previous writings, his return to a medieval setting for his fourth novel, *Baudolino*, might seem as inevitable as was his choice of it for his first.[7] Once again, representation of medieval history and culture enables Eco to articulate in fiction his theoretical and philosophical interests. By invoking the Letter of Prester John and the journey to the East, *Baudolino* aligns past and present intellectual structures and conceptions of textuality and truth. At the same time, *Baudolino* frames its idea of the Middle Ages in terms of the writing of history itself, a process that it depicts as rendering suspect all representations of the past. In a lighter vein, Eco also unabashedly renders the Middle Ages of *Baudolino* more explicitly personal. Eco makes the eponymous hero of *Baudolino* hail from the region of his hometown, Alessandria, whose foundation in the twelfth century contributes one of the important historical anecdotes in the novel.[8] The medieval traveler and raconteur Baudolino, who possesses the "gift of tongues" (Umberto Eco, *Baudolino*. Trans. William Weaver. Orlando, FL: Harcourt Brace, 2000, p. 7) and is "capable of retaining in his memory everything he heard" (p. 43) also bears an intriguing resemblance to his creator himself.

Still, in *The Name of the Rose* and *Baudolino*, the Middle Ages do not simply provide the intellectual architecture – or "theater" to use their author's metaphor – for Eco's ideas about history, language, and interpretation. What inevitably strikes the reader who is also a serious student of the Middle Ages is the precision with which Eco represents even the most idiosyncratic elements of medieval life and culture. For some critics, this attribute has even complicated theoretical classification of *The Name of the Rose* as an instance of postmodern historical fiction, or "historiographic metafiction," to use Linda Hutcheon's term, since that novel's commitment to representing the medieval world would appear to align its narrative technique with that of more traditional historical novels.[9] Indeed, no contemporary fiction writer approaches the period with the breadth of knowledge and command of medieval discursive idioms as does Umberto Eco. His mastery of the latter in particular uniquely inflects his narrative vision of the Middle Ages and conveys a sense of that vision's historical authenticity. This authenticity is largely a function of Eco's regular habit of quoting, obviously or surreptitiously, from medieval texts themselves and his ability to mimic modes of representation and habits of thought articulated by medieval cultural discourses. In *The Name of the Rose*, for instance, Eco's polyglot historical and linguistic sensibility keenly distinguishes the logical idiom of William of Baskerville, the Franciscan nominalist, from the exegetical ruminations of Adso, the Benedictine novice. The assertion that

"Adso thinks and writes like a monk" (Eco, *The Name of the Rose*, p. 4) is a key narrative device of *The Name of the Rose*: the division of the monastic day according to the cycle of prayer known as the canonical hours structures Adso's story, in which monastic modes of understanding, methods of interpretation, and appropriations of biblical language make frequent appearances.

Although *Baudolino* exhibits the same exuberant citation of medieval texts that distinguished *The Name of the Rose*, the later novel only intermittently imitates particular medieval social and institutional discourses. In fact, Baudolino and his companions more often employ a discursive idiom that is as reminiscent of the twentieth-century interlocutors Belbo, Casaubon, and Diotallevi in *Foucault's Pendulum* as it is of any medieval habits of verbal representation. Instead, *Baudolino* reaches for authenticity by opening with an imaginative glimpse at a foundational moment in the history of medieval textuality. Baudolino's struggle to "write down what I want which is my own story" (Eco, *Baudolino*, p. 1) enacts in miniature the emergence of a written vernacular language, a historical development of sweeping consequences for medieval culture and, as it happens, for Baudolino's own tale. Eco represents that singular event in terms of the linguistic and cultural categories by which we retrospectively understand it. Baudolino's first attempt at writing in his native Frascheta, an invented language comprising his "memories of other speech that I had heard around me" (p. 38), performs a complex drama of medieval literate practices, enacting the differences between reading and writing, orality and literacy. His historic endeavor – "I was maybe the first to try to write the way we talked" (p. 29) – bears witness to the social and material conditions that shaped the emergence of medieval vernacular writing. Baudolino's personal narrative is already compromised by the circumstances under which it comes into being, inscribed on a stolen parchment scraped clean of the text that had previously covered it: Otto of Freising's *Chronica sive Historia de duabus civitatibus*. Traces of that prior text remain in the palimpsest of Baudolino's writing ("ncipit prologus de duabus civilitatibus historiae…" [p. 1]), asserting the authority of Otto's fugitive Latin chronicle as official history and thereby its difference from the vernacular author's idiosyncratic story.

This erasure of textual and cultural hegemony that must occur if the vulgar peasant is to tell his tale effectively figures the historical perspective on the Middle Ages that we encounter in *Baudolino*. Eco has described his latest medieval fiction as an "antistrophe to *The Name of the Rose*" because the latter is the story of pompous intellectuals whereas the former is a tale of common people who speak dialect.[10] But the changes wrought by the later novel on representation of the medieval historical world are more far-reaching than Eco's metaphor suggests; it might be just as accurate to claim that *Baudolino* turns *The Name of the Rose* inside out. The displacement of Otto's *Chronica* by Baudolino's entrance into vernacular writing reverses the ideological priorities and social investments of *The Name of the Rose* and bestows upon cultural voices marginalized by the earlier novel the later fiction's narrative center. The opening narrative of *Baudolino* represents precisely the rhetorical and ideological event that Jorge works so hard to prevent in *The Name of the Rose*: "The simple," he declares, "must not speak" (Eco, *The Name of the Rose*, p. 478). Whereas Eco's first novel demonstrates how subaltern medieval voices of poverty and heresy are suppressed by forces of inquisitorial prosecution, *Baudolino* gives such marginal voices a free rein, showing what the vox populi that Baudolino represents might say if given the opportunity to infiltrate the worlds of learning and power. As narrator, Baudolino brilliantly mediates between these realms. A twelfth-century Horatio Alger whose talents for languages and lying lead to his adoption by Emperor Frederick Barbarossa, Baudolino retains sympathy with his common origins even as he triumphs in the schools of Paris, mastering the rhetorical arts of *disputatio, dictaminis,* and *poetria,* and earning a post as an imperial ambassador. What *The Name of the Rose*'s Adso can only observe about the relationship between power and discourse, Baudolino regularly practices through arts of verbal manipulation that make him a one-man medieval culture machine.

Baudolino's more expansive interactions with the medieval historical world, and the historical vision of the Middle Ages resulting from them, find a parallel in a narrative structure that also significantly departs from that of Eco's earlier medieval fiction. The entire action of *The Name of the Rose* takes place in a single week in 1327, confined to the localized, even claustrophobic setting of a Benedictine monastery. *Baudolino* paints a larger historical and geographical canvas; its story toggles between the present moment of narration in 1204 and adventures going back to the middle of the previous century, all recounted by Baudolino to Niketas Choniates during the fall of Constantinople. Although the historical world of *The Name of the Rose* is by no means parochial, the reach of *Baudolino* is global, albeit in medieval terms. The later novel's preoccupation with maps, actual and fictitious, underscores an interest in the world beyond Byzantium, in the wonders and riches of the mysterious East that captured the imagination of writers and explorers from antiquity to the early modern period. The cultural map traced by the sequence of

Eco's two medieval historical novels – from the institutional confines of Western monasticism and mendicant history of the high Middle Ages to the geopolitics of East/West relationships and the world stage upon which Baudolino charts his personal quest – importantly coincides with related developments in academic medieval studies during the decades that separate the publication of the two works (1980/2000). In this interval scholars and teachers of the medieval West have increasingly approached the period from larger geopolitical perspectives. As a novel, *Baudolino* speaks to conceptions of a traditional as well as a postcolonial Middle Ages.

MEDIEVAL FICTIONS/MEDIEVAL HISTORY

Eco's medieval novels fully acknowledge postmodern historical fiction's critique of the prospects for historical knowledge, addressing fundamental issues raised by that critique. The genre recognizes, for example, the dependence of historical narrative on a contingent textuality; the fragmentary traces through which the past endures in the present; the tension between the historically real and its fictional representation; and the complex relationship of history and narrative fiction to truth and falsehood.[11] Although *The Name of the Rose* and *Baudolino* both illustrate how the medieval past motivated Eco's theoretical and philosophical interventions in historical fiction, the two novels differently inflect their respective encounters with the capacity of narrative to represent the historical world.

The Name of the Rose embeds its scrutiny of historical fiction and narrative history in a detective novel and thereby critiques both forms of writing in terms of paradigms of that popular genre. In his *Postscript to The Name of the Rose* Eco argues that the plot of a detective novel focuses upon metaphysical and philosophical questions. Efforts by William of Baskerville and Adso to solve the mysterious murders in the abbey – the whodunit – put into play a "structure of conjecture" that aligns modes of narrative organization such as chronology and causality with detective fiction's inherent epistemological concerns. As the murder investigation unfolds, William and Adso's frequent colloquies probe the interpretation of signs. These conversations are devoted especially to determining how such interpretation may impose logical order upon the chaos of evidence and events by using available linguistic and cognitive tools. The processes of detection employed by the philosopher and novice monk parallel the processes for organizing the past entailed in writing history. For the fictional detective and the historian, the past offers up a chaos of information on which order must be imposed, whether that past comprises the events of the fictional crime or actual events performed by human actors in real time. The work of William and Adso as detectives implicitly comments on the work of producing history; both enterprises involve the construction of narratives that purport to offer an accurate response to the question: what happened? The denouement of *The Name of the Rose* makes clear that such activity puts at risk notions of a transparent truth. When William at last understands the motivation for and manner of the deaths in the abbey, he earns Adso's praise for having uncovered Jorge's crimes by correctly interpreting the clues that William discovered. But as the abbey goes up in flames, William makes this anticlimactic observation on their effort: "There was no plot…and I discovered it by mistake" (Eco, *The Name of the Rose*, p. 491). Articulating the paradox of the false pattern that arrives at some truth, William's remark recognizes the contingency of all acts of interpretation and the provisional nature of the truth-claims that result from them; he offers a chastening parable for all makers of narrative committed to truthful representation, including, perhaps especially, writers of history.[12]

If *The Name of the Rose* uses conventions of detective fiction to critique narrative's contingent patterning of events, *Baudolino* employs a different "structure of conjecture" to organize similar suspicions about narrative's truth-value. As historical fiction, *Baudolino* trumps the earlier novel by regularly calling into question the entire enterprise of writing a history that can make only dubious claims to represent the past truthfully. Because it emphasizes the discursive, textual construction of the past, such a preoccupation might be seen to expose the postmodern undergirding of the novel's medieval historical architecture, thereby confusing the theoretical relationship between history and fiction, truth and falsehood. Yet, as scholars of medieval historical writing increasingly note, writers of that history were themselves profoundly aware "that narrative history is a verbal construct, a textual artefact with its own poetics rather than a direct, uncomplicated reflection of events."[13] Even as *Baudolino* takes its suspicions about the truth claims of history to their most extreme – and often hilarious – conclusions, Eco's novel inventively animates such a medieval understanding of historical writing to underscore, as does *The Name of the Rose*, the rich potential for dialogue between past and present that the historical novel affords.

Baudolino ingeniously deploys representations of actual medieval historians to undermine the concept of written history as a factual record of human events (or as the historical novelist's raw material). As we have seen, the transgressive text that opens the novel, Baudolino's macaronic personal narrative, exists only because its author has "stolen many pages" from the cabinet in which his teacher, Otto of Freising, has (Eco, *Baudolino*, p. 1) stored the parchments containing his *Chronica*. The novel fashions a fitting mentor for Baudolino in the learned Otto, who counsels his protégé: "If you want to become a man of letters and perhaps write some Histories one day, you must also lie and invent tales, otherwise your History would become monotonous" (p. 43). When the young man's theft prompts Otto to rewrite his somber world history while he simultaneously composes the more upbeat *Gesta Frederici*, Baudolino discerns "the extent of Otto's lying, seeing how he contradicted himself" as he passed from the *Chronica* to the *Gesta* (p. 43).

This image of the medieval historian, self-reflexively aware of the truth-claims of his enterprise, further resonates at the novel's conclusion when Niketas Choniates, Byzantine historian and interlocutor of Baudolino, discusses with Paphnutius the vexed possibilities for truth in historical writing. Wanting to record Baudolino's story even while recognizing its author as the consummate liar, Niketas seeks advice on the role that Baudolino should play in his historical account of the last days of Byzantium. None at all, Paphnutius recommends, because "a writer of history cannot put his faith in such uncertain testimony" (p. 520). But Paphnutius also belies his insistence on the historian's need for accurate sources when he further advises Niketas how to handle the relic-faking Genoese who had assisted him and Baudolino. They too should be omitted, Paphnutius asserts, because exposure of their deception will make "your readers…lose faith in the most sacred things. It won't cost you much to alter events slightly; you will say you were helped by some Venetians. Yes, I know, it's not the truth, but in a great history little truths can be altered so that the greater truth emerges" (p. 520–1).

Paphnutius' willingness to dispense with inconvenient facts for the sake of a grander historiographic enterprise highlights the ideological and political biases that inevitably shape such endeavors. His preference for the "true story of the empire of the Romans" and disparagement of the "little adventure that was born in a far-off swamp, in barbarian lands, among barbarian peoples" points to the contingency of his historical truth (pp. 520–1). His choice also circles back to Baudolino's struggle, in the novel's opening pages, to overwrite Otto's world-historical *Chronica* with his "own story." *Baudolino*, the novel, materially fulfills its character Paphnutius' prediction that "sooner or later, someone – a greater liar than Baudolino – will tell his 'beautiful story'" (p. 521).

This ultimate conflation of written history's unstable truth-claims with the yet-to-be realized history of Baudolino that in fact comprises the novel obviously blurs whatever distinctions remain among these ostensibly different forms of narrative. Baudolino's self-identification as a liar is central to this conflation and to the eponymous novel's meditation on historical writing and historical fiction. Otto of Freising makes this very connection when he favorably assesses Baudolino's potential as a historian by observing, "You are a born liar" (p. 43). The novel takes the idea of history as "humanity's recorded past" and shows it to be an "ingenious illusion, something that Eco describes through the artifice of lies."[14] Baudolino's inventions as a liar are no mean achievements; indeed, he unwittingly provokes or masterminds the creation of textual and legendary phenomena that post-medieval generations have embraced as quintessential cultural evidence of the historical Middle Ages: the grail legend, the correspondence of Abelard and Heloise, the Letter of Prester John. It is the nature of Baudolino's mendacious gift to expose these and other medieval cultural artifacts either as accidental and unexpected outcomes of contingent circumstances, such as the history of the deeds of Emperor Frederick that comes into being because Baudolino had scraped away the first text of Otto's *Chronica*; or as hoaxes initially perpetrated for what seem like good reasons, such as Baudolino's embellishing the legend of the Magi to accompany the supposed bodies of the same that Baudolino acquires during the sacking of Milan in Chapter 10.

Although Baudolino's adventures in reconfiguring the origins and significance of medieval historical phenomena reveal the naiveté of believing in the transparency of historical writing, they neither give the lie to history nor completely erase the divide between history and fiction. No one would confuse Eco's novel with a work of history. The novel does take seriously the creative work of writing history that Otto of Freising commends to the youthful Baudolino; and our hero, as Raffaele De Benedictis observes, "portrays not only...a ludicrous and sly boy who takes pleasure in lying only for the sake of lying, but...the historical critic who tries to put into perspective the dynamic forces that dominate history in its making. Eco's approach appears to be paradoxical, yet objectively accurate...It is very original and somewhat exceptional to propose an awareness of historical truth based on the strategy of lying for the sake of telling the truth."[15] In *Baudolino* Eco places the explanatory power of historical fiction on an equal footing with narrative history; rather than denigrate history, such a position instead makes a plea for the cognitive value of fiction and its capacity to influence the ways we think about reading and writing history.

MEDIEVAL TEXTS/MEDIEVAL FICTIONS

Why are representations of the Middle Ages so well suited to Eco's post-modern project for the historical novel? The sheer temporal distance that inevitably frames any contemporary encounter with medieval history and culture underscores the already shaky possibilities for historical knowledge emphasized in postmodern historical fiction. Those instabilities, more-over, are writ large in features of medieval textual culture that felicitously coincide with some of this fiction's central concerns. Uncertainties about the authorship, origins, and readers of texts; obscure patterns of textual transmission; and the fragile material conditions for textual circulation were more often the rule than the exception in the Middle Ages. These attributes offer a fruitful context for the postmodern historical novel's critique of the epistemological bases for truth claims about the past. Illustrating how the very ground of such claims is no more stable than the texts that articulate them, historical circumstances of medieval textual production and reception thus inevitably play a role in the creation of narratives about the past that nonetheless may have been, and even still be, regarded as true. If such contingent practices furnish the necessary conditions of medieval historical writing, Eco's *Baudolino* asks, what in fact will distinguish these "true" accounts of human events from the narrative flights of fancy that the novel's eponymous hero so consistently situates in relation to medieval textual culture – for instance, obsessively revising his Letter of Prester John or overseeing a scriptorium in which the imaginary document is produced in multiple languages (p. 208)? *Baudolino*'s common grounding of the processes for elaborating fictions and for producing narrative history enables the novel's audacious play with the idea of historical origins: what if a medieval cultural symbol such as the grail, which centuries of tradition had dignified as a precious relic of the Last Supper and the Crucifixion, was actually born of hearsay and intellectual sparring by a cohort of young twelfth-century Parisian scholars? What if the Letter of Prester John, which motivated Eastern journeys by actual medieval wanderers and explorers, resulted from a drug-induced, hallucinatory effort to elevate the status of Emperor Frederick over the Pope by putting him in contact with a magnificent Eastern kingdom?

Problems of medieval textual culture animate the plots as well as the metahistorical critiques of Eco's medieval novels. In *The Name of the Rose*, conditions and conventions of manuscript production, cultural habits of reading, and medieval modes for the textual organization of knowledge provide the crucial context for William of Baskerville's effort to identify and locate the homicidal text: the lost second book of Aristotle's *Poetics*. Furnishing the object of the detective's search and hence a focal point of the mystery, *Poetics II* also serves the novel's larger historical and semiotic agendas. As partially reconstructed in the novel, Aristotle's lost work speaks directly to the binary model of culture that *The Name of the Rose* critiques and offers an aesthetic and symbolic purchase on the novel's linguistic and political commitments.[16] The medieval textual practices epitomized by the lost book of the *Poetics* in *The Name of the Rose* make an even more prominent appearance in *Baudolino*. Here conditions of textual production and manuscript transmission as well as ambiguities about textual authorship and origins conspire to create the genuinely medieval text that prompts much of Baudolino's narrative production: the Letter of Prester John.

The legend of Prester John enters Eco's novel via the same route it took in the twelfth-century medieval West, the *Chronica* of Otto of Freising. Therein Otto reports the existence of a prosperous Eastern realm ruled by *Presbyter Iohannes*, a Nestorian Christian priest king descended from the Magi who seeks to assist the Church and Jerusalem in overcoming Islam.[17] Around 1165, this Prester John is credited with sending to Western rulers a letter detailing the wealth, power, and marvels of his highly idealized kingdom and asserting his Christian virtue.[18] By all accounts Prester John's Letter was a medieval best seller: through a complex process of transmission, the text survives in over two hundred Latin manuscripts. It was translated into French, German, English, Russian, Hebrew, and Serbian; between 1483 and 1565, it appeared in fourteen printed editions.[19]

Precisely how the legend of Prester John came to be incarnated in the famous Letter is the historical mystery that Eco's novel ingeniously unpacks, making the portrait of that Eastern kingdom and the Letter itself the collaborative creation of Baudolino and his friends. They undertake this labor with the full encouragement of the dying Otto, who has advised Baudolino: "if you have no other news of that realm, invent some...To testify falsely to what you believe true...is a virtuous act because it compensates for the lack of proof of something that certainly exists or happened" (p. 56). Addressing his fabricated epistle to Frederick, Baudolino at first has largely political motives. He expects the Letter to bolster the emperor's international profile by identifying him as Prester John's handpicked ally in the battle with the infidel; the rhetorical alliance of the two rulers, he thinks, will offer the appealing vision of a vast, unified Christian kingdom. But the writer's plans for his creation go awry. The letter never reaches Frederick, and the novel elaborates a circuitous web of deception and power-grabbing to explain how it came to be diverted to Byzantine emperor Manuel Comnenus, who, according to the medieval historical record, was the letter's probable recipient.[20]

The representation of Prester John's Letter and legend in *Baudolino* invokes other important details of that admittedly sketchy record. For instance, the novel provides for the purloined Letter to make its way to Pope Alexander III at a moment when Frederick's political fortunes are waning and those of the papacy are rising; and it acknowledges the Letter's broad medieval circulation by having those copies originate in the scriptorium that Baudolino organizes to provide for the text's wide dispersal throughout the Christian world.[21] But Eco's novel also differently realizes the historical significance of Prester John's Letter, elaborating complex narrative and symbolic functions for it that are nonetheless fully in keeping with its medieval reception. If the Letter is an ideological and cultural construction that focused rival claims to power by various players in the twelfth-century political field, it is also a complex sign upon which Baudolino and his friends inscribe their most deeply held desires: Abdul for an absent beloved, Boron and Kyot for the Grasal, Rabbi Solomon for the ten lost tribes and the origins of an Adamic language, Baudolino for the alluring elsewhere of the priest's mythic kingdom. Through these characters' fixations on Prester John's kingdom, Eco's novel importantly acknowledges the historical position that legendary realm occupied in Western utopian thought; it was "the geographical wishful image of all wishful images [that] played on the hopes of medieval people and…shone before them in a superstitiously moving, hopefully overhopeful way: the earthly paradise."[22] Medieval and early modern appropriations of Prester John are consistently marked by these utopic fantasies, even if their nostalgic longings take shape in anachronistic or actual dreams of conquest.[23]

Like *The Name of the Rose*, then, *Baudolino* demonstrates Eco's gift for crafting historical fiction that makes explicit the internal logic of medieval historical circumstances and medieval texts. Among such texts, the Letter of Prester John provides excellent material for this endeavor because it is, as modern scholars have recognized, "one of the biggest literary hoaxes ever attempted," a "wondrous concoction," an "authentic lie."[24] This point is not lost on the Letter's fictional author: even Baudolino deems his effort "a fine exercise in epistolary rhetoric, a *jocus*" (p. 169). Still, as the Letter's record of manuscript production and transmission demonstrates, the fact of its forgery by no means presented obstacles to its medieval popularity; the fictional Letter's impact on Baudolino, for example, is writ large in the historical Letter's medieval and early modern fortunes in the West. Just as these afterlives demonstrate the Letter's capacity to function as a document considered to be true, Baudolino comes fervently to believe in the kingdom that the Letter describes, even though it is of his own manufacturing. As a character inhabiting the twelfth-century fictional universe of a postmodern historical novel, Baudolino simultaneously anticipates and mirrors the Letter's documented medieval readers. Western envoys and missionaries such as Plano Carpini, William of Rubruck, Oderic of Pordenone, and, most notably, Marco Polo set off for the East expecting the possibility of encountering the Christian priest's kingdom.[25] If twelfth-century Baudolino is a kind of Marco Polo *avant la lettre* (no pun intended), these historical predecessors of their precocious fictional avatar themselves bear witness, after a fashion, to Otto of Freising's assertion that "to testify falsely to what you believe truth...is a virtuous act" (p. 56).

The last third of Eco's novel situates Baudolino in the tradition of these medieval travelers as the hero and his companions "set out...like the Magi...to reach finally the land of Prester John" (p. 322). Just as the detective novel generically shadows the postmodern historical fiction of *The Name of the Rose*, medieval travel writing and its near companion, the narrative of Eastern marvels and wonders, provide generic counterpoint in *Baudolino* from the moment that this entourage takes to the road. Here the novel leaves behind the historical realm represented in narrative chronicles such as Otto's and enters the realm of fantasy. Eco's appeal to medieval travel writing and the textual tradition of Eastern wonders is perfectly compatible with the larger narrative and theoretical designs of *Baudolino*; for the "literary situation" of the traveler, as Mary Campbell notes, offers "a limit case for such intertwined literary issues as truth, fact, figure, fiction, even genre" – the very issues that inform the novel as an instance of postmodern historical fiction.[26]

Through this shift in narrative form and perspective, *Baudolino* maintains its engagement with historical phenomena of medieval textuality. Focusing the story of Baudolino's journey to the East through the lens of medieval travelers' tales enables Eco to open up this historical fiction to an aspect of medieval textual culture that has long fascinated him: its preoccupation with the grotesque and fantastic, its hybridizing of categories of nature, and its attraction to monstrosities.[27] In their quest for the kingdom of Prester John, and especially during their sojourn in its putative outlying province Pndapetzim, Baudolino and his companions encounter sciapods, panotians, blemmyae, giants, pygmies, cynocephali, and other incarnations of the monstrous races that since antiquity had been identified as natural marvels inhabiting a geographically indeterminate land called India. Deriving especially from Pliny's *Natural History*, which drew upon earlier Greek sources, the monstrous races attained widespread popularity and secured their hold on the medieval cultural imagination through works such as Solinus's *Collectanea rerum memorabilium*, Isidore of Seville's *Etymologiae*, and the natural histories and encyclopedias that draw upon these texts, as well as *Alexander's Letter to Aristotle* and the Alexander romances. Not surprisingly, these are among the texts that appear on the reading list perused by the youthful Baudolino at the library of Saint Victoire in Paris (p. 72–3).[28]

The concept of the monstrous races bears witness to the complex processes of transmission, borrowing, and cross-fertilization that characterized circulation of knowledge about the East in the Middle Ages. As the Letter of Prester John illustrates, this knowledge "existed only in textual form." "Most medieval people," as Iain Higgins observes, "had no way of distinguishing what was really there from what was not – indeed, even genuine travelers sometimes had this difficulty, and acquired information about things that they could not personally confirm, but passed on anyway."[29] In an essay on Marco Polo's *Il Milione* (Umberto Eco, *Serendipities: Language and Lunacy.* Trans. William Weaver, New York: Columbia University Press, 1998, pp. 53–75), Eco invokes this classic example of medieval travel writing to tease out the semiotic and theoretical implications of such knowledge, especially as it involves the relationship of written authority to perceived and manufactured truths. Rocco Capozzi has argued that Eco's reading of *Il Milione* anticipates what the novelist would eventually do with his own medieval pilgrim and travel writer, Baudolino.[30] But another medieval tale of Eastern travel offers even richer possibilities for dialogue with both the theoretical commitments and the narrative investments of Eco's postmodern historical novel: *The Travels of Sir John Mandeville*.

Positing the intertextuality of these two works does not require the novel's deliberate look back to *The Travels of Sir John Mandeville*. Although roughly 650 years separate their composition, both draw upon a common archive of exotic Eastern lore and even share some specific sources.[31] Thus, like Baudolino, Mandeville reports encounters with monstrous races such as blemmiae, panotians, and cynocephali, as well as marvelous ones such as anthropophagi and gymnosophists. This common archive doubtless also accounts for other intriguing similarities between *Baudolino* and *The Travels of Sir John Mandeville*: for example, both Mandeville and Baudolino discover a river of stones (p. 357–60), experience funeral practices in which the skull of the dead person is turned into a drinking cup (p. 328–9), and report the existence of women with snakes in their vaginas (p. 333). Whereas Mandeville simply acknowledges the location of the Ten Lost Tribes in the Caspian hills, Baudolino's companion, Rabbi Solomon, is actively seeking them. In Eco's recasting of the story of the Old Man of the Mountain, which made its way to *The Travels of Sir John Mandeville* via Odoric of Pordenone's *Relatio*, Baudolino and his friends find creative inspiration in the pot of green honey that Abdul has stolen from Alo-eddin's garden (pp. 90–1).[32] At least part of the novel's account of Hypatia and her all-female community resembles Mandeville's report on the Amazons.[33] And the point certainly bears mentioning that *The Travels of Sir John Mandeville* surpasses other thirteenth- and fourteenth-century Eastern travelers' tales in the importance it accords to the kingdom of Prester John.[34]

More significant than such illustrations of these works' intertextual relation to traditions of medieval travel writing is the fact that Mandeville's *Travels* seems to have been the Letter of Prester John of its day. Manifestly a fabrication, *The Travels of Sir John Mandeville* was probably the most successful literary hoax of the Middle Ages. It was the most popular prose work of the period; over three hundred manuscripts document the text's circulation in two main variants, as well as its translation into Latin and the major European vernaculars.[35]

Perhaps all medieval travelers are liars, or so it must have seemed to post-Enlightenment readers who expected greater objectivity from these travelers' narratives, a more careful parsing of fact and fiction. For mendacity, though, the armchair traveler Mandeville surpasses them all, deliberately "making use of a form devised to transmit facts and never previously used with any antifactual intent."[36] The Mandeville author exhibits a marked self-consciousness, if not skepticism, regarding the "truth value of his inherited data,"[37] and the uncertain epistemological status of that data neither obstructs his argument for social and ecclesiastical reform in the Christian West nor the rhetorical pleasure he seems to have taken in making it. The human guide that *The Travels Sir John Mandeville* constructs, as Higgins notes in a description that resonates with Eco's novel, "is not a real person" but "a textual fiction written into others' writings and sometimes depicted as doing their deeds." He is "an entertainer, teacher, moralist, and geographer, as well as a trickster and an artist."[38]

This analogy between *Baudolino* and *The Travels of Sir John Mandeville* could be profitably extended; but it also only goes so far. For all the empathetic response that Baudolino's fourteenth-century fellow traveler expresses towards his exotic subjects of observation, Mandeville never ceases to be an observer, even when he sojourns with the Great Khan and

Prester John himself. In the brilliant interlude in which Baudolino and his companions set up housekeeping with Pliny's monstrous races, however, Eco's hero goes native, breaking the temporal, geographical, cultural, and even biological boundaries as no medieval traveler could have done. That he does so has as much to say about Eco's fictional vision as it does about formal and theoretical intersections between medieval travel writing, medieval textuality, and the postmodern historical novel. Yet *Baudolino*'s implicit dialogue with Mandeville's *Travels* remains provocative. With its narrative and intertextual complexity, troping of the storyteller as liar, and playful destabilizing of the ground of historical knowledge, *Baudolino* aptly meets generic expectations for the postmodern historical novel. In so doing, the novel echoes Mandeville's play with truth and lie, empirical bases for knowledge, and the capacity of texts to inspire belief and create new worlds. Rather than see these emphases simply as the contemporary novel's meaningful links to medieval textual traditions, however, it may be more productive to think of Mandeville's *Travels* as the *Baudolino* of its time. This rhetorical figure underscores the full reciprocity of past and present, medieval and (post)modern, showing how revised understandings of these categories may respond to the pressures of and opportunities for thinking and writing historically.

NOTES

1 See, for example, Ruth Glynn, "Presenting the Past: The Case of *Il nome della rosa*," *The Italianist* 17 (1997): 99–116; and Martha Tuck Rozett, "Constructing a World: How Postmodern Historical Fiction Reimagines the Past," *CLIO* 25 (1996): 145–50.
2 George Lukács, *The Historical Novel* (London: Merlin Press, 1962).
3 Umberto Eco, "How I Write," in Charlotte Ross and Rochelle Sibley (eds.), *Illuminating Eco: On the Boundaries of Interpretation* (Aldershot: Ashgate, 2004), p. 176.
4 For a discussion of this topic, see Theresa Coletti, *Naming the Rose: Eco, Medieval Signs, and Modern Theory* (Ithaca, NY: Cornell University Press, 1988).
5 *Ibid.*, pp. 17–31.
6 For an important corrective to this view, see Bruce Holsinger, *The Premodern Condition: Medievalism and the Making of Theory* (Chicago: University of Chicago Press, 2005).
7 See Umberto Eco, "A Response by Eco," in *Illuminating Eco*, pp. 194–5. See also Rocco Capozzi, "The Return of Umberto Eco. Baudolino *homo ludens*: Describing the Unknown," *Rivista di Studi Italiani* 18, 2 (2000): 214; and Peter Bondanella, *Umberto Eco and the Open Text: Semiotics, Fiction, Popular Culture* (Cambridge: Cambridge University Press, 1997).

8 Umberto Eco, "The Miracle of San Baudolino," in *How to Travel with a Salmon & Other Essays*, trans. William Weaver (New York: Harcourt Brace, 1994, pp. 234–48).

9 Linda Hutcheon, *A Poetics of Postmodernism* (London: Routledge, 1988), pp. 105–23, discussed by Glynn in "Presenting the Past."

10 Eco, "How I Write," in *Illuminating Eco*, p. 183.

11 See Glynn, "Presenting the Past"; and Rozett, "Constructing a World."

12 See Cristina della Coletta, *Plotting the Past: Metamorphoses of Historical Narrative in Modern Italian Fiction* (West Lafayette, IN: Purdue University Press, 1996), pp. 163–4.

13 Monika Otter, "Functions of Fiction in Historical Writing," in Nancy Partner (ed.), *Writing Medieval History* (London: Hodder Arnold, 2005), p. 109; in the same collection, see also Robert M. Stein, "Literary Criticism and the Evidence for History," pp. 67–87.

14 Raffaele De Benedictis, "That History Which is Not in Umberto Eco's *Baudolino*," *Forum Italicum* 36 (2002): 407; see also Capozzi, "Baudolino *homo ludens*."

15 De Benedictis, "That History Which is Not," 403–4.

16 Coletti, *Naming the Rose*, pp. 142–4.

17 For the relevant passage in the *Chronica*, see Vsevolod Slessarev, *Prester John: The Letter and the Legend* (Minneapolis: University of Minnesota Press, 1959), pp. 27–8.

18 For overviews see Slessarev, *Prester John*; and Charles E. Nowell, "The Historical Prester John," *Speculum* 28 (1953): 435–45.

19 Slessarev, *Prester John*, p. 5; Bettina Wagner, *Die "Epistola presbiteri Johannis" Lateinisch und Deutsch* (Tübingen: Max Niemeyer Verlag, 2000), pp. 2–25.

20 Nowell, "Historical Prester John," 435.

21 *Ibid.*, 444–5.

22 Ernst Bloch, *The Principle of Hope*, trans. Neville Plaice, Stephen Plaice, and Paul Knight, 2 vols. (Oxford: Basil Blackwell, 1962), vol. II: p. 769; quoted in Michael Uebel, "Imperial Fetishism: Prester John Among the Natives," in Jeffrey Jerome Cohen (ed.), *The Postcolonial Middle Ages* (New York: Palgrave, 2001), p. 281, n. 36.

23 Uebel, "Imperial Fetishism," pp. 444–5.

24 Sir E. Denison Ross, "Prester John and the Empire of Ethiopia," in Arthur Percival Newton (ed.), *Travel and Travelers of the Middle Ages* (London: Routledge and Kegan Paul, 1926; rpt. 1949), p. 179 (literary hoaxes); Nowell, "Historical Prester John," 435 (wondrous concoction); L. N. Gumilev, *Searches for an Imaginary Kingdom: The Legend of the Kingdom of Prester John*, trans. R. E. F. Smith (Cambridge University Press, 1987), p. 4 (lie).

25 Slessarev, *Prester John*, p. 5; Ross, "Prester John," pp. 182–3. On Marco Polo, see also Mary B. Campbell, *The Witness and the Other World: Exotic European Travel Writing, 400 – 1600* (Ithaca, NY: Cornell University Press, 1988), pp. 87–121.

26 Campbell, *Witness and the Other World*, p. 2.

27 On the implications of the monstrous, see Cristina Farronato, "Umberto Eco's *Baudolino* and the Language of Monsters," *Semiotica* 144 (2003): 319–42.

28 See Campbell, *Witness and the Other World*, chapter two, "The Fabulous East: 'Wonder Books' and Grotesque Facts," pp. 47–86; Rudolf Wittkower, "Marvels of the East: A Study in the History of Monsters," *Journal of the Warburg and Courtauld Institutes* 5 (1942): 159–97; and John Block Friedman, *The Monstrous Races in Medieval Art and Thought* (Cambridge, MA: Harvard University Press, 1981).

29 Iain MacCleod Higgins, *Writing East: The "Travels" of Sir John Mandeville* (Philadelphia: University of Pennsylvania Press, 1997), p. 189.

30 Capozzi, "Baudolino *homo ludens*," 222–6.

31 Mandeville's *Travels* was written in French around 1357; *Mandeville's Travels*, ed. M. C. Seymour (Oxford: Clarendon Press, 1967), p. xiii. For sources of the *Travels*, see *The Travels of Sir John Mandeville*, trans. and intro. C. W. R. D. Moseley (Harmondsworth: Penguin, 1983), p. 19. Eco mentions Mandeville in "How I Write," p. 183.

32 Abdul's green honey makes "tangible that which has never been seen" (Eco, *Baudolino*, p. 92). In *The Travels of Marco Polo*. Aloeddin cultivated an earthly paradise staffed by damsels; he captured young men, drugged them with opium, and exposed them to these delights upon their awakening. In this way Alo-eddin controlled his captives, who served him as assassins because they were convinced that such a paradise would be their reward. See *The Travels of Marco Polo*, intro. John Masefield (London: Dent and Sons Ltd; New York: E. P. Dutton, 1908; rpt. 1954), pp. 73–7.

33 For the corresponding discussions in Mandeville, see *Travels of Sir John Mandeville*, p. 169 (river of stones); pp. 186–7 (skull as drinking cap); p. 175 (snakes in vagina); pp. 165–6 (lost tribes); pp. 171–2 (green honey); pp. 116–17 (Amazons).

34 Higgins, *Writing East*, pp. 189–90.

35 Campbell, *Witness and the Other World*, p. 122. A comprehensive study of the manuscript variants appears in Higgins, *Writing East*.

36 See Campbell, *Witness and the Other World*, p.139.

37 *Ibid.*, p. 146.

38 Higgins, *Writing East*, p. 8.

CHAPTER 6

Eco and the tradition of the detective story

Peter Bondanella

The editors of a recent collection of essays on the history of the metaphysical detective story from Poe to the postmodern era suggest three variants of the contemporary metaphysical detective story that may be usefully applied to Eco's five novels.[1] The first type, in the tradition that begins with Poe and runs to the present with such writers as Sir Arthur Conan Doyle, Jorge Luis Borges, Eco, and Paul Auster, merges the historical novel with the metaphysical and produces a relatively minimalist, labyrinthine work where plural identities or suspects are reduced to one (the case of *The Name of the Rose*). The second type, juxtaposed to the first, reflects a maximalist style, is replete with loose ends and a chaotic plot, and includes characters whose identities are extremely uncertain, multiple, and remain open to question at the novel's conclusion (the editors place *Foucault's Pendulum* into this category). Finally, a third and relatively little studied postmodern variant of the metaphysical detective story, the pseudobiographical "research novel" where the search for the missing person leads to the surprising conclusion that we are he or she, is proposed. While the editors do not consider the other three of Eco's novels, *The Island of the Day Before*, *Baudolino*, and *The Mysterious Flame of Queen Loana* might well be placed in this category. Regardless of how critics organize Eco's literary production, there is little doubt that his fiction owes its inspiration, its popularity, and its originality to its creative engagement with the entire tradition of the literary detective story.

The link between Umberto Eco's literary career and the tradition of detective fiction may be said to reflect one facet of the writer's interest in popular culture. In the immediate postwar period in Italy, the country's literary and intellectual culture was dominated by remnants of the prewar idealism identified with Benedetto Croce, on the one hand, and the Marxist literary theories of George Lukács or Antonio Gramsci, on the other. In the first case, writers and critics under Croce's sway were profoundly uninterested in anything that smacked of popular or mass culture – they were, in Eco's terms, the highest expression of apocalyptic intellectuals. However, many Marxists who were opposed to Crocean idealism identified mass or popular culture with America and often, therefore, felt obliged to oppose many forms of popular culture on ideological grounds during the height of the Cold War. Eco, as his future fascination with popular song, film, television, and literature would demonstrate, approached these topics from an entirely different angle. In an early article in *Gioventù cattolica* (*Catholic Youth*) written at the beginning of his career (January 17, 1954), he declared: "If we went to dig through the library of a famous man, of a man of culture, or a scientist, perhaps we would discover there a series of detective novels. The detective novel is not only a youthful sin; it is a perpetual temptation."[2] This precocious appreciation of a popular literary genre's value as the reading fare of not only distracted travelers and bored housewives but also cultured intellectuals reflects Eco's early critical independence from the predominant schools of criticism in Italy at the time, both of which took themselves very seriously and refused to deal with anything but "high" culture. Among Italian intellectuals, Eco was not alone in his admiration for the detective story. Eugenio Montale, the winner of the 1975 Nobel Prize for Literature, is said to have declared that "I only read detective novels,"[3] but these sentiments were not commonly expressed until after the appearance of *The Name of the Rose* in 1980, the astounding critical and commercial success of which all over the world may be taken to mark the coming of age of the Italian detective story as a legitimate literary genre.

In Italy, unlike the rest of the continent or in the Americas, detective fiction between the mid-nineteenth and mid-twentieth centuries was virtually abandoned to foreign writers. Italian readers had very little interest in the few detective novels or novelists that existed. The writer most critics cite as a possible founder of a tradition that never developed in the peninsula is Emilio De Marchi (1851–1901), whose novel *Il cappello del prete* (1888, *The Priest's Hat*) recounts the murder of a priest by a nobleman, a very successful book that was inspired by a true crime. But the circumstances surrounding the book's creation underscore the general poverty of true detective fiction in Italy some several generations after the appearance of Edgar Allan Poe (1809–49), Émile Gorboriau (1832–73), and Sir Arthur Conan Doyle (1859–1930): De Marchi wrote the novel after a friend challenged him to show that a decent example of such a popular genre could be produced in Italy without importing a French author's creation! Clearly Italian readers expected their detective fiction to come from abroad.

De Marchi's example was not followed by many other Italians. In the United Kingdom and the United States, great detective fiction was produced in a variety of subgenres. The original links between detective fiction and metaphysical or philosophical questions arose immediately in the relatively small number of detective stories written by the universally recognized inventor of detective fiction, Edgar Allan Poe.[4] Poe identified his creations with the analytical faculty, a topic that would occupy Eco's semiotic theory and would influence other subsequent writers such as Jorge Luis Borges (1899–1986) and Eco himself. Following Poe's heuristic generic innovations, Sir Arthur Conan Doyle created the world's most famous detective – Sherlock Holmes – in a series of stories that underscored a more positivistic approach to crime, the detective as scientist rather than as analytical philosopher. Conan Doyle's literary creation would have a profound impact upon Eco's fiction. The "Golden Age" of English detective fiction identified with such figures as Agatha Christie (1890–1976) and Dorothy-Sayers (1893–1957) who departed from both of these analytical or positivistic traditions to create the subgenre often called the "cozy" or the puzzle mystery that flourished between the wars primarily in English-speaking countries. The famous detectives created by Christie and Sayers – Hercule Poirot and Lord Peter Wimsey – often solved crimes that took place in small English towns among the aristocracy of the period and that were unraveled as if they were puzzles. In fact, in Christie's *The Boomerang Clue* (1937), the solving of a murder is compared to working a crossword puzzle (another popular pastime of the era). Like Conan Doyle's Victorian sleuth Sherlock Holmes, their protagonists rarely raised questions that upset the status quo. The essence of this kind of fiction may be found in the popular parlor game *Clue* that was invented in 1949: it presented six suspects (Colonel Mustard, Professor Plum, Reverend Green, Mrs. White, Miss Scarlett, and Mrs. Peacock), and the players sought to discover who committed a crime, in what room it was committed, and by what weapon. The fact that this tremendously popular game was a "parlor" game underscores the kind of plot resolution typical of the mystery in this period: in general, the puzzle-solving detective, such as Poirot, assembled all the suspects in a room, reviewed the evidence, and fingered the guilty person in a public display of deductive virtuosity where the crime was defined as a kind of intellectual game. Conceived of in this fashion, these mysteries stressed plot over either action or character. The mystery in the hands of such writers generally followed the practice of making the "most surprising suspect" or the "least likely suspect" the guilty party.

The great prewar tradition that stood in direct contrast to such polite fiction was the hard-boiled detective fiction produced by a number of important American detective writers: Raymond Chandler (1888–1959), James Cain (1892–1977), Dashiell Hammett (1894–1961), and countless imitators. In the case of the two most famous detectives created by this genre – Chandler's Philip Marlowe and Hammett's Sam Spade – Hollywood's films noirs immortalized an action-packed, violent, sexy detective story and changed the direction of the genre from the polite, aristocratic atmosphere of such English fiction to the gritty, lonely, pessimistic, and cynical American variant. Both hard-boiled novels and films noirs introduced psychological themes into detective fiction (often influenced by Freud's theories), and treated important social problems, such as the Depression or the economic causes of crime. In particular, the *femme fatale* character – already popular in sentimental novels or opera – now often became a real killer, compared to the black widow spider in duplicity and guile. Humphrey Bogart's memorable performances as Sam Spade in the adaptation of Hammett's *The Maltese Falcon* (novel published in 1930; John Huston's film by the same name released in 1941) and as Philip Marlowe in the adaptation of Chandler's *The Big Sleep* (novel published in 1939; Howard Hawks' film by the same name released in 1946) represent a high-water mark in the popularity and the artistic quality of the detective genre in American literature and film.

In Italy, the relative paucity of home-grown detective fiction created an important publishing phenomenon, the foundation in 1929 of an important series of translated detective stories by Arnoldo Mondadori, one of Italy's most influential publishers. The titles in this series were almost exclusively French, English, or American, since those literary cultures possessed a robust detective fiction culture, and these popular books appeared with bright yellow covers. As a result, the term "giallo" ("yellow") became synonymous with the detective novel and came to include not only detective novels but crime stories in general, thrillers, suspense novels, as well as hard-boiled fiction. Its popularity as a term would later be transferred to the Italian postwar crime and horror film, as "giallo" in Italy also refers to the kind of B film with relatively low production values and criminal or horror themes that appeared in great numbers in Italy from the late 1950s into the 1970s (many of which were based upon non-Italian fictional sources). The most authoritative history of the giallo in Italy underscores the fact that even with the popular success of the Mondadori series, the detective novel remained identified with foreign culture. Even though the most successful detective novelist of the era, Augusto de Angelis – a figure of great importance in Eco's latest novel – argued that Italy deserved its own tradition of Italian detective stories, critics of the period argued that an Italian detective story was "absurd," that the detective genre required the "criminal Romanticism of Anglo-Saxon culture," and prejudices of this type would eventually inspire the Fascist government to suppress the Mondadori Giallo series in 1941 and 1942 precisely because its foreign nature supposedly stood in conflict with the sound moral character of Italian middle-class culture.[5] This same historian notes that those literary critics who shared this opinion that Italian culture was inhospitable a priori to the detective genre would find it incomprehensible that so many contemporary English-speaking authors have created extremely popular Italian detectives in the past several decades. Covi cites the most obvious cases that prove detective fiction may thrive in Italy in the hands of inventive narrators: Michael Dibdin and Donna Leon, the inventors of two series of detective novels set in Venice with Vice Questore Aurelio Zen and Commissario Brunetti as their respective protagonists; Magdalen Nabb's Maresciallo Guarnaccia detecting crimes in Florence; and Thomas Harris' Commissario Pazzi, also of Florence, who meets death at the hands of the monstrous Hannibal Lector, executed by being hanged from the Palazzo Vecchio in imitation of the demise of his more illustrious ancestors after the failure of the Pazzi Conspiracy in the fifteenth century.[6] These same negative critics would be even more astounded at the flourishing state of Italian detective fiction over a quarter of a century after the appearance of Eco's first novel.

Eco had a few important precursors in his own literary tradition. Carlo Emilio Gadda (1893–1973) published *Quer pasticciaccio brutto de via Merulana* (*That Awful Mess on Via Merulana*) first in magazines in 1946 and then as a novel in 1957. Like Eco's *The Name of the Rose*, Gadda's work appeals to very different audiences – those for whom the whodunit means an exciting murder mystery as well as for those more advanced readers who appreciate Gadda's linguistic experimentalism and use of various dialects. Perhaps the most popular detective writer in Italy before Eco's best seller appeared was Giorgio Scerbanenco (1911–1969), who wrote detective fiction (short stories as well as novels) close in tone to the hard-boiled American tradition, such as *Venere privata* (*Private Venus*, 1961) and *Traditori di tutti* (*Duca and the Milan Murders*, 1966). Scerbanenco's works focused upon Milan as the capital of crime during the Italian "economic miracle" in the 1960s and produced a notable anti-heroic figure, Duca Lamberti. A number of novels about the Mafia set in Sicily by Leonardo Sciascia (1921–89), such as *Il giorno della civetta* (1961,

Mafia Vendetta), *A ciascuno il suo* (*To Each His Own*, 1966), or *Il con-testo* (1971, *Equal Danger*) exploited the traditional mysterious workings of organized crime in Sicily as a metaphor for a world without justice. But while Gadda's popularity was limited to a tightly restricted elite of read-ers and Sciascia's works were generally interpreted as political tracts, only Scerbanenco's brand of hard-boiled detective stories was ever very popular and this, of course, meant that Italy's elite critics and academics largely ignored them. For apocalyptic intellectuals of Eco's generation, however, the identification of detective fiction with popular, mass culture guaran-teed that detective fiction of any quality would not be taken seriously.

When *The Name of the Rose* achieved not only best-seller status in Italy (a relatively small market) but international success, selling tens of mil-lions of copies in most of the major languages of the world, it became more and more difficult to relegate the detective novel to the status of pulp fiction designed for reading at vacations by the seashore or while waiting for flights at the airports. Eco was universally regarded by 1980 as Italy's most influential and original intellectual who had already achieved the impossible in Italy by writing a serious work of cultural theory (*The Open Work*) that had achieved best-seller status. Moreover, Eco was rec-ognized as one of the country's most serious and thoughtful writers of social and cultural essays published in major opinion-leading periodicals and newspapers. He was, in short, anything but a popularizer, although he was widely read for his works on popular culture, and his essays on James Bond, Superman, popular music, and other forms of mass culture that many of his colleagues treated with contempt had won him a wide following among the educated general reading public in Italy.

With *The Name of the Rose*, Eco succeeded in educating the Italian reading public to appreciate the kind of metaphysical detective fiction that characterizes such writers as Poe and Borges and that stood outside the Italian literary tradition. In the process, he helped to inject the best of Italian fiction into the mainstream of world literature. His ability to raise the level of this kind of generic literature was accompanied by a con-temporaneous analysis of the essence of detective fiction – the detective's epistemological quest for information or knowledge – that influenced his more esoteric theoretical works on semiotics. Between the 1960s and the publication of his first novel, Eco's fame as an analyst of popular culture had expanded into more theoretical inquiries into the nature of language itself. With the publication of *A Theory of Semiotics* in 1975 and a number of essays that appeared within the decade before this work (publications that were often linked to his interest in popular culture), Eco had become perhaps the world's most famous semiotician whose theory of semiotics was grounded squarely upon the ideas of the American philosopher Charles S. Peirce. Even before his first novel appeared, Eco recognized that an important intellectual link existed between the detective fiction of Poe and Conan Doyle, on the one hand, and the philosophical theories of Peirce, on the other, that bolstered his own discussions of semiotics. Moreover, during the time *The Name of the Rose* was gestating, Eco discovered that as early as 1978 these connections had begun to attract the attention of other linguists, semioticians, and philosophers of language, including Thomas A. Sebeok, Carlo Ginzburg, Jaakko Hintikka, and others.[7]

For Eco in *A Theory of Semiotics*, interpretation of a text was simply a specific example of more universal acts of comprehension or understanding, acts he preferred not to be defined as "decoding" but rather "understanding, on the basis of some previous decoding, the general sense of a vast portion of discourse," what Peirce labeled as a specific kind of philosophical inference he called 'abduction' or sometimes defined as 'making an hypothesis'" (Eco, *A Theory of Semiotics*, p.138). Since the popular imagination universally identifies Conan Doyle's Sherlock Holmes, the archetypal literary detective, with deductive logic, Peirce's distinctions between various kinds of inferences and Eco's acceptance of his distinctions, would have important consequences for his fiction. Deduction, properly defined, moves from a general rule (all the beans from this bag are white), and given a case (these beans are from this bag), it infers a result (these beans are or must be white). Induction, on the other hand, infers a probable rule (all the beans in this bag are white) from a plurality of results (all the beans I picked up were white) and a plurality of cases (they all came from this bag). Abduction invents or hypothesizes a general rule from a single result: these beans are white; now, if I suppose that there is a rule according to which all the beans in this bag are white, then the result could be a case of that rule.[8]

The Sign of Three: Dupin, Holmes, Peirce (1983) is a collection of essays that Eco co-edited with semiotician Thomas Sebeok. It appeared three years after the success of *The Name of the Rose* but originated from discussions and exchanges with like-minded scholars beginning as early as 1978, the period in which Eco was composing *The Name of the Rose*. It examines the implications of this definition of various kinds of logical inferences for the detective novel. As its title suggests, and as Eco believed, the detective fiction often denigrated as pulp entertainment actually contained a far more serious philosophical foundation. One contributor to the anthology, Marcello Truzzi, studied the entire corpus of Conan Doyle's Sherlock Holmes stories and concluded that there existed "at least 217 clearly described and discernible cases of inference (unobtrusive measurements) made by Holmes" and that "although Holmes often speaks of his *deductions*, these are actually quite rarely displayed in the canon. Nor are Holmes' most common inferences technically *inductions*. More exactly, Holmes consistently displays what Charles S. Peirce has called *abductions*."⁹ In his own contribution to *The Sign of Three*, Eco accepts Truzzi's conclusions that Sherlock Holmes' success at stopping crime grew out of his skill at making abductions, not deductions, and Eco goes even further to identify the third chapter of Voltaire's *Zadig* (1747) – a philosophical tale recounting how the hero of Voltaire's tale identified a horse without ever having set eyes upon him by means of abduction – as the fountainhead of all detective fiction, a hint that Poe picked up and turned into the genre that we all recognize today. Because abduction, as opposed to either deduction or induction, plays a crucial role in the creation of language and meaning through the process defined by Peirce and popularized by Eco as universal semiosis, it is abduction – and not the mythical deduction erroneously linked to Conan Doyle's detective fiction – that he highlighted in the detection practiced by the protagonist of *The Name of the Rose*. Because abduction lies at the heart of an epistemological inquiry aimed at making inferences about our world without having complete information, we shall see that all of Eco's fiction, and not just his first novel, rely upon plots that are ultimately detective plots – all rest upon a search for evidence or conclusions typical of the literary detective.

Eco himself composed the blurb on the cover of the first Italian edition of *The Name of the Rose*, and this document (unfortunately not reproduced on subsequent Italian or English editions) announced Eco's desire to appeal to three different audiences – the largest market, the mass of relatively unsophisticated readers who concentrated upon plot and precisely those readers ignored by apocalyptic intellectuals; a second public, readers who examined historical novels to find connections or analogies between the present and the past; and a third and even smaller elite audience, postmodern readers who enjoyed ironic references to other literary works and who assumed that a good work of fiction would produce what Eco calls a " 'whodunit' of quotations."¹⁰ After the initial success of this first fictional work, Eco published his *Postscript to "The Name of the Rose"*, what amounts to a "revisiting" of Poe's technique in writing "The Philosophy of Composition" to explain his poem "The Raven." In this auto-critique and analysis of his own novel, Eco defines the detective novel as "the most metaphysical and philosophical" literary form (Eco, *The Name of the Rose*, p. 524), an obvious reference to Poe's own definition of his own stories as examples of the analytical faculty.

In Eco's account of the investigation of the deaths of a number of monks in an Italian Benedictine monastery in 1327 by a Franciscan, William of Baskerville (a nod to Conan Doyle's Sherlock Holmes and *The Hound of the Baskervilles*) and his Benedictine novice Adso of Melk who is the book's narrator (another nod to Dr. Watson, the narrative voice of the Holmes stories) a number of the conventions from the history of the detective story are exploited and sometimes parodied. William's dramatic confrontation with the villain of the story, a blind fanatic named Jorge of Burgos, not only reminds the reader of Holmes' confrontation with his arch-enemy, the evil Moriarty called "the Napoleon of Crime" by Conan Doyle, but also points the reader in the direction of the detective fiction of Jorge Luis Borges (1889–1996). Borges is the ultimate source of the labyrinth theme in Eco's novel, and it is no accident that the maze-like labyrinth is a geometrical structure that also lies at the heart of discussions of the production of language in Eco's semiotic works. Eco was certainly aware of one particular essay by Borges, "On the Origins of the Detective Story," and he would have agreed with Borges' assertion in that piece that "the literature of our time is exhausted by interjections and opinions, incoherences and confidences: the detective story represents order and the obligation to invent."[11] In reporting William of Baskerville's first important demonstration of his bravura as a detective, Eco imitates Voltaire's tale of Zadig's description of a horse he has never seen, a passage he analyzes later at length in *The Sign of Three*: William not only describes the lost horse of the abbot but he even guesses his name (Brunellus) by an exercise of abductive logic. William thus becomes Eco's willfully anachronistic semiotician, employing Peirce's logic equally as skillfully as Sherlock Holmes.

Conan Doyle's world rested upon fundamentally conservative assumptions: he considered the British Empire a benevolent force in the world; he judged English society as fundamentally fair in spite of the many class distinctions it reflected; he more often believed crime derived from some evil genius than from degraded social and economic conditions in Victorian England; and, most importantly, he shared the positivistic faith of his era and was convinced that the universe was knowable through science. In typical postmodern fashion, Eco reverses these somewhat Victorian assumptions. In William's analysis of the crimes in the monastery, the monk discerns a pattern he believes comes from the Book of Revelation

(8:6–10:10): William concludes that the murderer (soon to be revealed as Jorge of Burgos) has based his crimes on this text. He discovers that only people who knew Greek died (a true conclusion) but falsely concludes that the Book of Revelation provides a pattern for their deaths. Since Jorge is from Spain, the producer of the most famous commentaries on the Book of Revelation, William assumes rightly that Jorge is the murderer. However, all his intellectual attempts to discover the truth arrive at an impasse: or, more correctly, William arrives at the discovery of the murderer by completely erroneous processes of abduction. The beginning of the pattern (Adelmo's death) results from suicide, not homicide; subsequently Malachi, and not Jorge, kills Severinus; after the fifth death, Jorge becomes convinced, like William, that a divine plan is repeating the pattern found in the Book of Revelation, and he then imitates it. As a result, William concludes: "there was no plot…and I discovered it by mistake" (Eco, *Name of the Rose,* p. 491). This is hardly a conclusion that Sherlock Holmes, or even Sam Spade for that matter, would reach, although the world of the American hard-boiled novel certainly offers very little philosophical consolation.

William's abductions falsely assume the existence of order and purpose in his world and in the universe. We as readers fall into the same logical trap experienced by William because detective fiction of a certain type – that popularized by Conan Doyle or by the English tradition of the Golden Age of detection – trains readers to seek out patterns and to resolve mysteries as if they were puzzles. For example, Agatha Christie's *The ABC Murders* presents a series of murders following an alphabetical pattern; Ellery Queen's *Ten Days Wonder* exploits a murder plot involving the Ten Commandments; and so forth.[12] A large number of the elements in Eco's plot owe their origins to Poe's fiction: the use of secret coded messages that must be decoded by cryptography (exploited by Poe in "The Gold Bug"); the mysteriously locked room (invented by "The Murders in the Rue Morgue"); the concealment of the important missing manuscript of Aristotle's lost treatise on comedy by hiding it in plain sight (invented in Poe's "The Purloined Letter"). These elements of his narrative recalling Poe, combined with the reminiscences of Conan Doyle and Borges, make *The Name of the Rose* the perfect combination of erudition and fiction. As Eco wrote on the cover of his book, his novel represents an important intellectual discovery for him: with it, he came to the realization "upon reaching maturity, that those things about which we cannot theorize, we must narrate" (Umberto Eco, *The Name of the Rose,* First Italian edn. Milan: Bompiani, 1980). What Eco's first novel concludes magnificently is that humanity is obliged to live without any single unequivocal Truth. Like the rose to which the last line of the novel in Latin refers ("Stat rosa pristine nomine, nomina nuda tenemus" – "Yesterday's rose endures in its name, we hold empty names"[13]), words or signs may contain within themselves a wide range of meanings, historical associations, symbolisms, and yet they remain only signs, not fixed truths. Only fanatics like Jorge of Burgos, blind not only physically but philosophically by searching for a single Truth, do not consider Truth a tenuous concept, something that human beings approach but which is never anything but a hypothesis, a working theory that will soon be undermined by different perspectives and conflicting evidence.

Compared to the plot of *The Name of the Rose*, which reflects a rather traditional, minimalist structure leading up to a Sherlock Holmes–Moriarty type showdown and the discovery of the villain in spite of its overwhelming erudition and generous sprinkling of Latin quotations that were inaccessible to most readers of the book, the detective narrative in *Foucault's Pendulum* is even more complex and maximalist, as Merivale and Sweeney note.[14]

Its narrator, Casaubon – named after Isaac Casaubon (1559–1614), a Swiss philologist who proved that the Corpus Hermeticum, a body of works supposedly written by Hermes Trismegistus before the time of Moses, was actually written after the Christian era – is described in the same way as Sam Spade, whose task is "exploring the mean streets – that's your job." This description manages in postmodern fashion to join Dashiell Hammett's famous detective with Raymond Chandler's famous essay on the detective genre, "The Simple Art of Murder," and it conjures up the violent world of Martin Scorsese's first important film, *Mean Streets*, which was also inspired by Chandler's essay (the term "mean streets" is Chandler's invention). But whereas the medieval semiotician-detective in *The Name of the Rose* had to contend with only one villain, in Eco's second novel, the narrative becomes even more involved with theoretical issues that occupied Eco at the time.

While Eco's second novel appeared in 1988, several works that were published subsequently – *The Limits of Interpretation* (1990) and *Interpretation and Overinterpretation* (1993)–contain the results of Eco's theoretical thinking during the time *Foucault's Pendulum* gestated in his mind, particularly his reaction to the deconstructionist ideas associated with the French philosopher Jacques Derrida. Eco asserts that much "so-called 'post-modern' thought will look very pre-antique" if carefully examined (Eco, *Interpretation and Overinterpretation*, p.25), and he essentially identifies deconstructionist theorists with second-century hermetic thinkers who rejected the classical Greek rationalist law of the excluded middle and believed that many things may be true at the same time even if they stand in obvious contradiction to each other: "where the coincidence of opposites triumphs, the principle of identity collapses. *Tout se tient*" (p.32). *Tout se tient* – everything is connected – is also the key to the plot of Eco's second novel, appearing numerous times in the text (Eco, *Foucault's Pendulum*, pp.179, 289, 618). Lunatics, as Jacopo Belbo – one of Casaubon's fellow editors at the publishing house where he works – says, always believe everything is connected and inevitably bring up the topic of the Templars, the Freemasons, the Jesuits, the Rosicrucians, and the Elders of Zion, and any number of supposedly conspiratorial groups in order to explain the chaotic universe. Casaubon, Belbo, and Diotallevi edit so many insane manuscripts on the occult and conspiracy theories at their publishing house that they decide to invent what they call "the Plan" after a meeting with an old Fascist officer who claims that the Templars had a plot to conquer the world and that after the suppression of their order in 1307 by the King of France, the Templars went underground. However, a strange document in Old French that this officer has salvaged leads him to believe that the Templars planned to meet every 120 years in six different locations. Beginning with this idea, the three editors invent an elaborate parody of the various conspiracy theories, creating a mega-conspiracy theory in which every possible conspiratorial group mentioned above (plus the seekers of the grail and the Nazis) are all connected. As Casaubon summarizes the rules of their Plan: "Rule one: Concepts are connected by analogy... Rule Two says that if tout se tient in the end, the connecting works ... Rule Three: The connections must not be original... But if you invent a plan and others carry it out, it's as if the Plan exists. At that point it does exist" (p. 618). The Sam Spade narrator in the novel and his friends have ignored a basic principle of human behavior: things perceived as real are real in their consequences. As a result, every lunatic in the world who believes that there is a conspiracy behind every human enterprise concludes that the three editors possess some universal Truth, and they seek to obtain that information from them. This pompous assumption that every social phenomenon obscures a conspiracy is deflated easily by Casaubon's girlfriend Lia, who examines the Old French document upon which the Plan is based and easily proves, through a combination of common sense, traditional philology, and reading a guide book about the town in which the document was discovered, that this mysterious clue suggesting an occult conspiracy in reality is nothing but an old laundry list drawn up by a merchant of the period! As one critic of conspiracy theories has put it, Eco's characters "play detective to their own virtual crime. They decipher and justify their own tampered evidence. They play all the parts in the detective drama – those of the author and of the characters, of the conspirators, and of the victims of conspiracy theory."[15]

If William of Baskerville's accidental discovery of the truth behind the murders in the abbey undercuts any confident belief in an orderly universe like that of Sherlock Holmes' Victorian universe, Casaubon's terrifying experience with what he calls "Diabolicals" – people whose belief in conspiracy theories is so intense that they will kill for non-existent information – calls into question the very logic of abduction or making informed inferences that lies at the basis of every form of detection. Real abductions require reality checks, but those who believe that everything is connected to everything else (an absurd parody of the "unlimited semiosis" that both Peirce and Eco promote in their semiotic theory) leave out this important link in making correct inferences about the universe. Eco surely suggests that the only true secret is that no secret exists (a version of the view Socrates held, that the only wise man is he who understands that he is not wise). It is not by accident that the password to Belbo's computer only opens when the question "Do you have the password?" is answered by the proper response of "No" instead of devising a complicated code to enter the program (p. 42).

In Eco's tale, the three friends – amateur detectives and semioticians working as editors (and therefore wordsmiths) – all end badly. Diotallevi dies of cancer and escapes any reckoning with the Diabolicals who pursue his friends. Belbo refuses to reveal the "secret" of the Plan – that there is no secret – to the Diabolicals who have captured him in the Musées des Arts et des Métiers in Paris, and he dies literally lashed to Foucault's pendulum, an instrument that was invented in the nineteenth century by Léon Foucault (1819–68) to prove experimentally that the earth rotates on its axis. However, Eco identifies another Foucault – literary theorist Michel Foucault (1926–84), the author of *The Order of Things* (1966) and, with Derrida, one of the key figures in French theories of interpretation at the time – as a philosopher whose paradigm of similarity resembles the conspiracy theories of his novel's characters that Eco criticizes (Eco, *Interpretation and Overinterpretation*, pp. 81–3). Even though Eco claims he had the scientist Foucault rather than the theorist Foucault in mind when he wrote his novel, it is significant that Belbo dies the day before Michel Foucault died (June 25, 1984), while Casaubon waits for the Diabolicals to come for him on the day after Michel Foucault died (June 26 1984).[16] The last act of Eco's narrator, then, ultimately is shaped by a long, inter-connected chain of overinterpretations or paranoid interpretations where *tout se tient* and where any hint of a reasonable inference based on sensible abduction to understand the universe has been abandoned by fanatical non-logic. The narrator-detective, like the policemen in Sciascia's Mafia novels or many characters in Kafka's stories, is rewarded by death for learning the "Truth" – that there is no Truth.

In some respects, Eco's latest three novels all embody the author's ideas on the nature of subjectivity (a topic that other semioticians, such as Patrizia Violi, have argued Eco perhaps treated far too sparingly in his early semiotic theory).[17] In this respect, they fit nicely into the third category of the postmodern metaphysical detective story discussed by Merivale and Sweeney – the pseudobiographical "research novel." In *The Island of the Day Before, Baudolino*, and *The Mysterious Flame of Queen Loana*, the protagonists all seek knowledge like a detective in the vast encyclopedia of the universe, attempting to find meaning in what appears linguistically and historically to be a chaotic world. They are rarely as suc-cessful as Sherlock Holmes, Sam Spade, Maigret, or Philip Marlowe, their literary predecessors. *The Island of the Day Before* contains a bewildering collection of facts about the Baroque period, particularly its scientific and speculative thought. Like the two novels that precede it, this third foray into narrative by Eco contains a dominant image as Eco replaces the labyrinth of the monastery library and the gigantic pendulum in a Paris museum with what the Spanish called the "punto fijo", the fixed point where precise measurements of longitude could be made. The search for a practical method of determining longitude, in an era when ships at sea lacked a nautical clock that would enable navigators to join a precise lon-gitude to their ability to determine their latitude, was a serious scientific problem until it was resolved by the nautical chronometers invented by John Harrison. Without such an instrument that could keep good time in spite of temperature change and the violent pitching of a ship's deck, ships were virtually without a clue as to their precise location. Following Eco's habitual method of filling his novels with a storehouse of lore about the past, creating a true "research novel" of seventeenth-century infor-mation, Eco introduces a number of strange scientific instruments that bear some resemblance to those employed today but are truly bizarre. He enjoys describing these Rube Goldberg-type machines, all of which are now footnotes to the history of scientific progress, since their solutions to important technological problems were passed by when other, more sensible technical solutions were developed. But Eco wants to under-score the fact with these machines that even scientific geniuses had weird ideas: Sir Isaac Newton, whose model of the universe would revolution-ize the world Eco represents in the seventeenth century, was also a firm believer in alchemy. Even Galileo worked out an astronomical solution to determining longitude that was based upon the predictable eclipses of the moons of Jupiter, producing a series of astronomical tables known as ephemeredes and also designed a "celatone" which apparently resembled a brass gas-mask with a telescope attached to an eye hole! Once Harrison's nautical chronometer appeared, such a cumbersome instrument as that invented by Galileo was simply discarded as impossible to operate from a practical perspective.

The most interesting scientific and philosophical concepts in Eco's novel turn our attention to one of his favorite concepts – unlimited semiosis. In *Foucault's Pendulum*, a corrupted notion of unlimited semiosis produced the Diabolicals' belief that everything is connected. The seventeenth cen-tury, the period of the Baroque in art and literature, was fascinated with affinities and metaphors: its definition of the marvelous in poetry involved connecting things that seemed unconnected with the rhetorical figure of metaphor and features an Aristotelian Telescope, a machine one critic has compared to both the modern computer and the slot-machine in Nevada casinos.[18] Unlike its modern counterparts, however, this device uses the gyration of a drum to associate words and Aristotelian categories, produc-ing a plethora of unexpected metaphorical associations that mimic unlim-ited semiosis. The seemingly ridiculous "Powder of Sympathy" theory (described in detail in Guy Raffa's chapter in this anthology) is yet another parody of the notion of unlimited semiosis based on the spurious assump-tion that "sympathy," the term employed to define the connection between unlikely things, derives from a "conformity or sympathy that connects things among themselves" (Eco, *The Island of the Day Before*, p. 165).

This fascinating and exotic world of seventeenth-century correspond-ences, what Michel Foucault described in *The Order of Things* as "the bur-ied kinships between things, their scattered resemblances,"[19] constitutes much of the charm of Eco's third novel and is the basis for making any critical claim that the work represents a research novel variant of the meta-physical detective story. In fact, Eco put so much research into writing the novel that a year after its appearance, he produced a CD-ROM guide to the entire Baroque period: *Il Seicento: Guida multimediale alla storia della civiltà European diretta da Umberto Eco (The Seventeenth-Century: A Multimedia Guide to the History of European Civilization Directed by*

Umberto Eco). But an important difference marks off *The Island of the Day Before* (and Eco's two subsequent novels) from his first two metaphysical detective narratives – the focus upon a pseudoautobiographical theme where much of the mystery revolves around the identity (or lack of identity) of the central protagonist of the book. In *The Island of the Day Before*, Eco creates a hero that might be found in any number of novels written since the age of Cervantes, whose *Don Quixote* was the ultimate metaliterary work of the Baroque period and Foucault's best example of the kind of literature that bases itself upon resemblances, no matter how strange. Roberto de la Grive is a minor nobleman of the period whose epistolary love affair displays the whole array of Petrarchan conceits based upon the improbable metaphors of the time. His adventures as a soldier at the siege of Casale and his discovery that he has a double who is his brother even confined in a prison behind an iron mask most certainly is lifted from a wide variety of popular fictional works that Eco had already examined in some detail in *The Role of the Reader* or *Six Walks in the Fictional Woods*: Alexandre Dumas' swashbuckling *The Three Musketeers* (1844) and *The Man in the Iron Mask* (1848–50) furnish obvious material for Eco's depiction of France in the age of Cardinals Richelieu and Mazzarin, but the more important feature of Eco's protagonist – the existence of a doppelganger or double – refers not only to Dumas but to a wide variety of authors – Poe's "William Wilson" (1839); Dostoevsky's *The Double* (1846), and Robert Louis Stevenson's *The Strange Case of Dr. Jekyll and Mr. Hyde* (1886). Italo Calvino's *Six Lectures for the Next Millennium* (1988) was an important influence upon Eco while he was writing this novel: *Six Lectures* and the book it inspired, Eco's *Six Walks in the Fictional Woods*, were both originally Norton lectures at Harvard University. Eco's consideration of inferential walks in literature (the literary parallel to inferences in abductions in his semiotic theory) in *Six Walks in the Fictional Woods* focuses upon Alexandre Dumas, a major influence upon *The Island of the Day Before*, and both *Six Walks* and *The Island* appeared in the same year – 1994. The link to Calvino in Eco's theoretical considerations of literature also suggests that the bifurcated narrator of Eco's third novel – Roberto de la Grive and his doppelganger brother Ferrante – owes a great deal to the example of Calvino's fantastic tale of *The Cloven Viscount* (1951): in both Calvino and Eco, the two sides of the same protagonist represent respectively good and evil. As Robert Louis Stevenson's *Treasure Island* inspired both Calvino's work and Eco's stranded narrator on a desert island in the Pacific in *The Island of the Day Before*, the numerous references to other literary classics in Eco's third novel, like his first two, fit easily within the postmodern pastiche mode Eco had already described brilliantly in his *Postscript to "The Name of the Rose."*

Roberto's search for the truth concerns his own identity rather than a traditional crime. As he believes all his troubles arise from his hatred for his twin brother Ferrante, Roberto decides to create a romance narrative in which he can resolve his obsession with his doppelganger: in his story, Ferrante appears at the siege of Casale as Captain Gambero, fighting the French army in which Roberto serves; Ferrante and Roberto oppose each other (at least in Roberto's mind) in a duel of secret agents, each serving a different master, and it is inevitable that because of their physical similarity, Ferrante becomes Roberto's rival in lovemaking with his mistress Lilia and Ferrante even sails into the South Seas to follow Roberto. Roberto's romance should have ended in the traditional conclusion of the swashbuckling novel: a duel to the death, *mano a mano,* between the two brothers as in Poe's novella about William Wilson. But Roberto's search for his identity dissolves at the end of the book and is never resolved. Eco's narrator brings the tale of Roberto's frantic search for his identity to a close by announcing that his novel really has no ending: "Finally, if from this story I wanted to produce a novel, I would demonstrate once again that it is impossible to write except by making a palimpsest of a rediscovered manuscript – without ever succeeding in eluding the Anxiety of Influence" (Eco, *The Island of the Day Before*, p. 512). Eco's narrative dissolves just as Roberto's pseudobiographical quest for his identity concludes without result. Once again, at the conclusion of a narrative, Eco suggests that any absolute search for "Truth" will lead to failure, even one that focuses solely upon the subjective world of personal identity.

If *The Island of the Day Before* introduces the subjective world of personality into Eco's fiction, *Baudolino* links this subjectivity to the process of creating history. Once again, the form of the novel resembles a mystery or detective story: Baudolino is a simple man from Eco's home town of Alessandria in Piedmonte during the twelfth century whose goal is "to write down what I want which is my own story" (Eco, *Baudolino*, p. 1). Baudolino is adopted by the Emperor Frederick Barbarossa, and in his travels Baudolino observes the fall of Constantinople to Christian Crusaders and many other historical events that he is perfectly willing to recount in various chronicles, blending fact and inventive fantasy. As Teresa Coletti observes in her chapter in this anthology, "for the fictional detective and the historian, the past offers up a chaos of information on which order must be imposed, whether that past comprises the events of the fictional crime or actual events performed by human actors in real time," (pp. 77–8) but in Baudolino's narrative (unlike Adso's description of William of Baskerville's investigations), the entire enterprise of writing true history is called into question, thereby also calling into question the relationship between truth and falsehood, real life and invented fiction. Baudolino is a self-confessed fabricator of historical untruths and half truths, all mixed in with some facts: "You are a born liar," he is told by one of Eco's characters (Eco, *Baudolino*, p.43). The end result of his mendacity as an historian results in some amazing literary inventions. Baudolino's lies manage to make important contributions not only to the legend of the Holy Grail, but also to the historical account of his adopted father, Emperor Barbarrosa, and to the myth of Prester John (the belief that there existed a Christian kingdom south of the lands controlled by the Muslims in the East). In the process, Eco employs this postmodern novel about medieval history to cast doubts upon the claims of historians that their investigations only aim at uncovering the "Truth" about the past. Part of the appeal of *Baudolino* as a novel resides in Eco's clever unraveling of a completely fictitious account of how the legend of Prester John results from Baudolino's creative fabrication. In both historical fact and in Eco's novel, this strange legend appears through the *Chronica* of Otto of Freising, an author who advises Baudolino that he may invent things that he believes to be true in historical writing (Eco, *Baudolino*, p. 56). But even though Baudolino obviously knows that the myth of Prester John derives not from fact but from his own manipulations of history, Baudolino nevertheless believes in the kingdom's existence and sets off on a quest to find it.

Eco's fourth novel thus explores the subjective world of the intellectual whose quest for meaning begins with a completely ahistorical belief in a world that he has himself created. The final third of the novel, largely based upon *The Travels of Sir John Mandeville*, describes a universe filled with monsters, strange peoples, and even stranger places, something quite typical of the travel literature of the Middle Ages, perhaps best known in the accounts of Marco Polo. Now Eco's protagonist resembles a detective operating in comic imitation of a semiotician making a daring abduction, an inference about the existence of a mysterious kingdom in the Orient: he first posits the fact that there is such a place as the Kingdom of Prester John (in fact, he literally invents the documentary evidence for its existence) – an inference – and then attempts to complete a reality check of his abduction by searching for the very place he has fabricated! In the process, Eco's parody of abductive logic in his fourth novel once again casts doubts upon the authenticity of historical narration, upon the very nature of historical "Truth" when history is so closely related to fictional storytelling.

Eco's fifth and final novel to date, *The Mysterious Flame of Queen Loana*, continues the writer's conflation of the detective figure engaged in abductions in a universe shaped by universal semiosis with an increased interest in the realm of the subjective. It is evident that this interest in the subject in Eco's work was encouraged by the critique of his early semiotic theory provided by Patricia Violi, among others.[20] Clearly, Eco's lastest venture into the realm of fiction directly engages the topic of subjectivity within the framework of the postmodern mode of narrative fiction and the genre of the metaphysical detective story (for a complete discussion of this question, see Farronato's chapter in this anthology). Once again, his fiction grounds itself upon important considerations linked to his semiotic theories.

When Yambo, a dealer in the rare books so dear to Eco's heart, awakens from a coma, he finds himself unable to remember anything of his personal memory: while he may remember aspects of the cultural memory of members of his generation (the same generation to which Eco belongs who lived through the Second World War as young children), he knows nothing of his self. In semiotic terms, he retains links to the encyclopedia of shared experience but no connection to the personal data that forms his psyche. Thus, while he may not recognize members of his own family, Yambo understands the popular music of the Fascist period when he was a boy and recognizes the comic strips that everyone read before the war: "My life as an encyclopedia continues. I speak as if I were up against a wall and could never turn around. My memories have the depth of a few weeks. Other people's stretch back centuries" (Eco, *The Mysterious Flame of Queen Loana*, p. 49). Rather than having personal recollections, Yambo's mental musings tend to be reminiscences of books he has read: when he thinks of going to bed late, all that comes to mind is the first line of Marcel Proust's *In Search of Lost Time*, but nothing of his own particular late night retirements to rest can be conjured up.

Yambo is a truly subjective narrator (in the sense that the world described in the novel is seen from his personal perspective), yet his narrative "subjectivity" has been emptied of what normally constitutes personal, particular subjectivity in fiction. But his search for his identity clearly resembles the detective-like quest for answers typical of all Eco's novels. Yambo's first thought as he awakens from the coma that begins the novel turns to three famous literary detectives – one explicit reference to Georges Simenon's Inspector Maigret, and two implicit references to

Agatha Christie's Hercule Poirot and Conan Doyle's Sherlock Holmes by virtue of the mention of two famous book titles associated with these two mystery writers (respectively *Ten Little Indians*[21] and *The Hound of the Baskervilles*): "Maigret? Elementary, my dear Watson, there are ten little Indians, and the hound of the Baskervilles vanishes into the fog" (Eco, *The Mysterious Flame of Queen Loana*, p. 4). Yambo retires to a family villa in the country and spends over a week reading, particularly visual and popular culture materials from his childhood. Of particular interest to him is one detective novel that appeared during Yambo's and Eco's childhood – *L'albergo delle tre rose* (1936, *The Hotel of the Three Roses*) by Augusto de Angelis (1888–1943). This mystery was actually included in the Mondadori Giallo collection, and de Angelis represents one of the few genuinely Italian detective novelists who obtained popularity among Italian readers while remaining almost completely unknown abroad. Without any memory of his own, Yambo attempts to relate the plot of the book to the three loves or "roses" of his life (also playing with the obviously autobiographical links between Eco and the rose of his first best seller).

The dominant image of Yambo's loss of identity is fog, precisely the popular image of Victorian London we retain from even a superficial familiarity with the universe of Sherlock Holmes in literature and especially, visually, in film. As a rare-book dealer, Yambo discovers in his family country villa not only original editions of the Conan Doyle books but also the original numbers of *The Strand* magazine in which the Sherlock Holmes stories first appeared before being bound together in book form. In particular Yambo peruses the Sidney Paget illustrations of Watson and Holmes in their study, or in a train compartment, discussing the crimes that they are investigating:

Those images said to me: *de te fabula narratur*. At that very moment Sherlock Holmes was me, intent on retracing and reconstructing remote events of which he had no prior knowledge, while remaining at home, shut away, perhaps even in an attic. He too, like me, motionless and isolated from the world, deciphering pure signs. He always succeeded in making the repressed resurface. Would I be able to ? At least, I had a model. And like him, I had to combat the fog. (p. 152)

In citing the Latin phrase that Eco also employed in *The Name of the Rose* (p. 241) – "the story is about you" – postmodern Eco clearly points the attentive reader to the fact that Yambo and Eco are alter egos.

Umberto Eco never strays too far away from his beloved Middle Ages. At the conclusion of *The Mysterious Flame of Queen Loana*, Yambo's musings in the attic culminate in a phantasmagoric vision that recalls not only the drug-induced vision of Adso in *The Name of the Rose* but also the conclusion of Dante's *Paradiso* XXXI (the vision of the Celestial Rose in Paradise) as well as the visionary images from the Book of Revelation in the Bible (the subject of the most important illustrated manuscripts popular in the Spain of his arch-villain in *The Name of the Rose*, Jorge of Burgos). It combines both high-culture images and those from Yambo's adolescence and includes not only the entire range of Italian and American comic strips (particularly *Mandrake the Magician* and *Flash Gordon*) but popular songs (including a Latin version of the greatest song to emerge from the Second World War, the German "Lilli Marleen"), and Walt Disney's Seven Dwarfs. These figures from what Yambo calls his "paper imagination" stride down an enormous staircase like the vaudeville number made famous by Wanda Osiris (1905–94), a musical hall dancer and singer active in Italy from the 1930s through the 1950s whose characteristic number consisted in walking down an enormous staircase, a performance parodied in Federico Fellini's first film, *Variety Lights* (1950). As *The Mysterious Flame of Queen Loana* concludes, the reader must wonder if this search for identity will ever end in the discovery of Yambo's true self, the essence of his personal subjectivity, or will it forever involve a process of pop-culture transitions from one image to another, a visual dramatization of Eco's favorite concept, unlimited semiosis:

I cannot let myself go, I want to know who I am. One thing is certain. The memories that surfaced at the beginning of what I believe to be my coma are obscure, foggy, and arranged in patchwork fashion, with breaks, uncertainties, tears, missing pieces…Those of Solara, however, and those of Milan after I woke up in the hospital, are clear, they follow a logical sequence… (p. 419)

Eco leaves to our imagination, I believe, whether Yambo dies at the end of his novel or whether he comes out of his coma. Does Yambo fail to recover from the shock of discovering a first folio of 1623 containing all of Shakespeare's works in Chapter 14 of the novel entitled "The Hotel of the Three Roses"? The chapter title contains a telling reference to the most popular novel by Italian detective novelist Augusto de Angelis from the 1930s. Or does the dark sun and the returning foggy mist that concludes the novel refer, rather, to the end of Yambo's postmodern quest for identity like the Maigret or the Sherlock Holmes that he hopes to imitate? The reader is left, like Eco's detective protagonists, to solve this final mystery alone.

Regardless of the literary merits of Eco's five novels (and they are numerous), Umberto Eco's narratives have succeeded in legitimizing the detective story within Italian literary culture. This was accomplished fundamentally by his heuristic discovery that the detective and the semiotician share similar mental habits and that their inferential abductions lie at the heart of an epistemological operation that is fundamental to human thought. By embracing the particular form of the detective story that is the metaphysical detective genre, Eco made the whodunit respectable. Without Eco's pioneering example, it would be difficult to imagine the serious critical and popular reception of Andrea Camilleri (1925–), who must certainly be considered Italy's greatest living novelist and the inventor of the detective stories with Salvo Montalbano as their protagonist that have sold millions and millions of copies not only in translation but in Italy itself. One of Eco's colleagues at the University of Bologna, Giorgio Celli, paid Eco the greatest compliment possible to a clever inventor of detective stories: in his novel entitled *Chi ha ucciso Umberto Eco e altri piccolissimi omicidi* (*Who Killed Umberto Eco and Other Very Tiny Homicides*) Celli imagines Sherlock Holmes on vacation in Cattolica (the small Adriatic vacation town famous not only for its beaches but also having been for many years the home of the Mystfest, a summer celebration of the giallo originally sponsored by the Mondadori publishing house). Eco is found dead in the inevitable locked room in the most prestigious hotel on the coast, but Holmes suspects that murder is afoot in the Italian provinces: a fitting tribute to Italy's postmodern genius and one that he must certainly have relished.

NOTES

1 My outline of this typology is indebted to Patricia Merivale and Susan Elizabeth Sweeney, "The Game's Afoot: On the Trail of the Metaphysical Detective Story," in Merivale and Sweeney (eds.), *Detecting Texts: The Metaphysical Detective Story from Poe to Postmodernism* (Philadelphia: University of Pennsylvania Press, 1999), pp. 17–21. Their discussion contains a diagram of what they term a "tentative genealogy" of the metaphysical detective story, locates Eco's first two novels squarely within the most important novels in this tradition, and describes the tradition as an important subcategory of postmodernist literature.

2 Cited in Francesca Pansa and Anna Vinci, *Effetto Eco* (Arricia: Nuova Edizioni del Gallo, 1990), p. 23 (author's translation).

3 Cited by Stefano Benvenuti and Gianni Rizzoni, *Il romanzo giallo: Storia, autori e personaggi* (Milan: Mondadori, 1979), p. 148 (author's translation).

4 For an extremely learned and enlightening treatment of this subject, see John Irvin's *The Mystery to a Solution: Poe, Borges, and the Analytical Detective Story*, (Baltimore: The Johns Hopkins University Press, 1994).

5 See Luca Covi, *Tutti i colori del giallo* (Venice: Marsilio, 2002), pp. 9 – 10 and 59 – 60 for this information.

6 *Ibid.*, p. 10.

7 For the chronology of the development of this interest, see the "Preface" by Eco and Sebeok in Umberto Eco, *The Sign of Three: Dupin, Holmes, Peirce* (Bloomington: Indiana University Press, 1983; original Italian edn., Milan: Bompiani, 1983).

8 This definition of deduction, induction, and abduction represents a verbatim recount Eco provided to me in a letter of January 30, 1996.

9 Marcello Truzzi, "Sherlock Holmes: Applied Social Psychologist," in Eco, *The Sign of Three,* p. 69.

10 For a complete English translation of this important blurb, see Walter E. Stephens, "Ec(h)o in Fabula," *Diacritics* 12 (1983): 51.

11 Jorge Luis Borges, *Borges: A Reader* (New York: Dutton, 1981), p. 148.

12 See David H. Richter, "Eco's Echoes: Semiotic Theory and Detective Practice in *The Name of the Rose," Studies in Twentieth-Century Literature* 10, 2 (1986): 213–36.

13 From Bernard of Cluny, *De contemptu mundi* (I: 952) – trans. Adele J. Haft, Jane G. White, and Robert J. White in *The Key to "The Name of the Rose"* (Ann Arbor: University of Michigan Press, 1999), p. 176.

14 Merivale and Sweeney, "The Game's Afoot." See note 1.

15 Svetlana Boym, "Conspiracy Theories and Literary Ethics: Umberto Eco, Danilo Kis, and *The Protocols of Zion," Comparative Literature* 51, 2 (1999): 109–10.

16 Thomas Stauder, "*Il pendolo di Foucault*: l'autobiografia segreta di Umberto Eco," *Il lettore di provincia* 23 (1991): 5, argues this point.

17 For Violi's analysis of this topic in Eco's work, see Chapter 7 in this anthology.

18 Norma Bouchard, "Umberto Eco's *L'isola del giorno prima*: Postmodern Theory and Fictional Praxis," *Italica* 72 (1995): 197.

19 Michel Focault, *The Order of Things* (New York: Vintage, 1971), p.49.

20 See, for example, Patrizia Violi's essay, translated into English as "Individual and Communal Encyclopedias" in Norma Bouchard and Veronica Pravadelli (eds.), *Umberto Eco's Alternative*, pp. 25–38; or Violi's chapter in this volume. As Eco himself suggested to me that Professor Violi be included in this anthology, there is little doubt that Eco has very carefully considered her critique of subjectivity in his semiotic theory.

21 Christie's novel was originally titled *Ten Little Niggers* (1939); for obvious reasons it was subsequently retitled most famously as *Ten Little Indians* and also as *And Then There Were None.*

CHAPTER 7

"The subject is in the adverbs." The role of the subject in Eco's semiotics

Patrizia Violi

After the publication of *The Name of the Rose*, in response to a question from a journalist who asked him if he was able to locate the subjectivity of the author in his novel, Umberto Eco replied: "The subject is in the adverbs." It would be an error to interpret this reply as a mere witty quip, a playful sidestep to avoid a rather silly question. On the contrary, I believe his reply efficiently synthesizes an articulated theoretical position on the theme of subjectivity that we can trace throughout the entire body of Eco's theoretical works. In this chapter I should like to reinterpret this body of work, reconstructing several crucial parts of it and proposing an interpretation that is perhaps a bit unorthodox.

Eco's first theoretical discussion of the subject may be found in *A Theory of Semiotics* (Italian edition) from 1975. At first glance, subjectivity plays a marginal role in this work, since its focus is primarily on the modalities of production and representation of signs. Only a few pages (less than five, to be exact, in a volume of more than three hundred pages) are devoted to the subject, but a more careful reading quickly overturns this initial impression. In fact, these few pages are the final pages of the volume representing Eco's theoretical conclusions, and constitute a closing chapter entitled "The Subject of Semiotics" where, in Eco's words, this "sort of ghostly presence, until now somewhat removed from the present discourse, finally makes an unavoidable appearance. What is, in the semiotic framework, the place of the *acting subject* of every semiosic act?" (Eco, *A Theory of Semiotics*, p. 314).

In reality, throughout this entire volume Eco always, even if only implicitly, had been speaking of this "absent" subject. It was first evoked at the moment in which he affirmed the social practice character of the labor of sign production, as well as when he insisted upon the communicative nature of all cultural phenomena. In the concluding chapter of *A Theory of Semiotics*, asking what the role of the subject would be in the framework of the theory outlined in the course of his entire work, Eco

113

writes: "*the subject of any semiotic enquiry being no more than the semiotic subject of semiosis, that is, the historical and social result of the segmentation of the world that a survey on Semantic Space makes available*" (p. 315, Eco's italics). The subject is thus essentially a way of seeing the world, and "can only be known as a way of segmenting the universe and of coupling semantic units with expression-units: by this labor it becomes entitled to continuously destroy and restructure its social and historical systematic concretions" (p. 315).

The subject of *A Theory of Semiotics*, in its double role of argument and protagonist, is thus nothing other than semiosis itself, coinciding with meaning-creation and production processes in accordance with an inherently Peircean perspective. It is Peirce to whom Eco explicitly refers, and his notion of man as a sign that subsumes both thought and semiosis.

A similar formulation can be found in *Semiotics and the Philosophy of Language* from 1984, where the theme of the subject is again revisited in almost the same terms. It is important to underline – and the reasons for this will soon become clear – that the question of the subject is connected to Eco's proposal to rethink the concept of the sign in an inferential perspective. If the sign – understood as identity and equality – presupposes, along with a stronger, more objective notion of code, a more sclerotic subject, then a sign that functions as inference, involving continuous shifts between the planes of language, necessarily implies a much more mobile and omnipresent subject:

The sign as the locus (constantly interrogated) for the semiosic process constitutes...the instrument through which the subject is continuously made and unmade...The subject is constantly reshaped by the endless resegmentation of the content...As subjects, we are what the shape of the world produced by signs makes us become...And yet we recognize ourselves only as semiosis in progress, signifying systems and communicational processes. The map of semiosis, as defined at a given stage of historical development (with the debris carried over from previous semiosis), tells us who we are and what (or how) we think. The science of signs is the science of how the subject is historically constituted. (Eco, *Semiotics and the Philosophy of Language*, p. 45)[1]

Already on the basis of these first few excerpts, we are able to begin to draw a rough sketch of what for Eco is, and is not, the subject. The subject is a diffuse configuration, neither circumscribed nor circumscribable. It is not reducible to a single instance determined once and for all, nor to any other predetermined semiotic entity as was the code. It is not static but dynamic, and linked to practices of construction and transformation of meaning. But since these practices are historical and integrated into the practices and the work of mankind, subjectivity is also a product of history and is materially based.

If these are its positive characteristics, its negative ones are perhaps even more interesting, since they may help us understand what the subject is *not* in Eco's thought. The subject is neither a form of the individual nor an instance of the transcendental. These two spaces really do appear to be the borders that delimit the territory of subjectivity in Eco's work, borders that will never be crossed – neither in Eco's theory nor in his literary writings. We shall return later to the question of individuality, but for now I want to linger over the transcendental aspect of subjectivity, a topic that deserves further analysis. In the semiotic paradigm there exists another important model of subjectivity, inscribed in the theory of enunciation as developed in linguistics by Émile Benveniste, and subsequently in A. J. Greimas' poststructuralist school of generative semiotics. The subject of enunciation is a general, universal principle, an abstract function of the linguistic mechanism with its theoretical roots in the transcendental "I" of Edmund Husserl's philosophy. In the phenomenological approach, both discourse and meaning derive from a judgment, an act of predication on the part of the subject. Through this predicative operation, the judging consciousness at one and the same time establishes the being, signifying object and the conscious subject. According to Husserl it is in fact consciousness that constitutes external objectivity: sense objects and significations that come into existence only at the moment in which the "I" causes them to do so through an act of judgment. Consciousness thus comes to be identified with the very act of signifying, which in its turn is made possible only by the existence of a transcendental subject. The possibility of signification rests therefore on the assumption of an "I" as a synthesizing consciousness, which is precisely what Benveniste's subject of enunciation is based on too. Only in so far as the "I" is transcendental can it render possible the advent of discourse in language, putting into operation a passage from the system understood as a classifying inventory towards enunciation. Transcendence, guaranteeing the appearance of an abstract and universal subjectivity, creates that space in which Being can emerge in language. And it is in this sense that the reality of the "I" is, as Benveniste observes, the "reality of Being."

We can now better gauge the distance that separates this latter subject from the mobile figure in constant transformation described by Eco that is not a transcendental consciousness, but rather a loose collection or network of multiple, dynamic relationships that, just like the semiosis with which it is identifiable, has the open and rhizomatic form of the encyclopedia, "with the debris carried over," from the history that produced it.

Eco has been criticized for not having given much attention in his the-
orizing to the problematic issues of enunciation and, thus too, for a lack
of sufficient instruments to fully articulate the unfolding of semiotic subjectivity. What I should like to suggest is that it is, paradoxically, precisely
this lack of a theory of classical enunciation that permitted Eco (perhaps
in spite of himself) to avoid the dead ends of the transcendental position and develop an alternative theory of subjectivity that today, in the
first decade of the third millennium, has been rediscovered as extremely
topical, in that it presents unexpected affinities with more recent developments in post-Greimassian semiotics.

To clarify this point, it is necessary to depart from a notion central to
Eco's theoretical reflections that has not received the attention it deserves,
nor been further developed, even by Eco himself in his later works: the
typology of modes of sign production. Born of taxonomic exigency in
order to substitute numerous unsatisfactory sign typologies, such a model
was perhaps set aside because it was perceived as being too tied to an
idea of the sign considered in isolation, in a time where semiotic research
was progressively moving in more textually oriented directions. This is a
misleading reading, in my opinion, since the modes of production do not
classify signs as such, but outline an ordering of possible processes and
thus, too, complex actions that may, virtually, become possible texts. That
the text/sign opposition in reality is a false problem ought to be clear,
since Eco himself on more than one occasion has posited the principle of
reciprocal implication between sign and text: an entire text can be seen as
an expansion of a single sememe, and the sememe is nothing but a virtual
text.

The problem as such is another: more precisely, it regards the articulation of a zone of convergence between the text as a product of a process,
and the process itself as a practice of textual production. In the structuralist tradition, system is opposed to process, the latter being identified
directly with the text which ought, however, more appropriately, to be
seen as the product of the processes that actualize the system. The typology of modes of sign production tries to account exhaustively for how
process enters into the system structure or, in the words of *A Theory of
Semiotics*: "the theory of sign production and the mutation of codes is
interested in the process by which the rule is imposed on the indeterminacy of the source."[2]

From this point of view, the theory of sign production has more than
one trait in common with the notion of enunciatory praxis developed

recently in post-Greimassian circles by Fontanille and Zilberberg, precisely in order to move beyond the transcendental problems implicit in classical enunciation theory. Enunciatory practice focuses on conversion of "forms" into "operations," and this is "a practice to the precise degree that it provides a certain reality status – definable – to the products of language activity."[3] This is not at all unlike how practices of sign production function for Eco.

An interesting question worth posing at this point regards the relationship between production and interpretation practices that, at first glance, would seem to stand in a reciprocity relationship to one another as contrary terms. In Eco's semiotics, the text/sign appears, initially, to be the result of a double movement, or, more precisely, a twin series of practices: on the one hand, productive practices with their complex varieties of modes of production, and, on the other, interpretative practices with their inferential movements. The text thus presents itself as the zone of intersection between practices of production and practices of interpretation, which appears to be the model emerging in, for example, *The Role of the Reader*.

In reality, it is perhaps incorrect to oppose production and interpretation as though they are two clearly distinct and articulated practices. Interpretation seems rather to be just one of the modes of sense production involving the construction of interpretants and thus, too, of signs and semiosis. The fact that interpretation may be attributed full rights as a mode of production is already implicit in the typology of sign production developed in *A Theory of Semiotics* (Chapter 3.6), where signs produced "by recognition" are discussed. Interpretation is certainly an inferential, abductive practice of "recognition," where meaning is constructed in the production of new interpretants. But if one accepts the idea of the sign as inference, also the other modes of production[4] – not only invention but also ostension and even replica – are constitutively production practices that imply interpretative work. In other words, production and interpretation are co-extensive terms: nothing but two different ways of looking at *exactly* the same activity that is, semiosis in action.

The subject, as we have already seen, coincides with these production and interpretation practices, since it is, in Eco's words, "the social result of the segmentation of the world" (p. 315). We are here very far from an idea of the subject as a trace left in a text, and are instead dealing with a diffused subjectivity, inscribed in practices (both interpretative and productive) or, in other words, with semiosis in action.

To declare that subject and semiosis coincide means, however, to operate with a radical shift in the way of thinking about the foundational notion of the sign, and the relationship between expression and content, the two constitutive planes in every semiotics. The moment the sign is opened up to inferential mobility, there is no longer any code, nor is there any pre-established rule to guarantee the connection. Then, what allows us to suture and bring signifier and signified, expression and content together – that is, to set semiosis in motion – can only be the subject. In this respect, Eco anticipates, already in 1975 in *A Theory of Semiotics,* a critical rethinking of formalist and logical structuralism that only recently has emerged in the poststructural, generative traditions. In classical structuralism, at least in its vulgarized version, the correlation between the two planes of semiosis was established by a uniquely logical operator, a function – the sign function – that brings into relation and correlates expression and content functives. Today, within the generative tradition that more than any other is heir to structuralism, there is a large consensus on the need to rethink the relationship binding together the two planes of semiosis, and to discuss its very foundations. This tendency can be seen reflected in the work of François Rastier, Jean-Claude Coquet, and, from a rather different perspective, recent work by Jacques Fontanille. Fontanille individuates in the body, rather than in the subject, the operational center of semiotic relations, but this difference is not so relevant, since the subject in Eco (contrary to my own beliefs of some years ago)[5] is, or could be, massively embodied, and deeply rooted in perceptual and sensorial bodily processes. I shall return to this point later. For the time being it is sufficient to underline the fact that Eco, in making the subject coincide with the activity of semiosis – that is, with the foundational relationship between expression and content – reinstalls the subject at the center, not only of the text itself, but also of the processuality of the selfsame practices that produce it.

In this way, with a single stroke, Eco distances himself simultaneously from both the transcendental nature of the subject of enunciation and a rigidly text-based position. In fact, there is a close connection between the classical theory of enunciation and the textual perspective. The transcendental subject and the textual perspective imply one another, given that a strong delimitation of the text presupposes a strong enunciating subject and, in its turn, that the subject of enunciation has its locus of manifestation in, and solely within, the text. In Eco, the diffusive nature of the notion of subject that makes it factually coincident with practices of semiosis in the broadest sense produces a simultaneous shift from traditionally conceived textuality to the openness of the encyclopedia.

Just as the subject is in the practices of production and interpretation rather than in traces left in texts, meaning is diffused throughout the endless intertextual network that is the encyclopedia. In such a perspective, individual texts can be seen as nodes in the encyclopedic network: points of connection and intersection of the rhizome that comprises it. Texts are points of stability that we can – and must – interrogate (and Eco has done so constantly in his works), but it is only in the encyclopedically constitutive dimension of their intertextuality that they can be grasped through a full unfolding of their meaning.

I believe this particular formulation is, paradoxically, not only compatible with, but also very close to, the fundamental inspiration animating the founding fathers of structuralism, in particular Saussure and Lévi-Strauss.

In Saussure, as has recently been observed (R. Simone, *Il sogno di Saussere*. Bari: Laterza, 1992), there is a co-presence of two different paradigms that have given rise to two divergent readings. On the one hand, there is a paradigm centered on the language system, generally accredited to the received Saussaurian view, where the status of the speaker is relegated to the role of a variable. On the other hand, another – this time user-centered – paradigm is discernible, in which linguistic facts are not mere data in the objectivity of the system, but rather that which is perceived and reconstructed by the speaker.

Curiously, in this reading of Saussure, objectivity and subjectivity appear to invert their respective roles: it is objective data that become relegated to variables, while subjectivity lies instead at the foundations of the system, permitting the establishment of order in a universe of objectively chaotic entities. Consider how Saussure defines the signifier plane: it is certainly not the physical existence of an infinite variety of sounds in their material objectivity that permits linguistically organized phonic form. Rather, phonic form is an acoustic image, a subjectively constructed mental entity, not pure objective materiality. In short, subjectivity creates system – in a way what makes us equal – while it is precisely in the objectivity of matter that we differ.

This type of perspective generates an unexpected (but only up to a certain point) short-circuit with Peircean semiotics. For Peirce, too, it is the subject that institutes semiosis, just as for Eco it is the subject that brings together expression and content. We could say that semiotics – both in its interpretative and structural versions – from the very beginning has been concerned with the question of subjectivity, which lies at its center as its constitutive core. It is within this tradition that Eco situates himself and must be situated. There is also another similarity worth underlining: in *Semiotics and the Philosophy of Language*, discussing the question of subjectivity, Eco advances the suspicion that we are not dealing with a singular subject but always a "collectivity of subjects," thus shifting focus from the individual to the collective sphere. Indeed even for Saussure, subjectivity does not coincide with the individual but is, on the contrary, collectively regulated; a certain type of social subjectivity that seems very similar to Eco's diffuse "adverbial" subject.

Together with the idea of socially distributed subjectivity in a community of speakers, the other fundamental notion that Saussure offers us is that of relation: no entity exists solely in itself, but always and only in relation to other elements. Incidentally, the notion of relation is of extraordinary topicality and applicable to many questions of central concern today, such as that of identity: perhaps if we were to remember to think and feel in terms that are more relational and less essentialistic, we might avoid many of the horrors that our present time holds for us. But to return to more limited questions, applying the idea of relation to texts suggests a perspective marked strongly by intertextuality, where each individual text becomes analyzable and comprehensible only within the network of intertextual relationships that it establishes with other texts – in other words, within the complex encyclopedia that delimits the horizon of a culture. A similar perspective on textuality is explicit in Lévi-Strauss, who underlines the constitutive character of intertextual links in his analyses of myths: the analysis of a single myth, of a single text, isolated from the network-system of all the other myths and texts, is impractical, since a single element remains opaque if analyzed only on its own. There are no self-defined texts and *then* transformations; on the contrary what occurs is the reverse: a myriad of different practices and transformations embed themselves within individual texts, the intelligibility of which always requires reference to the background of intertextual transformations that have produced them.

Such an approach is inherently encyclopedic, and quite distant from the postulates of a textualism that considers only the internal structure of the individual text, objectivizing it and isolating it. We might wonder why structural semiotics, born with a focus on the notion of subjectivity and intertextual relations, became objectivist and textualist in the most traditional sense, considering the text as a closed object, turned in towards itself. It is probably more interesting to note that even within the latter tradition, we are today witnessing a significant transformation of the notions of text and enunciation, with a move to an opening up for practice and enunciation in action, much more mobile, dynamic concepts. This shift has probably also been effectuated by the need to deal with new objects of analysis, ranging from the potentially open network of the internet – itself a marvelous metaphor for the encyclopedia – to social practices and phenomenological and corporeal experiences that are pushing the envelope of the traditional confines of textuality. In the theoretical model developed by Eco, a vocational encyclopedic grounding and close attention to the process of semiosis have been present right from the very beginning, since the 1970s, and this has produced openings towards many different forms of textuality and intertextuality, as well as a dynamically diffused, processual idea of subjectivity.

We can therefore single out two macro-paradigms in semiotics: the first tied to a more objectivist idea of text that sees subjectivity as a form of textual inscription, a trace of text production left behind inside the text; the second intertextual and encyclopedic, where the subject is the operative instance establishing the semiosis. I believe it is extremely important to underline that these two paradigms are not homologous, and neither do they coincide in a simplistic manner with the interpretative and generative approaches but, rather, they straddle both in a transversal way, as suggested by our close reading of Saussure and Lévi-Strauss.

More specifically, regarding the idea of the subject, I should like to question both these paradigms from a slightly different point of view, by shifting focus to the different relationships they establish between subject and action. In fact, in structural semiotics the subject, apart from existing in the form of a transcendental subject of enunciation, appears as actant at the level of the text: a syntactic role that lies at the center of the very idea of narrativity. We know that the Greimassian model is first and foremost a model of narrativity which accounts for the ways in which narrative structure underlies all texts. According to Greimas, narrativity is nothing more than the most general form of meaning, our way of giving meaning to life. At its deepest level, narrativity is reducible to a series of states and transformations among states, carried out by the abstract, syntactic configurations that actants represent. From the point of view of the theory of action, at the heart of the narrative generation of texts, the two principal actants are subject and object. Subject and object are not ontologically definable per se, but are intrinsically relational: a subject is what it is only in relation to an object endowed with a given value, just as an object is definable only insofar as it has a relationship of juncture (conjuncture or disjuncture) with a subject. The model of action underpinning this type of relationship is of a subject as agent of a transformation, in correspondence with the linguistic model of transitivity. Transitivity – over and above being a grammatical form in some specific languages – is a particular way of conceptualizing action and the role of the subject in it, centered upon the idea of causativity: that the process in action is caused by a subject. It presumes, in other terms, a causative, intentional agency.

There exists, however, another way of conceptualizing action, that is well known in linguistics, and this is the model known as ergativity. Transitivity and ergativity are two distinct ways of thinking about the relationship between subject and action, and as such they exist in all languages, independently of their explicit forms of grammaticalization. The principal difference between these two typologies resides in their respective ways of looking at the origin of action, which can be seen either as internal to the process itself, or as external to it. The ergative schema combines in one case what we are used to thinking of as the subject of an intransitive action ("the *man* runs") and the object of a transitive action ("the man" in a sentence like "the lion chases the *man*" therefore causing him to run).[6]

A similar distribution can appear bizarre only if we stay within the schema of transitivity and its related idea of causativity. To understand the ergative perspective, we must restructure our thinking, in a similar way to what we do when we look at a double figure that may alternatively appear first concave, then convex. In the ergative schema, as opposed to the transitive one, action is internal to the subject but is not caused by it. It takes place, to put it another way, by way of the subject but without its intentional causality. Also in our languages that are not ergative languages, some processes are conceptualized and comprehended within this framework: consider sentences such as "the pasta is cooked," "the machine stopped," "the thread broke," "the glass broke," "the ice melted," and so on, all constructed according to an ergative point of view. Certainly, someone or something must have caused this given process (somebody cooked the pasta, broke the thread, broke the glass; something caused the machine to stop, etc.), but language describes it as something that occurs without external intervention. We can say that the action is internal to the subject but not caused by it.

If we turn now to the words that Eco employed to define the subject, we note a curious similarity: "The subject is constantly reshaped by the endless resegmentation of the content...As subjects, we are what the shape of the world produced by signs makes us become" (Eco, *Semiotics and the Philosophy of Language*, p. 45). Here, too, we see a subject involved in a process (the process of content resegmentation), internal to this process, but not actively causing it as agent. Here we are confronted by a subject enacted by semiosis ("we are what the shape of the world produced by signs makes us become"), which, however, is not either identifiable with a position of passivity.

This intermediate configuration, neither active nor passive, appears to outline a subject that is involved but not an agent, enacted by signs and culture, constructed by the encyclopedic network without ever being its omnipotent intentional creator, a subject that corresponds more to an ergative schema rather than a transitive one. It is certainly a quite different form of subjectivity from the one that underlies Greimas' narrativity, where the subject is the agent of a transitive action over the object and tends to join it with an intentional movement. In this framework, the transcendental background that we have already seen underpinning the theory of enunciation re-emerges, where the subject is foundational at one and the same time for both action and cognition, establishing significa-tion through an act of consciousness, and through action by way of its intentional project in the world.

Some time ago while working on Zen texts from Japanese culture,[7] I suggested using the ergative model to account for the particular config-uration of the subject that Zen practices tend to produce – a subject that succeeds in emptying itself of its own conscious intentionality, of its own nature as an active agent, transforming itself into a vehicle that is recep-tive of an action that takes place through it. A good example is the Zen archer with the bow who strikes the target only when he stops aiming at it, arriving at a state of suspension of his own intentionality and will. At this point, "the action occurs" with no intentional action on the part of the archer, but only "by way of him." In this case, too, we have an enacted subject rather than an agentive subject, a subject without an "I." At this point the "I" disappears from the scene, also from the linguistic scene: the bow bends, the arrow is released, the target is struck, but it is not "I" who draws the bow, who releases the arrow, who strikes the target.

This comparison between Umberto Eco and Zen culture is perhaps less paradoxical than might appear at first glance. Let us not forget that in 1959, Eco dedicated an essay to "Zen and the West,"[8] and this parallel will serve to confront the final point I wish to treat here, the question of individuality.

One accusation that has been raised many times against Eco's posi-tion is that his subject is a purely mental subject, a thinking subject, but deprived of a body or an unconscious. Since I have held a similar position in the past, I feel authorized to review this position critically today. In reality, nothing prohibits the subject diffused in semiotic processes from being equipped with a body and an unconscious. We recall that for Peirce, it is precisely within the body that semiosis begins: it is sensible perceptual processes that allow us to construct our first interpretative conjunctures, to give sense to the world around us, to develop our first interpretants. In such a perspective, perception is far from being a passive registration of reality, it is rather a semiotic inferential process that constructs it. In *Kant and the Platypus* (1997, Italian edition), Eco returned to consider visual perception in precisely this vein, and there can be no theoretical reasons preventing extension of such research to the level of the whole sensory apparatus, a theme much discussed in contemporary semiotics.

Also as far as the unconscious is concerned – a topic perhaps less conso-nant with the sensibilities (not merely theoretical) of Eco – this too could, I believe, be treated using the instruments offered by interpretive semiot-ics, at least regarding certain aspects. The reading of the unconscious is an interpretative practice that can be fully inscribed within the inferential paradigm evoked by Ginzburg,[9] establishing an explicit link with the sem-iotics of Peirce. This theme would require greater depth of investigation than is possible here, but there exist no theoretical reasons that prevent the integration of the unconscious into the interpretative perspective suggested by Eco, as long as it is seen as a general device, a mode of psychic function-ing with its own features, parallel to and co-agentive with consciousness, rather than interrogating its individual, highly idiosyncratic organizational aspects. Indeed, this is precisely the kind of approach Eco has privileged wherever he has confronted, even marginally, such themes. Let us consider the entry "Symbol" for the Einaudi Encyclopedia, published in *Semiotics and the Philosophy of Language* (pp. 130–63), where he refers to the mystical experience of a symbolic vision described by Jung, that of Brother Klaus von der Flue. What most interests Eco with regard to this particular experience is the moment in which the individual symbol enters into contact with the collectivity and becomes translated into the encyclopedia of its time, which, so to say "normalizes" it. Brother Klaus comes to inscribe his personal visionary experience in the Trinitarian dogma, thus saving himself from that excess of individual subjectivity that might have carried him over into heresy or madness. Here Eco is especially attentive to the regulatory modal-ities that inscribe the individual subconscious with its "excessive" symbols in the encyclopedic network. The encyclopedia is an inventory of knowledge that has been, and is, collectively established, and thus socially acceptable, while the individual component in the cultural process remains more in the shadows. It is not, therefore, so much the unconscious or the body that poses a problem for Eco's theory of subjectivity, but the subjective individuality of single bodies, or single unconsciousnesses. It is the individual that is the unexpressed residue of theory: that which opposes resistance, and that which remains as an opaque background and is definitively not speakable.

Eco has affirmed on more than one occasion that he has written novels in order to be able to express "that which cannot be theorized." It is not, therefore, by chance that in what seems to be the most personal and autobiographical of all his novels, his latest narrative work *The Mysterious Flame of Queen Loana*, the protagonist Yambo is precisely a man without individuality, an encyclopedic subject par excellence who handles with perfect command the knowledge shared by his culture, but who has lost the network of his own most intimate and secret assonances. But without the trace of one's own singularity, the unlimited encyclopedic network is nothing but a senseless and chaotic unfolding of associative links deprived of real meaning. It is certainly not the peaceful and composed Zen emptiness that Yambo experiences in his bewilderment, but rather an anguishing loss of his own authenticity.

The encyclopedia was tumbling down on it, its pages loose, and I felt like waving my hands the way one does amid a swarm of bees. Meanwhile the children were calling me Grandpa, I knew I was supposed to love them more than myself, and yet I could not tell which was Giangio, which was Alessandro, which was Luca. I knew all about Alexander the Great, but nothing about Alessandro the tiny, the mine. (Eco, *The Mysterious Flame of Queen Loana*, p. 20)

Through the entire course of the novel, Yambo will search for the mysterious access to his own individual history that symbolically assumes the face of Lila, his lost love. But the secret of the individual appears truly to be the epitome of the unspeakable: as for Martin Eden, one can know only when one ceases to know. For Yambo, at the very moment his beloved's shining face is about to reveal itself, finally giving meaning and peace to his angst-ridden search, the vision draws away forever, smoke hides it, and the sun turns black.

NOTES

1 The last sentence of this passage is not actually included in the English translation of this work (see p. 54 of the Italian edition for the original sentence).
2 This sentence occurs on p. 179 of the original Italian edition of *A Theory of Semiotics* but does not occur in the corresponding chapter ("The format of the sematic space") of the English version.
3 J. Fontanille and C. Zilberberg, *Tension et signification* (Hayen: Mardaga, 1998), p. 128.

4 Eco's typology of modes of sign production is found in a diagram in *A Theory of Semiotics* (p. 218).

5 See Patrizia Violi, "Individual and Communal Encyclopedias," in Bouchard and Pravadelli (eds.), *Umberto Eco's Alternative.*

6 Examples are taken from M.A.K. Halliday, *An Introduction to Functional Grammar* (London: Arnold, 1994).

7 See Patrizia Violi, "A Semiotic of Non-Ordinary Experience," *Versus. Quaderni di studi semiotici,* 83/84 (1999): 243–280.

8 The essay first appeared in the Italian edition of *The Open Work* (1962).

9 Carlo Ginzburg (1939–) is a learned professor of micro-historical narratives who has been one of Eco's colleagues at the University of Bologna for many years and presently also holds a chair at the University of California at Los Angeles. He is the author of a number of famous books, including: *The Cheese and the Worms: The Cosmos of a Sixteenth-Century Miller* (1980); and *Night Battles: Witchcraft and Agrarian Battles in the Sixteenth and Seventeenth Centuries* (1983). The link in question, Ginzburg's treatment of abductive reasoning in the works of an art historian, a psychoanalyst, and in the detective tales of Conan Doyle, may be consulted in Carlo Ginzburg, "Morelli, Freud, and Sherlock Holmes: Clues and Scientific Method," in Eco and Sebeok (eds.) *The Sign of Three*, pp. 81–118.

CHAPTER 8

Double coding memorabilia in *The Mysterious Flame of Queen Loana*

Rocco Capozzi

In five important novels, Umberto Eco has pursued his art of instructing and entertaining with thought-provoking, hybrid, encyclopedic fiction. Masterful, playful combinations of erudition and popular culture, his fiction consistently demonstrates his love of writing double-coded fiction that allows for several levels of interpretation. The dust cover of the first Italian edition of *The Name of the Rose* contained an important warning that this novel was difficult to define and was a mixture of very different literary genres (gothic, historical, detective, essay) that could be read by three different categories of readers, a work in which story and history were interwoven.[1] The warning is undoubtedly applicable to all his hybrid novels that are constructed with multiple levels of meaning in order to appeal to and stimulate different types of readers who appreciate astute and playful pastiches of intertextuality, detective stories, Bildungsroman, historical novels, essay novels, and puzzles, to mention only a few of the elements that go into his fiction. Eco's hybrid novels often challenge the definition and structure of traditional novels, by embedding manuscripts, digressions, and micro-stories within larger narratives. For the most part these digressions are of a philosophical or historical nature, but, at times, they may serve a metafictional purpose, as does the protagonist of *The Island of the Day Before*, Robert, who purports to be writing about his double, Ferrante.

With *The Mysterious Flame of Queen Loana*, Eco seems to have set aside his treatments of palimpsests, found manuscripts and parodic reconstructions of other texts, but he continues his practice of composing hybrid fiction in which digressions play an important role. In Eco's account of the strange story of his protagonist (Giambattista Bodoni, nicknamed Yambo) and his attempts at reconstructing his memory and personal identity, there is a novel within another novel that falls within the pictorial and multimedia genre of storytelling. The work is divided into three parts: Part I, "The Incident"; Part II, "Paper Memory";

and Part III, "OI NOΣTOI" – Greek for "The Nostos," meaning "the return" or "the homecoming." Part II of the novel provides a long historical digression made up of words and images: this section of the work should be considered a hypertextual, historiographic, graphic novel that a postmodern reading can link to the postwar Italian neorealist narratives treating Fascism and the Resistance. It certainly justifies the subtitle of the book, "An Illustrated Novel."

Such an emphasis on graphic or visual materials comes as no surprise from Eco, because ever since the early 1960s, he has studied popular culture and its iconographic representations in film, television, popular song, comic books, and comic strips, producing famous essays on the film *Casablanca*, and on such comic strips as *Steve Canyon*, *Superman*, and *Snoopy* reprinted in such works as *Apocalyptic and Integrated Intellectuals*, *Home Customs*, and *The Superman of the Masses*.[2] Eco's early semiotic readings of these pop images underscore his expertise in filling the gaps between the said and the left-unsaid-but-visually-implied. It is not by accident that in Eco's fifth novel, Yambo points out how *Steve Canyon* played an important role in his childhood (Eco, *The Mysterious Flame of Queen Loana*, pp. 234–6). Eco has combined very cleverly intertextual allusions to the world of writing and illustrated novels in his choice of names. Another Giambattista Bodoni (1740–1813) – engraver, typographer, and editor – designed the famous Bodoni font. Yambo is also the pseudonym of Enrico Novelli (1876–1943), a famous journalist, writer, and illustrator of children's books, including one entitled *The Adventures of Ciuffettino* about a boy with a strange quiff of hair, which explains why the protagonist calls himself Yambo (p. 134). Eco employs such images to provide the historical and cultural background within which Yambo's second (re)awakening – that is, the temporary reacquisition of his autobiographic memory – occurs along with his rediscovery of his anti-Fascism.

The Mysterious Flame of Queen Loana contains over one hundred illustrations to complement his protagonist's stories, illustrations that advance the narrative's hypertextual strategies on different levels. The illustrations in Part II, for instance, provide an additional cognitive framework for the reader. Depending on the reader's ability to perceive, recognize, remember, and interpret several of these images (potentially loaded with historical and ideological realism), such images of memorabilia can function simply as documentary sources. On another and more sophisticated level of reading, however, they may serve as micro-narratives that can produce numerous other stories and anecdotes by readers who wish to generate their own stories. In general, Eco's images are not intended to illustrate words, and by the same token, Yambo's personal stories are not always meant to explain the images. After examining the first few illustrations in the novel, the astute reader realizes that in the myriad of images, only a few are directly related to Yambo's personal life. Consequently, the reader's task is not so much a question of perceiving and interpreting the illustrations strictly in relation to Yambo's private stories, as it is concerned with applying his or her own encyclopedic competence to the exploitation of the dynamics of visual and auditory stimulations provided by the hypertext facing him. Thus, the perceptive reader soon appreciates how *The Mysterious Flame of Queen Loana* provides the material for the generation of thousands of different stories.

Eco focuses upon Yambo's visual memorabilia primarily as artifacts of the popular culture of his protagonist's past (the past of Eco's generation, one that came of age under the Fascist regime but grew up in the post-war period of constitutional democracy). The author underscores popular and mass culture rather than high-brow Italian culture from the past because he wishes to document a specific period of Italian history and to illustrate how cultural hegemony was achieved during the Fascist era (1922–45). Ever since Eco turned to fiction, he has constructed ingenious possible worlds with at least two types of "model readers" in mind: one erudite or academic audience that is knowledgeable about strategies of intertextuality (references to other works), intratextuality (references to Eco's own works), metafiction, semiotics, and current discussions on literary, theological, and philosophical issues; and another, general audience perhaps more familiar with comic books, pop music, the movies, and television than with learned discourse on the nature of narrative. One category certainly does not exclude the other, and to paraphrase a famous essay by Leslie Fiedler, Eco has made both audiences very happy by "crossing the border" and "closing the gap" between these two usually separated worlds.[3]

What is most impressive in Eco's novels is the way the author integrates important texts, events, and ideas from the past within stories that are concerned with key critical issues of our times. In Eco's familiar paradigmatic vision of history and culture (both visual and textual), readers have in fact become accustomed to looking for revealing analogies and associations that bounce back and forth between the Middle Ages, the age of the Baroque, and our own times. In essence, all of Eco's novels are double coded for different model readers who are able to test their encyclopedic competence against the author's overwhelmingly erudite mind, and are constructed, by the author, as "narrative machines" for generating other texts. Traditional thought on memory associates a locus (a room or place) with material to be memorized: this kind of interest in the "art of memory" begins with Aristotle's *De memoria et reminiscentia* and has traditionally exploited key metaphors such as the cave, the palace, the museum, the theater, the Wunderkammer, or the library. It has been celebrated by such academic works (all certainly known to Eco) as Frances Yates' *The Art of Memory*, or Lina Bolzoni's *The Gallery of Memory*. The traditional "art of memory" played an important role in *The Island of the Day Before*, and in *The Mysterious Flame of Queen Loana* Eco adds another contemporary metaphor to the traditional images of cave or palace: the attic or storage space that all his readers own, crammed to the roof with memorabilia.

The Mysterious Flame of Queen Loana abounds with double-coded hypertextual strategies that make the novel less about the personal story of Yambo's quest for identity than about the history of a generation that Yambo frequently defines as "schizophrenic" (pp. 205, 231, 242). The juxtaposition of images and words in Parts II and III – the reason Eco subtitles his work "An Illustrated Novel" – employs a masterful fusion of ekphrasis, icons, and verbal signs with emphasis on the visual elements of the narration. Here, Yambo's personal story blends with his generation's experience and combines fiction, truth, documentary, anecdotes, and history. The wealth of memorabilia items extracted from the seemingly endless attic rooms Yambo explores become an integral part of a clever hypertextual neorealist novel with a postmodern twist about social consciousness, cultural hegemony, and Fascism. The double coding of memorabilia assures that *The Mysterious Flame of Queen Loana* represents more than the beautifully illustrated coffee-table book on popular culture in the 1930s and the early 1940s that his subtitle might suggest. As Yambo declares:

What I had rediscovered were the things I had read, which countless others had also read. All my archeology boiled down to this: except for the story of the unbreakable glass and a charming anecdote about my grandfather (but not about me), I had not relived my own childhood so much as that of a generation. (p. 272)

Part I is dominated by a delightful pastiche of intertextual allusions to texts and movies dealing with awakening, fog, flames, and memory, while Part II, emphasizing history, images, and multimedia hypertextuality, presents a collage-montage of multimedia iconographic representations that invite the reader to construe smaller stories within a larger narrative. This process achieves completion in Part III where the boundaries between autobiography, history, and reality are masterfully blurred in order to give space to Eco's version of neorealist fiction. Here the reader encounters Yambo's traumatic experiences with war and love, a process not unlike that which occurs at the conclusion to *Foucault's Pendulum*. In this section of the novel, the mysteries surrounding the deadly "gorge" engulfed by real "fog," as well as Yambo's first love (Lila) are resolved: Yambo's unrequited love story contains echoes of Nerval's short story *Sylvie*, *Hypnerotomachia Poliphili*, *Cyrano of Bergerac*, as well as Dante's *Vita Nuova*, and his *Paradise*. In Part III, Eco's images come mainly from the world of entertainment, fiction, and comic books. In the concluding chapter of the novel, Yambo's brain becomes like a screen for the projection of the super-spectacular, theatrical parody of an apocalyptic vision that recalls a variety of finales ranging from Hollywood-style musicals to the Italian burlesque shows of Wanda Osiris, and to the literary works of authors as different as Dante and Elio Vittorini. It contains a theatrical stage-call of all the actors and protagonists in the performance. In this vivid, colorful, and theatrical scene, the whole array of figures from the comic strips, children's novels, adventure stories, and Yambo's memory all descend the stairs – except for his much awaited love interest, Lila.

The Mysterious Flame – an "open work" that speaks, among many other things, about semiotic strategies for reading words and images – elicits the reader's cooperation in perceiving, recognizing, and interpreting iconographic representations that function like photographic or filmic frames requiring additional montage[4] and additional words (scripts) from readers who wish to generate their own stories pertaining to the Fascist era. In other words, Yambo's digging in his attic provides memorabilia that must be edited by Eco's readers. Part II is the longest part of the novel and is appropriately named "Paper Memory." Here, memory functions as a cognitive process more than a narrative strategy or a process. And here, intertextuality and hypertextuality also function as a dynamic and interactive process in the montage and (re)construction of the anecdotes and stories recounted by Yambo. The collage-montage of illustrations that potentially contain numerous elliptical stories – as many potential stories as there are readers from Yambo's generation – and function like a film, or perhaps more accurately like a documentary slideshow, a PowerPoint presentation that historicizes Italian culture and events during the Fascist era. Part II also sets the stage for the neorealist-type stories recounted by Yambo in his recollections of his grandfather's activities, as well as those of his unrequited lost love and his heroics during the war. Hypertextuality may be defined in the context of Eco's novel as primarily non-linear reading, as an intricate web of possibilities of reading, and, above all, as a cognitive process of making associations among words and images as well as of connecting links, nodes, fragments, lexias, and texts selected by the

reader who may choose to follow a variety of paths in his search, depending on his curiosity, knowledge, and experience. Hypertextuality is thus a
process that illustrates Eco's familiar notion of taking "inferential walks"
that he describes not only in *The Role of the Reader* but also in *Six Walks
in the Fictional Woods*.

Hypertextuality, like intertextuality, requires going outside one text in
order to gather more information (and authority) before returning to the
first text with additional material that enriches the reading. Moreover, for
Eco a hypertext embodies the principle of unlimited semiosis as defined
by Peirce. Through intertextuality and hypertextuality, every act of reading theoretically becomes a rereading and a rewriting of the text being
read. In an appropriately placed online interview with David Ng, Eco
explains that he structured his novel in imitation of the free-associative
behavior typical when surfing the internet:

We've been reading books in a hypertextual way ever since Homer. We read a
page and then we jump, especially when we're rereading. Think of the Bible.
When people read it, they're always jumping here and there, constantly connecting various quotations.[5]

Thus in Chapter 1 of Part II, the reader encounters the first intertextual echoes of neorealist works – specifically Cesare Pavese's *The Moon
and the Bonfires* and Elio Vittorini's *In Sicily*.[6] The region made famous
by Pavese's novel (the area of Piedmont called "le Langhe" that is not far
from Eco's native city of Alessandria) is mentioned constantly by Eco.
Pavese's novel was centrally about memory. But Eco's references to this
region of Piedmont also provide intertextual echoes that send us back to
Foucault's Pendulum where Belbo and Casaubon speak, for different reasons, of the same hills in the Langhe region. In Pavese's and Vittorini's
novels, the theme of returning home, the moment of homecoming, and
recovering suppressed memories become topics treated by Eco in the
first three chapters of Part III. Like the phantasmagoric ending of *The
Mysterious Flame of Queen Loana*, Vittorini's *In Sicily* closes with all the
characters appearing one more time, just as if at the theater or at a circus,
but in Yambo's vision the figures appear on a stage shaped like a long,
ascending theatrical staircase. Eco's references to Pavese and Vittorini
are important because they point to the fact that on the subject of memory, Eco is not using Marcel Proust as a model, even though he makes
several explicit references to Proust and Combray. Eco is fully aware
that it has become a cliché to refer to Marcel Proust and the "madeleine"
whenever the topic of remembering surfaces in literature: "my character

has no personal memories, or madeleines, and is dealing with collective, mineral memorability. He's working with external material, not internal material."[7] Proust is therefore only one of hundreds of intertextual echoes throughout the novel.

Yambo's search is mainly of an archeological nature: rather than digging deeply into his soul, he is extracting and retrieving memories from images and objects discovered in an immense attic. Moreover, Yambo's recollections are physical, they primarily involve lifting, opening, and searching through boxes. And in Part II, Yambo's search is less about private memories than about public and collective or historic memories of his generation. Many of the illustrations bear witness to the extraordinary manner in which Fascist culture penetrated all aspects of Italian life without the use of force: the family, education, religion, sports, entertainment, the media, colonialism, patriotism, racism, and the war. Furthermore, in addition to specifying that he is dealing mostly with "paper memory" rather than with interior or subconscious memory, during Yambo's physical search among the hundreds of boxes containing the different items of memorabilia, the narrator refers to himself specifically as a detective, an historian, and an archeologist.[8] This is Eco's way of underlining Yambo's objectivity, or better yet his ability to maintain aesthetic and critical distance while recovering innumerable archived items from the past. Photos, images, and objects, just like words, are grounded into a specific era. Pictures make a long-lasting imprint in our brain. In Yambo's case, only a single image is required to recall an entire story. Indeed, the image of a woman's face on a magazine cover leaves a deep impression in Yambo's mind for the rest of his life, and on several occasions in the text (pp. 216, 242, 253), he declares that more than words, images have made an everlasting impression on him. That an important story can be narrated with and through illustrations, cartoon-like techniques, or a series of photos comes as no surprise to contemporary readers familiar with such illustrated works as Art Spiegelman's *Maus*, a cartoon treatment of the Holocaust. In fact, Eco has recently provided an introduction to a similarly controversial graphic novel, Will Eisner's *The Plot: The Secret Story of the Protocols of Zion*,[9] a topic that he treated extensively in the conspiratorial plots he satirizes in *Foucault's Pendulum*.

Once we recognize that Yambo's attic at Solara[10] functions as a metaphoric and cognitive imaginary structure where images, words, texts, and memory interact, it is necessary to establish the central images that complement Yambo's account of the heroic deed he executed in the company of his childhood mentor, Gragnola. Of the over one hundred illustrations, some twenty of them are explicitly linked to Fascism and the Second World War. The samples range from a children's book about young Fascists to illustrations of the *balilla* (the Fascist regime's substitute for the less bellicose Boy Scouts), the *brigate nere* or "black brigades" celebrated by Fascist folklore, Mussolini, war news, references to colonialism, the war in Abyssinia, war songs, soldiers, concentration camps, headline news of the downfall of Mussolini, and newspaper columns announcing the end of the war.[11] Rather than standing apart from the other items of memorabilia, these images actually complement the rest of the illustrations relating to advertising, entertainment, books, magazines, comic books, stamps, tin cans, popular songs, and movies of the era. Eco employs the combination of the images and Yambo's comments to furnish the socio-historical background necessary for contextualizing what constitutes what the novel defines as a "schizophrenic" generation.

From the beginning of Part II we notice a crescendo of references to Fascism. This becomes more evident in Yambo's discussions on his grade school days, his nationalistic education, his Fascist teacher, Amalia's fears of Fascists, the relationship between Fascism and religion, the anti-Fascism of Yambo's grandfather, and – above all – Yambo's confusion about his childhood days as a *balilla*. Yambo poses disturbing questions to himself or to his old faithful servant Amalia about his family, himself, and Italian society in general as he looks at specific images and searches through his school notebooks. But what exactly precipitates Yambo's rebellion? What leads him to participate in a partisan rescue mission with Gragnola? Was his choice based on an ideological stand? And, if so, how did he gain his socio-political consciousness? The answers to many of these questions surface throughout Part II as Yambo goes through hundreds of boxes, inside of which are catalogued the innumerable items of memorabilia. As he handles these carefully archived items Yambo slowly begins to remember some important events of his childhood days at school and at Solara.

Yambo's focus on social consciousness begins in Chapter 7 of Part II where he reminisces about his reaction in reading the children's book *Ragazzi d'Italia nel mondo* (*Italy's Boys in the World*). Yambo now recognizes that the story was nothing more than Fascist propaganda for promoting the heroic deeds of children who saved the Fascist headquarters in Barcelona. From this point on, Yambo's comments directed at specific items of memorabilia begin to develop a larger story about Fascist hegemony that permeated Italian culture. Yambo wishes to know what had influenced him the most. And when he finds a series of cardboard boxes with labels such as "Fascism," "The 40s," and "The War", which most certainly had been put together by his grandfather, a troublesome and important question keeps coming up: "Where did I stand?" (p. 150). Chapter 8 of Part II, "When the radio," contains an excellent example of multimedia hypertextuality as Yambo starts recalling a variety of songs and radio programs from the era. Capturing some contradictions of this powerful mass media instrument, he wonders how people reacted to popular songs like "Maramao" and "Pippo non lo sa" and to German and Fascist songs like "Lilli Marleen," "Giovinezza," and "Faccetta nera," as radio stations would play them in between war-news bulletins. Yambo questions if people were oblivious, indifferent, or simply apathetic to all that was happening. Were radio stations intentionally confusing appearances with reality? And thus in Chapter 8 Yambo begins to talk about a "schizophrenic society" by first describing his own "divided self":

Over the previous days I had been trying to imagine the divided self of a boy exposed to messages of national glory while at the same time daydreaming about the fogs of London where he would encounter Fantomas battling Sandokan amid a hail of nail shot that ripped holes in the chests and tore off arms and legs of Sherlock Holmes's politely perplexed compatriots. (pp. 169–70)

Yambo continues to ask questions about his grandfather's political stand: "Had my grandfather been fascist, or anti-fascist, or neither?" (p. 170). And he is not sure if the young *balilla* sang "Maramao" and "Lilli Marleen" actually knowing what the words in the songs meant.

Chapter 9 begins as Yambo returns to the attic and defines his activity of going through the gamut of memorabilia in terms of assembling a "montage": "I put disparate pieces of evidence together, cutting and joining, sometimes according to a natural progression of ideas and emotions, sometimes to create contrast" (p. 178). Eco is not speaking so much of filmic montage as of a multimedia hypertextual collage that he creates for his reader: the deplotted images/frames containing potential stories require montage and script (proper sequence and filling the gaps of the non-said) from readers who choose to undertake their own process of hypertextual research and story telling.

Throughout Chapter 9 the focus on hegemony intensifies. Yambo speaks clearly of following an "historical approach" (p. 179) as he introduces the topic of Fascist control and censorship. After giving us a sample of Fascist rhetoric in Mussolini's speech (taken from the famous declaration of war on June 10, 1940), Yambo examines some of the news that circulated in his days, underlining that "you have to know how to read between the lines" (p. 179). To find answers to his questions about "social consciousness" he realizes that he must go through the notebooks of his elementary and junior high school, between 1937 and 1945, and see exactly what he was writing at the time. He wants to know whether he had experienced the beginning of the war as a great adventure. His school notes make it clear that Fascist propaganda did not spare children who were often, like Yambo, instructed by Fascist headmasters:

Did I really believe all that, or was I repeating stock phrases? What did my parents think when I brought home (with high marks) such compositions? Perhaps they believed it themselves, having absorbed phrases of that kind even prior to Fascism. (p. 200)

And what about me, how did I experience this schizophrenic Italy? Did I believe in victory, did I love the Duce, did I want to die for him? Did I believe in the Chief's historic phrases, which the headmaster dictated to us? (p. 205)

Among his notes he finds a composition and two poems that tell a great deal about him. The composition, "Chronicle of the Unbreakable Glass," reveals how Yambo's optimism and faith in Fascism quickly crumbled. Yambo uses T. S. Eliot's concept of the objective correlative to explain how he linked the lies of Fascism to the lies about the unbreakable glass that his mother had dropped: "I had become the narrator of a failure, whose unbreakable objective correlative I represented. I had become existentially, if ironically, bitter, radically skeptical, impervious to an illusion" (p. 210). His illusions were shattered not only about Fascism but also about his first love that he loses not once but twice. The mysteries surrounding both of these important traumatic events are resolved in Part III where Yambo finally reconstructs his heroic actions during the war and what leads to his discovery of Lila's death.

The provocative questions that Yambo asks throughout Part II, Chapters 8–10, are questions Eco especially hopes his Italian readers will also ask about themselves: as he says, "It's a book for Italian people of my age. When I was in New York 30 years ago, I saw a shop with a sign that said it was selling 'Shoes for Spanish-Speaking Fat Ladies.' There was a special market for them! So I thought of my book in this way."[12] In Chapter 10 (with some winking at us as Eco alludes to the secret room in *The Name of the Rose*),[13] Yambo finds the trap door that leads to a secret room – to his grandfather's sanctuary – where he learns a great deal about his grandfather's confrontation with members of Fascist black brigades. With the help of Amalia, at the end of Chapter 12, he resolves the mystery about the cod-liver oil, the little bottle full of feces and cod-liver oil, and his grandfather's ultimate satisfaction in humiliating Merlo by forcing him to swallow the content of the bottle twenty years later (pp. 269–70).

As Yambo goes through stacks of his favorite comic books he finally finds what he describes as "the most insipid story every conceived by the human brain" (p. 251): "The Mysterious Flame of Queen Loana" that provides Eco with the title of his novel. This is a comic book version by Cino and Franco, based on Pierre Benoit's *Atlantide*, which in turn is based on (or allegedly plagiarized from) H. Rider Haggard's novel *She* (1887). However, as Yambo explains, what bewitched him was not the story or the images in the comic book but the title itself: "I had spent all the years of my childhood – perhaps even more – cultivating not an image but a sound. Having forgotten the 'historical' Loana. And years later, my memory in shambles, I had reactivated the flame's name to signal the reverberation of forgotten delights" (p. 253).

In the next two chapters Yambo reiterates the metonymic associations between the image of the profile of a woman on a magazine cover and first Queen Loana, then his first love Lila Saba, and his later fascination for Sibilla. Some missing pieces of the puzzle about his first love-flame come together when he finds the love poem he composed years ago, "Creature Contained" (pp. 281–3), a composition that with the assistance of his old friend Gianni, Yambo realizes refers to Lila Saba in the style of the Italian "sweet new style" poets of Dante's era.[14] A second key poem ("The Partisans," pp. 284–5) provides information about the development of Yambo's social consciousness and deals with the struggle and sacrifice of partisans battling the Fascist black brigades – allusions that in Part III are linked to Yambo's heroic act as a partisan.

In Chapter 14 of Part II ("The Hotel of the Three Roses"), the fog clouding Yambo's memory of the past lifts. Yambo's second awakening allows him to recall his partisan friend and mentor Gragnola. What follows are the kinds of digressive discussions we find in every novel by Eco: debates on God, the existence of evil, religion, and faith that in this context focus upon the relationships between the Church and Mussolini's regime. Yambo's heroism recounted in Chapter 15 of Part III ("Your're Back at Last, Friend Mist!") echoes a similar moment when the young Casaubon is playing the trumpet in *Foucault's Pendulum*: Yambo, the true partisan hero, leads a rescue team that must get to the village of San Martino in the dark and in treacherous surroundings to free eight Cossack soldiers held prisoners by the Nazis and their Fascist allies. Yambo undertakes the mission as if it were an adventure for superheroes: "…an adventure I would later be able to tell stories about. A Partisan thing, a coup unlike any of Flash Gordon's in the Forest of Arboria" (p. 364).

By the end of Chapter 16 in Part III ("The Wind is Whistling"), just before the beginning of his theatrical vision, Yambo finally unlocks his suppressed memories of his own heroism and unrequited love but only too late.

What follows is the colorful vision in the form of a theatrical setting, culminating with the lights dimming rapidly on the stage, that seems to send the reader back to the beginning of the novel. While perhaps allegorical, this vision is not like Dante's allegorical rose that dominates the closing cantos of *Paradise*, also recalled by Eco in the final chapter of the novel. The ending confers a circular structure to the novel as it brings us back to the beginning where Yambo first awakens and comes out of the darkness.

For Eco the practices and strategies of postmodernism, as first outlined in *Postscript to "The Name of the Rose*," are more about ironic, parodic, and intertextual treatment of the past than about revisiting history with nostalgia. The double codings of the historical memorabilia in Eco's fifth novel are not, however, focused upon a parodic, nostalgic, or ironic revisitation of Yambo's past or that of the generation who, like Eco, came of age during the Fascist period and immediately after the end of the Second World War. Now Eco is more concerned with historicizing and politicizing such memorabilia. There is little emotional engagement when the narrator handles the numerous objects and images. On the contrary, he behaves scientifically – like a detective, historian, or archeologist. And, I would argue, as a semiotician. In presenting the memorabilia from Italy's recent past, Eco aims at realism, documentary, truth, authenticity, and history, while the double coding, that in past novels focused upon parody and irony, now examines the hegemonic control exercised by a repressive regime that provides the necessary background to Yambo's rebellion against Fascism.

In each of his five novels and in many of his critical essays, Eco has invited his reader to consider the role that popular culture – and in particular pulp novels dealing with detection or historical themes – have played in forming an era's social and political consciousness. During his entire career, the question of cultural hegemony – that is, how popular ideologies are formed and shaped by political elites – has fascinated and attracted Eco. In his preface to *The Superman of the Masses*, Eco credits his inspiration for this interest in hegemony to Antonio Gramsci, one of the founders of the Italian Communist Party. Often echoing Michel Foucault, the author has examined the complexities and intricate webs of what constitutes hegemony: power, knowledge, and culture. In *The Mysterious Flame of Queen Loana*, the treatment of cultural hegemony addresses readers of Eco's generation most familiar with Fascist Italy during the 1930s and the early 1940s, an audience made up of people like Yambo who can still recognize and give life to the memorabilia assembled in the novel. Eco is a master at creating historical novels with postmodern techniques. In *The Mysterious Flame of Queen Loana*, he has supplemented his usual talents as postmodern narrator with iconographical representations. The choice of images that appear throughout the text reveals very well the society and culture that produced and consumed the memorabilia. And thus, as he examines the power of cultural and ideological hegemony in Fascist Italy, in what is perhaps his most autobiographic novel, Eco also allows himself to create his own version of neorealist war fiction, illustrating his art of thinking and narration through images, analogies, and metaphors. Over six decades after the fall of Fascism and the liberation of Italy in 1945, Eco seems to be asking his reader what progress Italian society has made in understanding the cultural and political hegemony conditioning Italian life. And what progress has been made worldwide, since the Second World War, in understanding how socio-economic and political forces exercise control over the masses?

Because *The Mysterious Flame of Queen Loana* is a novel about the memory of a generation and not simply about Yambo's personal recovery of memory, it is not by accident that at the beginning of the novel when Yambo comes out of his coma, the first date that comes to his mind is April 25, 1945 (the official date celebrated as Liberation Day in Italy) rather than the actual date of April 25, 1991. In the midst of an intense reconsideration of Fascist Italy's heritage that moves beyond the older ideological positions taken up immediately after the war by the traditional forces of the Left and the Right in Italy, Eco's novel adds to the national Italian debate about the nation's past.

NOTES

1 For an English translation of the entire text of the dust cover, see Walter E. Stephens, "Ec(ho) in Fabula," *Diacritics* 13, 2 (1983): 51–64.

2 Eco's analysis of *Steve Canyon* may be found in English in "A Reading of *Steve Canyon*," in *Comic Iconoclasm*, Shenna Wagstaff (ed.), (London: Institute of Contemporary Arts, 1988), pp. 20–5; his discussion of Snoopy and *Charlie Brown* is included in *Apocalypse Postponed*, pp. 36–44; Eco, *The Role of the Reader*, pp. 105–24, contains the often cited essay on *Superman*. The three essays were originally collected in *Apocalyptic and Integrated Intellectuals; Mass Communications and Theories of Mass Culture* (Milan: Bompiani) in 1964.

3 I am paraphrasing Leslie Fiedler's essay "Cross the Border-Close the Gap," a summary of a postmodern belief that these two worlds should not be separated by critics. See *The Collected Essays of Leslie Fiedler* (New York: Stein and Day Publishers, 1971).

4 Yambo speaks specifically of montage: "Other days...have blurred together in my memory, which is just as well, since what that left me with was, so to speak, the quintessence of a montage"(Eco, *The Mysterious Flame of Queen Loana*, p.178), but it is important to note that Yambo himself never edits the frames; they remain as episodic micro-narratives that Eco's readers can rearrange and expand at will in order to fit them in within their own stories about Fascism and the war.

5 See David Ng's "Eco and the Funnymen," pp. 1–2 in *The Village Voice*, June 28, 2005 (www.villagevoice.com/books/0527,ngeco,65582,10.html).
6 Eco has discussed the neorealist generation of readers of Pavese and Vittorini in a brief article/letter addressed to his friend Furio Colombo – "Il cuore rosso del sogno Americano" ("The Red Heart of the American Dream"), in *L'Unità* (November 10, 2001).
7 Ng, "Eco and the Funnymen," p. 2.
8 See, for example: "Sherlock Holmes was me" (p. 152); "I decided to proceed using the historian's method subjecting evidence to cross-comparison" (p. 179); "All my archeology…" (p. 272); and, "I felt like Lord Carnarvon setting foot in Tutankhamen's tomb" (p. 225).
9 New York: Norton, 2005.
10 In the Italian original, it is easier to see the link between Solara and solaio (attic).
11 Between the first chapter of Part II to Chapter 16 in Part II, references to Fascism and war appear on pp. 145, 172, 173, 181, 183, 186, 188, 193, 196, 199, 200, 268, 329, 332, 334, 347, and 361.
12 Ng, "Eco and the Funnymen," p. 3.
13 In *The Mysterious Flame of Queen Loana* (p. 152), the narrator alludes to being Sherlock Holmes after perusing a collection of *The Strand* magazines (the original source of Conan Doyle's publications about the famous detective) and implies that the pictures say to Yambo "de te fabula narratur" ("the story is about you") just as the narrator Adso remarks in *The Name of the Rose* (p. 241).
14 Eco frequently employs the poetics of the "sweet new style" to describe the angelic qualities of a woman and her face, as well as lost or unrequited loves: this occurs, for instance, when Adso recounts his adventure with the woman who is never named in *The Name of the Rose*; in the description of the love affair between Roberto and Lilia in *The Island of the Day Before*; and in a similar love affair between Baudolino and Ipazia in *Baudolino*. Again, Eco plays upon his audience's knowledge of this type of love poetry from the distant past, a tradition that would be particularly known among his Italian readers.

CHAPTER 9

Eco and Joyce[1]

Michael Caesar

Umberto Eco's career as a writer, scholar and philosopher reflects a life-long engagement with the writings of James Joyce. Eco's encounters with Joyce in his "pre-semiotic" phase were both critical and creative, occasional as well as substantial. Eco also made very specific semiotic uses of Joyce. Early in his career, Eco examined Joyce in an important essay that formed part of the original Italian edition of his *Open Work: Form and Indeterminancy in Contemporary Poetics* (1962), now entitled in English as *The Aesthetics of Chaosmos: The Middle Ages of James Joyce* (1989). The young Eco found aspects of Joyce's character Stephen Dedalus congenial, but the interaction of medievalism and modernism in the mature Joyce constitutes a model to which Eco constantly returns. Indeed, the patterning of cultural history discernible in Eco's first three novels, foreshadowed in his reading of Joyce's medievalism, lends a character of hesitancy to the history that is narrated there.

1954–68: CRITICAL AND CREATIVE ENCOUNTERS WITH JOYCE

Eco worked on Joyce during the 1950s. There are allusions to the Irish writer in his degree thesis of 1954 on Saint Thomas Aquinas (first published in 1956 in Italian, revised in 1970, and now available in English as *The Aesthetics of Thomas Aquinas* [1988]). Eco's principal points of reference in his thesis – understandably, in view of his focus on Thomas Aquinas – were the abandoned autobiographical novel *Stephen Hero* and its successor, *Portrait of the Artist as a Young Man*. Their use is evidence of Eco's interest in the Thomist, and more generally Aristotelian, foundations of Joyce's poetics. Eco struck a note which would characterize all of his subsequent Joyce criticism when he highlighted Joyce's ability to combine "faithful interpretation and the freedom to rework his scholastic sources."[2] His analysis of the fundamental themes of Joyce's poetics (the subdivision of literary art into the lyric, epic and dramatic genres, the objectivity and impersonality of the work, the autonomy of art, the nature of aesthetic emotion and the criteria of beauty) was at this point, however, still based largely on *Stephen Hero* and the fifth chapter of *Portrait*.

Eco's longer and more comprehensive essay on Joyce appeared as the second half (some 150 pages) of the original *Open Work* of 1962. Within the context of *Open Work* Joyce was restored to full modernist glory, as a chief exemplar of the poetics of the "open work", yet the medieval strand of Joyce's thought remained central to Eco's interpretation. Joyce's "medievalism" was stressed in the title both of the immediate, though partial, French translation in *Tel Quel* (1962–3)[3] and in the American version which appeared in 1982 in the reflected glow of the name of the author of *The Name of the Rose*.[4] In his "Author's Note" to the American edition, Eco declared the "central theme of [his] research" to be "the permanence of a medieval model, not only in the early writings, but also in the later work of James Joyce." Eco was not by this intending to argue for a "medieval" Joyce *against* a modernist one; on the contrary, it was the paradox implicit in the juxtaposition of the terms that attracted him. For Eco, Joyce was "the node where the Middle Ages and the avant-garde meet." Following on its partial translation in *Tel Quel*, the Joyce essay was included in its entirety in the important Seuil edition of *L'Œuvre ouverte* in 1965. But from the mid-1960s on, it led a separate existence from the rest of *Open Work*, despite its undoubted strategic importance to the first edition of that book, and in 1965 appeared in Italian as an autonomous text – *The Poetics of Joyce: From the "Summa" to Finnegans Wake*, – the title by which it has been subsequently known.

Not surprisingly, in view of their closeness in time to the principal Joyce essay, there are numerous echoes and traces of Eco's work on Joyce in the essays collected in *The Open Work*[5] and *The Definition of Art* (1968)[6], as well as the playful recollection of Joyce's summoning of his "twelve marshalls" under the command of Samuel Beckett in defence of *Finnegans Wake* in one of the spoofs collected in *Misreadings* (1993; originally published in *Minimal Diary*), a critical appreciation of Joyce's newly discovered last work, *The Betrothed*.[7] As this last example suggests, Joyce continued throughout the 1950s and 1960s to reverberate in Eco's creative and experimental work as well as in his scholarly and critical essays, especially in collaboration with the composer Luciano Berio. His life-long friendship with Berio began while Eco was working for the state broadcaster RAI in Milan and Berio for RAI's experimental "Phonology Studio"

(*Studio di fonologia*), founded in 1955. Their collaborative work on *Thema (Omaggio a Joyce)* was to take Berio's earlier experimentation with Joyce's work (*Chamber Music*) to a quite different level. The original idea had been for a radio programme on onomatopoeia in poetic texts, which included Joyce, but this narrowed to a focus on the opening of the eleventh chapter of *Ulysses*, the "Sirens" episode ("Bronze by gold heard the hoofirons, steelyringing Imperthnthn thnthnthn. Chips, picking chips off rocky thumbnail, chips. [etc.]"). With this material Berio, always interested in the musical potentialities inherent in the human voice and in the possibility of finding new meanings in words by analysing them acoustically and musically, could see a way of exploring the relation between the musical and the poetic, without entirely suppressing the one in favour of the other. The first version of this experiment, never broadcast, was a polyphonic composition, uniting not only the English text read dazzlingly by Cathy Berberian, but also a French translation read by two voices (one of which was Eco's) and an Italian translation read by three. The recorded voices functioned as raw material for a subsequent electro-acoustic reworking, through which Berio aimed to produce a kind of musical metalanguage based on the physical, phonic properties of the three natural languages but without reference to the semantic differences between them. In the second version, on tape but not at present commercially available, the role of the translated texts was reduced almost to nothing and Berio concentrated partly on extending the procedure already inherent in the Joyce text whereby sense is established by building apparently arbitrary bridges between the sounds rather than the strict semantic meaning of words, and partly on a more detailed and sophisticated electronic re-elaboration, and reinterpretation, of the Berberian recording.[8]

Eco's contribution to the *Thema* project was not limited to providing one of the French voices; indeed, Berio stated that "[w]ithout Eco *Thema (Omaggio a Joyce)* wouldn't exist."[9] What is important to note is that this creative and experimental engagement with Joyce on Eco's part – which was later to be continued in a further collaboration with Berio and the poet Edoardo Sanguineti in *Epifanie* (1959–61, 1965) – indicated that he was not only approaching Joyce from the cultural-historical (and personal) perspective which underlay his emphasis on Joyce's medievalism, but that he was also already committed to the challenge of analysing and elaborating the structural features of Joyce's language. In fact, these two approaches, the historical and the linguistic, would constitute the central pillars of Eco's reading of Joyce over the years.

SEMIOTICS AND THE *WAKE*

Eco's principal and substantial work on Joyce, then, as a critic and a historian of poetics, occured in the "pre-semiotic" phase of his activity. After 1968, Eco's use of Joyce in his theoretical work became highly selective, in terms both of what he used and how he used it. The trigger text for Eco's semiotic readings of Joyce was the dense chapter in *The Poetics of Joyce* on the "poetics of the pun" in *Finnegans Wake*, a poetics which, Eco stated, "could only be clarified by contemporary structural semiotics."[10] Reworkings and extensions of those few pages played a strategic role at key moments in the evolution of Eco's semiotics. This was true of both the initial phase, roughly that leading up to the attempted systematization of *A Theory of Semiotics*, in which Eco was concerned primarily with questions of semantics and syntactics, and the post-*Theory* phase in which his interests shifted, or shifted back, towards pragmatics and questions to do with inference, use and interpretation. To sketch the itinerary: the 1962 pages on the poetics of the pun were expanded in the chapter of *Le forme del contenuto* (1971) entitled "La semantica della metafora"; this chapter was in turn revised, as "The Semantics of Metaphor," for the English-language volume *The Role of the Reader* (1981) and, in reduced form, for *The Aesthetics of Chaosmos* (but not for subsequent editions of *The Poetics of Joyce*, in which the section on "La poetica del *calembour*" retained its original form). Eco returned to the same essay in the early 1990s and included an adapted version of it in *The Limits of Interpretation* (1990).

Finnegans Wake was seen by Eco as a crux for semioticians, and in this he did no more than confirm the centrality of Joyce's last novel for poststructuralism in general, and indeed for postmodernism. Building on the repertoire of puns established in *The Poetics of Joyce* (riverrun, [commodius] vicus of recirculation, scherzarade, meander[thall]tale, slipping beauty, sansglorians), which would be repeated with some variations and additions in the subsequent essays (Minucius Mandrake, Jungfraud['s] messonge[book]), Eco set out in "The Semantics of Metaphor" to use examples of Joyce's punning to show how a code could be enriched. According to Eco, the *Wake*

provides the model of a global semantic system in which metaphoric substitution can be traced back to a subjacent chain of metonymic connections... Metaphor is generated by the coupling of elements producing a short circuit, thus leaving out the underlying metonymic series and suggesting a kind of spontaneity and naturalness. The analysis of the Joycean pun, a particular form of metaphor, shows that the creativity of the metaphor does not reside in the series of connections, but in the decision of the short circuit [*sic*].[11]

"The Semantics of Metaphor" included an experiment, which had two purposes: "first, to see if, from a point outside Joyce's linguistic universe, we can enter into the universe; then, departing from a point internal to that universe, to see whether or not we can connect, through multiple and continuous pathways, as in a garden where all the paths fork, all the other points."[12] The outside point was the word/Neanderthal/, not found as such in the text, but which generated, through a phonetic association, three other lexemes: /meander/, t[h]al (German "valley"), and /tale/, which combined to form the pun/meandertale/ (or two puns, since /meanderthalltale/ also appears). Taking the "atomic element" of Joyce's novel, the pun, as the matter of his experiment, Eco hoped to demonstrate the hypothesis that a metaphor could be invented because language, in its process of unlimited semiosis, constitutes a multidimensional network of metonymies, each of which is explained by a cultural convention rather than by an original resemblance. As far as the novel is concerned, it should be possible to show that each metaphor produced in *Finnegans Wake* (and thus each pun) can in the last resort be made sense of "because the entire book, read in different directions, actually furnishes the metonymic chains that justify it."[13] There were two sides to the claim about metaphor. The first had to do with the self-referentiality of language. In this connection, Jonathan Culler rightly observed, in his commentary on Eco's essay, that to "maintain the primacy of metaphor is to treat language as a device for the expression of thoughts, perceptions, truths. To posit the dependency of metaphor on metonymy is to treat what language expresses as the effect of contingent, conventional, relations and a system of mechanical processes."[14] The second had to do with that principle of boundless but ultimately regulated creativity which Eco derived from the semiotics of Peirce. The process whereby metonymies generate metaphors, Eco wrote, is "the very characteristic of a language considered as the place of unlimited semiosis (as for Peirce), where each term is explained by other terms and where each one is, through an infinite chain of interpretants, potentially explainable by all the others."[15] The Peircean concept of "unlimited semiosis" is the lynch-pin of Eco's semiotics, and "*Finnegans Wake* is itself a metaphor for the process of unlimited semiosis."[16]

Eco's analysis had primarily to do with that part of his semiotics that was concerned with the general principles of signification. But the concept of unlimited semiosis, and its metaphorical expression *Finnegans Wake*, raised other questions: not only "*how* does it mean?" but "*what* does it mean?" or "can it mean anything at all, or whatever you want it to mean?," a question that was at the basis of Eco's reflections on the limits of interpretation in the 1980s and 1990s. Once again, as he prepared to do battle with what he regarded as that deregulated practice of interpretation which he associated with deconstruction, we find him turning to the familiar terrain of the Joycean pun for assistance. He reiterated the claim that the *Wake* is "a satisfactory image of the universe of unlimited semiosis precisely because it is a text in its own right. An open text is always a text, and a text can elicit infinite readings without allowing all possible readings."[17] In support of this view, Eco appealed to the seemingly old-fashioned principle of "internal textual coherence" to set the limits, a principle with which most readers can agree, but which leaves open the question as to where one can find "decisive theoretical rules."[18] This was a further affirmation that, in the unlimited semiosis that is *Finnegans Wake*, there are limits to interpretation.

There were other strands to Eco's reading of Joyce in the years after 1968. He retained, for example, an interest in "Irishness" in Joyce, for which he drew in particular on the early medieval Irish illuminated manuscripts (see the section below on "Patterns of Cultural History").[19] Also in the 1990s he returned to the problematics of the pun in a context that straddled his interests in "perfect" and artificial languages on the one hand and in translation theory on the other by addressing the challenges posed to translation theory by an author who translates, if that is what he does, from his own "invented" language. This is the case of the French and Italian versions of the "Anna Livia Plurabelle" chapter of *Finnegans Wake*, in whose composition during the years when the *Wake* was still in progress Joyce's own contribution was active.[20] Even so, it is difficult to avoid the conclusion that the Joyce who mattered to Eco, from the moment that his thought began to fashion and was itself fashioned by an evolving semiotics, became a highly focussed Joyce, one who was identified almost wholly with *Finnegans Wake*, and furthermore with a specific, albeit central, aspect of the *Wake*, namely the pun. The evidence presented so far, it is true, could be interpreted in one of two ways. It could be argued that for Eco Joyce has been a constant companion, one who has been alongside him at crucial moments in the development of his intellectual career, from an early (auto-)biographical identification, through the poetics of the open work, the principle of unlimited semiosis, the statement of the limits of interpretation and the critique of the search for a perfect language. A counterview would be that in fact Eco's reference to and use of Joyce became increasingly narrow and specialized, relying on little more than the pun in *Finnegans Wake*, the obsession with the

Wake being itself a sign that Eco was now simply taking his place at the feeding trough that the novel had become for every subdivision of post-structuralist thought. But it may be that the narrowing of Eco's interest in Joyce is something of an optical illusion, based as it is on consideration purely of Eco's theoretical writings and that there is, even in the later Eco, a thicker, denser presence of Joyce than may appear at first to be the case. In order to pursue this argument, however, we must go back again to *The Poetics of Joyce*.

PORTRAIT OF THE ARTIST AS A YOUNG PHILOSOPHER

The focus of Eco's essay, as the title declared, was on Joyce's "poetics" in the plural, seen as "opposite and complementary," through which we may discern "the history of contemporary poetics in the play of continuous opposition and interdependence."[21] Eco was interested in the conflictuality of Joyce's various poetics and above all he was intrigued by the vast historical canvas that they opened up, one upon which the modern and the premodern – or the medieval and the postmedieval – did battle. Thus, to follow the broad-brush picture sketched by Eco in his opening pages, the critic regarded Thomism, Ibsen and symbolism as the three defining influences of Joyce's youth, which would bear on all his later work, but at the same time he located Joyce's reading of Vico "in the framework of a sensibility inhabited by Pan and the Cabala, which has more in common with Renaissance influences than with those of modern historicism."[22] This recognition of a "Renaissance" or, rather, "hermetic" Joyce would be important later in the essay for Eco's reading of *Finnegans Wake*.[23] Joyce emerged from Eco's study as an eclectic thinker, who accumulated aesthetic positions from all ages and mixed or juxtaposed them, whose work was a "battleground" but which might also reflect Joyce's "constant taste for compromise."[24] Joyce's poetics, for Eco, rested on the continuing opposition between a classical conception of form and the need for a more flexible and "open" formulation of the work, on the dialectic between order and adventure, on the contrast between the world of the medieval *summae* and that of contemporary science and philosophy.

The analysis of *Stephen Hero* and *Portrait* asked what became of Joyce's Catholicism, his Thomism, his scholasticism. The question as to whether Stephen's scholasticism is real, formal or apparent is resolved in the underlying dialectic of order and adventure: modern culture is the continuous need (*esigenza*) for order and the need (*bisogno*) to find in the world "a changeable form, open to adventure, permeated with possibility"[25], but every time we try to define this new condition of our world we find ourselves working with the formulae, albeit disguised, of classical order. Joyce himself rejected the "absurdity" of Catholicism, while relishing throughout his life its formal "coherence." For the moment the struggle for the new, the attempt to find the language that will adequately define the condition of modernity, amounts to the attempt to create a space within the old language; and the young Eco, whose own writing in *Open Work* was itself a constant negotiation between a reassuringly familiar literary essayism and the signalling of new territories to be mapped out, showed a sneaking regard for Stephen's propensity to use Thomist categories "confidently (*con disinvoltura*), hiding new and worrying ideas behind the veil of traditional correctness."[26] There is cunning, we know, and also a certain *chutzpah*, in Stephen's proceedings.

The key example of the transfusion of new wine into old bottles was what Eco would later describe as Joyce's "contradictory" grounding of his doctrine of epiphanies, which was largely indebted to the symbolism of Walter Pater, on the teachings of Thomas Aquinas.[27] Eco traced the evolution of the idea of epiphany from *Stephen Hero* (where it represented those privileged moments in which reality is revealed, even through the seemingly most inconsequential of events, scraps of conversation, etc.) through *Dubliners* (each story seeming to be "a vast epiphany") to *Portrait of the Artist as a Young Man*, where the emphasis changes significantly: "… in the *Portrait* epiphany changes from a moment of emotion which the artistic word serves at most to recollect to one of action in an artistic process which lays the foundations of a way not of *experiencing* but of *shaping* life."[28] At this point the term "epiphany" itself disappears. According to Eco, "Aquinas's categories are revealed for how they had been understood by the young artist, a convenient launching-pad, an interpretative exercise that he might find stimulating provided he could use it as a starting point for a different solution."[29]

If cunning and irony are attributes that Eco acknowledged in the young Stephen, they were also weapons that the emerging writer who sometimes signed himself "Dedalus"[30] used to good effect in his own emancipation as a thinker and philosopher. There was an element of autobiographical identification in Eco's description of Joyce's absorption, cheerful utilization and partial overcoming of his Catholic education, but when it came to the major novels (the short stories and poems commanded little attention in Eco's study), the focus broadened considerably. The relationship between the modern world and the Christian Middle Ages was no longer a personal one; it was conceived within the broad sweep of a thousand years of cultural history.

PATTERNS OF CULTURAL HISTORY IN *THE POETICS OF JOYCE* AND ECO'S NOVELS

The discussion of *Ulysses*, which constitutes the central section of Eco's tripartite study, is underpinned by two guiding principles: the novel is read as an apocalyptic work, signalling the crisis of a culture, while Joyce's narrative procedures are justified by what I shall describe as a "perverse" recourse to medieval poetics. Eco, to be sure, devoted the first part of his analysis of the poetics of the novel to the "poetics of expressive form" (the message is in the form), and to the poetics of interior monologue and the stream of consciousness.[31] These were broadly the big themes of Joyce's modernism, for which Eco drew extensively on existing English and American criticism. Retrospectively, it can probably be stated that this high modernism was that which contributed least to Eco's own narrative procedures and which commanded least attention in his narrative theory. But *Ulysses* was not only the "demonstration and summation of the major features of the entire [modernist] movement."[32] The liminal status of *Ulysses* as a text that lies between modernism and a "something else" which in 1962 could not easily be named was latent if perhaps unexpressed in Eco's essay. Twenty years later, the original Italian version of *Postscript to "The Name of the Rose"* would return to Joyce as the exemplary demonstration of how "the modern and the post-modern can co-exist in the same artist or follow each other in quick succession," with *Portrait* and *Dubliners* as "modern" and *Finnegans Wake* as "post-modern," while "*Ulysses* is on the border."[33] *The Name of the Rose* shares with *Ulysses* at least the capacity to leave readers uncertain on which side of the modernist/postmodernist divide it stands or, more positively, to intrigue by its incorporation and mingling of devices and strategies that can be attributed to both modernism and postmodernism: it is not an accident that these are the two novels to which in his fundamental study *Constructing Postmodernism* Brian McHale allowed the "amphibious" label of "(post) modernist."[34]

Eco began his chapter on *Ulysses*, however, by quoting Jung's 1932 review of the novel, seen by the Swiss psychologist, who was reading from a strictly psychoanalytic point of view, as a destruction of the past, a representation of modern man liberating himself from the whole of the ancient world.[35] Eco endorsed Jung's stress on "the theme of the breaking and destruction of a world."[36] Rupture took the form of a radical and dramatic loss of cultural coordinates. The magma of experience, spoken in language laden with five thousand years of culture, was open to multiple readings and possibilities of symbolic relation. But such symbolism was

quite different from that of the Middle Ages in which meaning was activated on the basis of a shared repertory (of bestiaries and lapidaries, gram-
mars and encyclopedias). The difference was in fact a radical opposition,
as Eco made clear:

> The relation between signifier and signified is clear in the medieval symbol by
> virtue of a single culture, but the contemporary poetic symbol lacks this and is
> born instead of the multiplicity of cultural perspectives. In this multiplicity the
> marriage of sign and meaning is brought about in a poetically necessary but
> ontologically unforeseen and gratuitous short-circuit.[37]

These differences, and the corresponding characterization of contemporary culture, were the staple themes of essays like "La poetica dell,'opera
aperta," but there was an interesting game of mirrors going on. In his
writings of the 1950s and the 1960s, including this study of Joyce, Eco was
generally cautious and prudent in his dealings with the reader, not aggres-
sive or revolutionary. The overt programme of the essays of *Open Work*
and *The Definition of Art* (1968) (as well as those of *Apocalypse Postponed*
[1964]) was one of *aggiornamento* (bringing up to date), a word which, like
apertura itself (opening/openness), was quite acceptable to progressive circles, including Catholic ones, of the time. But along with the progressive
message ran an apocalyptic one, one that addressed the theme of cultural
crisis, of rupture between the old world and the new, which in this essay
was delegated to the discussion of *Ulysses*, albeit in a strangely telescoped
way. For the antagonist of the *contemporary* world is the Middle Ages,
as though there were nothing in between. The other side of Eco's argument was that, against the chaos of the world, Joyce established an
arbitary structuring order by recourse to medieval principles of beauty,
proportio and *ordo* borrowed (consciously or not) from the medieval
arts of rhetoric and producing results of which the masters of those arts,
insisting on their "iron rule," would have approved.[38] The novel has a
"medieval nature,"[39] but "while symbols and allegories exist in a medieval poem to give a sense to the Ordo which they try to define, in *Ulysses*
the Ordo serves to make sense of the relations between symbols."[40] In
keeping with the rules of modernist symbolism outlined previously, the
understanding of the symbol is conditioned by the structure of the work
and can only be understood within it.

I describe this recourse to the medieval "perverse" because it was a medievalism detached from medieval belief systems. Eco read *Ulysses* as a novel
of cultural crisis (and thus it may have been an indirect model for *The
Name of the Rose*, where the cultural crisis was more directly confronted
and historically located), and at the same time he privileged a "medieval"

reading of its order. The Middle Ages were thus doomed to destruction in the story. Eco's reading of Joyce's narrative procedures as a destruction of medieval order returns as if it had been repressed in the discourse.

The structure of Eco's analysis of the poetics of *Finnegans Wake* resembled that of the poetics of *Ulysses*, which is to say that about twenty pages that focussed on linguistic and structural questions, notably the section on the "poetics of the pun," were followed by a broader, cultural-historical perspective on the novel. This structure was not without its own significance. It is important to note that, alongside the specialized and detailed work in aesthetics, in information theory, and ultimately in semiotics, Eco has always kept open the wide historical perspective marked already by his decision to choose a topic from the history of philosophy for his thesis. Throughout his career Eco has always left himself the space to shift his gaze from the object under immediate critical or semiotic scrutiny and to create a history, or a story, around it. The Joyce essay of 1962 was a prime example of this narrativization of the world of signs even while its title pointed towards the potentially abstract aesthetic concept of "poetics." The emergence of Eco as a novelist in the 1980s, while unforeseeable, was a not entirely surprising augmentation of the story-telling disposition that had always been strongly present in the philosopher; it is inherent in the argument of this chapter, furthermore, that not only the story-telling but also in some measure the story that is told is foreshadowed in the young Eco's reading of Joyce. Thus the analysis of *Finnegans Wake* served in part to write the next chapter in Eco's story, or history, of the origins of modern culture.

The cultural history into which Eco inserted *Finnegans Wake* started from Vico and involved, as did the discussion of *Ulysses*, an assessment of the congruence of the novel with modern science and philosophy. But, if in this novel the memory of scholastic Ordo that was present in *Ulysses* has now "disappeared,"[41] Eco demonstrated yet again the continuing presence and crisis of Joyce's Middle Ages, this time, however, by evoking what came before it and what came after it. What came before was what Eco called "Hisperic poetics"– that is, the art of the Irish monasteries inherited directly from the late Empire, the Book of Kells first and foremost, which in Eco's own writing would produce not only the phantasmagoria of *The Name of the Rose* but also the drug-induced hallucinations of *Foucault's Pendulum*. From this "Hisperian" poetic derived a portrait of the artist as "the last of the medieval monks, protected by his own silence to illuminate illegible, fantastic words, not knowing if for himself or the men of tomorrow."[42]

What came after was Giordano Bruno and Nicholas of Cusa, the former in particular frequently alluded to by Joyce in the *Wake,* and seen by him as the philosopher who had awakened him from the slumber of scholastic dogma in his teens. The transition from absolute and authoritative certainty to a conception of the world, Bruno's, which itself passed from the acceptance of plurality to the idea of a unitary *anima* that sustained the whole was a transition which, in Eco's view, not only made possible the poetics of Joyce's last novel, but was also full of temptation – the kind that Eco would analyse forcefully again in *The Limits of Interpretation* and *Interpetation and Overinterpretation,* as well as in *Foucault's Pendulum.* Towards the end of his study Eco posed the question as to whether *Finnegans Wake* "remains as an example of a belated Middle Ages," whether "the reduction of the world to language and the struggle of cultural oppositions fought through words" was no more than nominalism, whether Joyce's overcoming of his medievalism in *Ulysses* was only apparent or what what he called "a renaissance by excess." In which case:

[Joyce] might have turned in his last book to the labyrinthine forms of a certain experimental and fantastic humanism and written a kind of *Hypnerothomachia Polyphyli,* or rather gone in search of a magical-cabalistic symbolism of the book along the lines of certain emblems of the fifteenth and sixteenth centuries (which Joyce glimpsed in Bruno...).[43]

If the novel tended towards the latter it was because the world of Bruno and his contemporaries was one of transition – you do not get from scholasticism to the new science in one step: "the book attempts paradoxically to define the new world by composing a dizzying, chaotic encyclopedia of the old."[44] Eco did not conceal his reservations about the validity of the exercise. *Finnegans Wake* was at best a possible solution, not a model.

THE HESITANCY OF HISTORY

Joyce's poetics, as articulated by Eco and as realized in his own work, were seen by Eco as the site of successive crises of an original medieval order. In *Stephen Hero,* Joyce founded his theory of epiphanies, which was largely indebted to Walter Pater, on the teachings of Aquinas, only to kick this pseudodoctrinal ladder away when he no longer needed it, in the *Portrait. Ulysses* was read as an apocalyptic text, one that stressed rupture in the form of a radical and dramatic loss of cultural co-ordinates, whose symbolism Eco put in sharp contrast with that of the Middle Ages in which meaning was activated on the basis of a shared cultural code;

yet it was a work that showed its "medieval nature" in the "iron rule" of its ordering. In *Finnegans Wake*, finally, the memory of a scholastic order that was present, however "perversely," in *Ulysses* had now disappeared. But the sense of a crisis had not. In Joyce's last novel, it was evoked for Eco by what came before and after that order: before; Joyce's indebtedness to the Irish monastic art of manuscript illustration from which derived a portrait of the artist as "the last of the medieval monks"; and after, Joyce's fascination with the liberating, and dangerous, potentially hermeticist, fantastication and experimentation of Giordano Bruno and Nicholas of Cusa, the Renaissance obsession with the "coincidence of opposites," and, later, not simply Vico's interest in historical recursiveness and the succession of human ages, but what Eco summarized as his "sensibility inhabited by Pan and the Cabala."

While the reader of Eco the philosopher and semiotician will notice the continuities between the theses concerning Joyce and the arguments of *Open Work* and the crucial role played by the poetics of the pun in the evolution of Eco's arguments concerning infinite semiosis and the limits of interpretation, the reader of the novels will be struck by the similarities between the thematic patterns discerned in Eco's reading of Joyce's medievalism and some of those that emerge from Eco's own fiction. Although Eco could not by any stretch of the imagination be called a Joycean novelist, there are Joycean moments in the novels (the "epiphany" of Belbo's boyhood trumpet solo in *Foucault's Pendulum*, for example). But the dialogue with Joyce continues in the overall conceptualization of the cultural and intellectual history that the novels dramatize: the late-medieval crisis of the scholastic, and monastic, order in *The Name of the Rose*; the cultural disintegration that occurs when interpretation of the world gives way to the construction of *a* world based on perceived similarities, the coincidence of opposites, and the conviction that even the simplest of signs point to bottomless mysteries, as happens, notoriously, in *Foucault's Pendulum*; and finally, the oddly contradictory world of *The Island of the Day Before*, which, set in 1643, is filled with glimmerings of the new science, but where the modern world refuses to come into being.

What is noticeable about this pattern is that its apparent dynamism is not a progressive one, but rather a shuttling back and forth, so much so that it seems frozen within a kind of immobility. "Beginning" never reaches its "end." The late medieval crisis of scholasticism is played out right to the end in Joyce's work, in Eco's assessment, but it is never resolved. You can never get out of this frame into another. The future that is always projected is always deferred. In the history that these novels relate (and, according to Eco, Joyce's do too), the present can never forget its past, the end can never turn its eyes away from its beginning. This fixity, the illusion of movement, when history is stuck, progress is denied, but there is certainly no going back, is the more hesitant, troubled definition of a space, elsewhere heralded affirmatively and optimistically as the scene of open semiotic adventure, in which Eco's medieval monks, his twentieth-century intellectuals tempted by hermeticism, and his shipwrecked scientists try, but also fail, to make sense of the world.

NOTES

1 First published, in a longer form, as "The node: Eco and the meaning of Joyce" in *Journal of Romance Studies* 1 (2001): 53–72, and adapted here with permission.

2 U. Eco, *Il problema estetico in Tommaso d'Aquino*, 2nd revised edn. (Milan: Bompiani, 1970), pp. 128–9, 152. Eco's more detailed discussion of the use of Thomist categories in *Stephen Hero* and *Portrait* will be dealt with later in the chapter.

3 U. Eco, "Le Moyen âge de James Joyce," trans. L. Bonalumi, *Tel Quel* 11: 39–52, and 12: 83–92.

4 Eco, *The Aesthetics of Chaosmos: The Middle Ages of James Joyce,* trans. Ellen Esrock (Cambridge, MA: Harvard University Press, 1989). Given that the American edition introduces a number of changes with respect to the Italian text (as explained in both the translator's and the author's forewords), I will generally for the purposes of this essay (especially in Sections 3 and 4) translate directly from the Italian original, drawing on the published English translation only where it adds significantly to the original.

5 Notably in "La poetica dell'opera aperta," (1959) and "Analisi del linguaggio poetico" (1961, containing a comparison between Joyce and Dante).

6 In particular, "Sperimentalismo e avanguardia" (1962) and "Due ipotesi sulla morte dell'arte" (1963); the second essay is included in the English translation of *The Open Work* as "Two Hypotheses about the Death of Art."

7 U. Eco, "My exagmination round his factification for incamination to reduplication with ridecolation of a portrait of the artist as Alessandro Manzoni," *Misreadings* (1993), 165–80.

8 Berio wrote a detailed account of his work with the "Sirens" episode in "Poesia e musica – un'esperienza," *Incontri musicali* 3 (1959): 98–111. His article is quoted from extensively in I. Stoianova, "Luciano Berio. Chemins en musique," published as the entirety of the triple number of *La Revue musicale* 375–376–377 (1985): 148–57. See also D. Osmond-Smith, *Berio* (Oxford University Press, 1991), pp. 61–3.

9 L. Berio, *Interviews with Rossana Dalmonte and Bálint András Varga* (London: Marion Boyars, 1985), pp. 139–56 (p. 142).

10 Eco, *The Aesthetics of Chaosmos*, p. 67.

11 H. Van der Heide, "On the Contribution of Umberto Eco to Joyce Criticism," *Style* 26 (1992): 327–39 (335).

12 Eco, *The Role of the Reader*, p. 74.

13 *Ibid.*, p. 72.

14 J. Culler, *The Pursuit of Signs: Semiotics, Literature, Deconstruction* (London: Routledge & Kegan Paul, 1981), pp. 201–2.

15 Eco, *The Role of the Reader*, p. 74.

16 *Ibid.*, p. 70.

17 Eco, "Joyce, Semiosis and Semiotics," in R. M. Bollettieri Bosinelli, C. Marengo and C. van Boheemen (eds.), *The Languages of Joyce* (Philadelphia, PA: Benjamins, 1992), pp. 19–38 (p. 34).

18 J.-M. Rabaté, "Pound, Joyce and Eco: Modernism and the 'Ideal Genetic Reader,'" *Romantic Review* 86 (1995): 485–500 (490).

19 Eco, "Foreword" to P. Fox (ed.), *The Book of Kells (Ms 58, Trinity College Library Dublin)* (Lucerne: Faksimile Verlag, 1990), pp. 11–16; and "A Portrait of the Artist as a Young Bachelor," in Eco and L. Santoro-Brienza (eds.), *Talking of Joyce* (University College Dublin Press, 1998), pp. 26–39.

20 Eco, "Ostrigotta, ora capesco," in J. Joyce, *Anna Livia Plurabelle*, R. M. Bollettieri Bosinelli (ed.) (Turin: Einaudi, 1996), pp. v-xxix.

21 Eco, *The Poetics of Joyce*, p. 6.

22 *Ibid.*, p. 9.

23 See C. Farronato, *Eco's Chaosmos: From the Middle Ages to Postmodernity* (Toronto: University of Toronto Press, 2003), pp. 23–31.

24 Eco, *The Poetics of Joyce*, p. 80.

25 *Ibid.*, p. 19.

26 *Ibid.*, p. 18.

27 Eco, *Art and Beauty in Medival Aesthetics* (Milan: Bompiani, 1987), p. 197.

28 Eco, *The Poetics of Joyce*, pp. 48–9.

29 *Ibid.*, p. 51.

30 In some of his contributions to *Il verri* and as the author of *Filosofi in libertà* (1958, then in *Il secondo diario minimo*, 1992), for example.

31 Eco, *The Poetics of Joyce*, pp. 68–77.

32 M. F. Beebe, "*Ulysses* and the age of modernism," in T. F. Staley (ed.), *Ulysses: Fifty Years* (Bloomington: Indiana University Press, 1974), pp. 172–88 (p. 176).

33 Eco, *Postille a "Il nome della rosa"* (Milan: Bompiani, 1983), p. 40 (the remark on Joyce was not included in the published English translation).

34 B. McHale, *Constructing Postmodernism* (London and New York: Routledge, 1992), Chapters 2 and 6.

35 Translated in R.H. Deming (ed.) *James Joyce. The Critical Heritage* 2 vols., (London: Routledge & Kegan Paul, 1970), pp. 584–5.

36 Eco, *The Poetics of Joyce*, p. 62.

37 *Ibid.*, p. 83.
38 *Ibid.*, p. 87.
39 *Ibid.*, p. 90.
40 *Ibid.*, p. 97.
41 *Ibid.*, p. 127.
42 Eco, *The Aesthetics of Chaosmos*, p. 81.
43 Eco, *The Poetics of Joyce*, pp. 157–8.
44 *Ibid.*, p. 160.

CHAPTER 10

Eco on film

Torunn Haaland

Let me only subreptitiously add that I do not believe it is possible to understand the social relevance and the aesthetics functioning of a movie without focusing it from a semiotic point of view. But…qui l'ho detto e qui lo nego, in this precise moment I say this and in this precise moment I deny to have said it. (Umberto Eco, "On the Contribution of Film to Semiotics," *Quarterly Review of Film Studies*, 2, 1(1977): 1–14)[1]

In Eco's *History of Beauty* – an excursus on aesthetic ideals of the beautiful, the sublime, and the marvellous from antiquity to the present – the author begins in the last chapter to discuss contemporary media as distinguished respectively by beauty of "provocation" and beauty of "consumption" (Umberto Eco (ed.), *History of Beauty*. Trans. Alstair McEwen New York: Rizzoli, 2004, pp. 413–18). Whereas the former category is associated with avant-garde artists such as Picasso, beauty of consumption belongs to the mass media and finds its privileged habitat in the cinema. Pictures of classic movie stars from Rita Hayworth and Anita Ekberg, flamboyantly featured in stills from *Gilda* and *La Dolce Vita*, to James Dean and Marcello Mastroianni, are displayed to underscore the "totally democratic" quality of film, offering "a model of Beauty" for everyone, whether they identify with the "svelte Audrey Hepburn" or the "blue-collar charm of Robert De Niro" (pp. 420–5). It is, however, not merely through the star system that the cinema invites the audience to participate in its aesthetic and communicative practices. More important are the interpretative possibilities it potentially offers, and for Eco, these present a visual field onto which he may project and demonstrate the value of his theoretical stance within the areas of semiotic and reception studies. If the signifying practices of the cinema illustrate the problems associated with iconic signs in relation to the viewer's connotation of images, it is precisely the notion of coded creation and culturally positioned readers that enables him to explain how one single film text may create opposed readings within two different audiences. Ultimately, Eco's study of the cinema points to the civic function that semiotic analysis should ideally serve in creating a public awareness about both the ideological implications and dialogic potential of art.

What role cinematic communication will play in Eco's semiotic theories is established in his first contribution to the field, *Notes on a Semiology of Visual Communications* (1967).[2] A more general study of visual and architectural signs,[3] the section devoted to "the cinematographic code" emerges more specifically as a response to the contemporary tendencies within film criticism, where "realist" approaches associated with Siegfried Kracauer and André Bazin are surpassed by attempts to apply a still developing "science of signs" to cinematic communication (Robert Stam, *Film Theory: An Introduction.* Oxford: Blackwell, 2000, p. 107). At the centre of the debate stands the question of whether cinema, being a system of signs organized by signifying practices, may not in fact be considered a language, and, if so, whether it presents a double articulation the way oral and written languages do (p. 107). Eco suggests that not all types of communication are based on the codes of verbal language and do not necessarily have a fixed double articulation. Thus, to Christian Metz's view that the cinema cannot be a language since it does not present a double articulation (the shot being the smallest "linguistic" unit) and to Pier Paolo Pasolini's far more radical affirmation that the cinema forms a language of reality with a double articulation (the objects comprised within the shot being the smallest unit),[4] Eco responds that the cinematic language presents a triple articulation, objecting in particular to Pasolini's faith in film's referentiality. Although the objects and actions included in the shot would share several features with the actual objects the image denotes, the correlation is still, according to Eco, culturally and not naturally coded.[5]

Contrary to the conception of the cinema as a language of reality, Eco defines the cinema as a "language that speaks another pre-existing language, both interacting with their system of conventions" (Eco, *The Absent Structure*, p.154). The cinema is too stylized and studied in its imitation of reality to be its spontaneous and natural transcription, and to see the cinematic language as consisting of a triple articulation the way Eco does, implies precisely that the sign and its significant ultimately are connected through the viewer's reading of the image. If images will tend to allow for a more immediate communication than verbal and arbitrary signs, this is due to the capacity of iconic signs to resemble the object they denote, but the process of denotations will in either case rely on an iconic code based on the "interaction between the stimuli of a given field and the perceptual schemes, learned and imposed by the subject" (Eco, "Towards a Semiotic Inquiry into the Television Image," in *The Absent Structure*, p. 112). Eco illustrates the function of iconic codes with reference to Antonioni's *Blow Up* (1966) where a photographer takes random photos of a park which he subsequently enlarges. The successive enlargements reveal a human body on the ground and, at last, a hand holding a revolver, but the enlargements are so distorted that only if there is a correlation between the iconic code and the narrative code would the figures be recognized as denoting a body and an armed hand (Eco, *The Absent Structure*, p. 154; Eco, "On the Contribution of Film to Semiotics," 7). The code for interpreting cinematic images may thus originate in the diegetic world and be narrative in nature, or it may be a cultural code external to the diegesis. Major discrepancies may, as we will see later, occur between intended codes and the ones that viewers actually will apply.

The ultimately unfixed nature of so-called iconic images stands at the focus of "On the Contribution of Film to Semiotics,"[6] where the cultural foundation of all signs is illustrated with reference to the interactive and inventive nature of film-spectatorship. What Eco now refers to as sign-function (rather than the simplistic sign) is the coded correlation between the independent elements of expression and its content, a correlation that also may be understood in terms of denotation and connotation. In the film *War and Peace* (Vidor, 1956), the image of a small fat man denotes nothing but "man" until he appears in a peculiar coat that connotes "Napoleon Bonaparte," a rather simple form of connotation which would be aided by a certain "iconographic subcode" (6). However, if the Russian nobleman Pierre Bezukhov's intention to shoot Bonaparte is interpreted as an act of justice (rather than the act of a "bad guy"), this would imply a more complex form of connotation in which the viewer's own "semiotic initiative" would interact with that of the film to create a new "subcode" (6). In this specific case, the addressee's initiative would be suppressed by the film's message (Pierre abandons his intentions), but such processes of connotation might just as well find support in the film's system of signification, or they may in fact modify them altogether:

when a different text introduces and reinforces new connotations (for instance, when in *Citizen Kane* the word – and the sled–/rosebud/ succeeds in connoting the memory of childhood and maternal tenderness) this connotation can last beyond the text that has imposed it…as a metaphor or an emblem. (6)

Ultimately, what conventionally is perceived as iconic images are neither arbitrary nor natural but cultural in their coded constitution, and only by acknowledging this may we account for the potentially complex nature of cinematic communication and for what Eco talks of as the "role of the reader" in selecting among and elaborating upon the interpretative possibilities that cinematic communication offers.

One director whose films Eco evokes to demonstrate what he refers to as the "referential indexical fallacy" (Eco, *A Theory of Semiotics*, p. 62; Eco, "On the Contribution of Film to Semiotics," 14) is Fellini, a figure who may speak with authority when it comes to the transformation of physical reality into a world of fantasy and dream-states. "Thoth, Fellini and the Pharaoh" is Eco's contribution to the collection of essays entitled *Fellini della memoria* (1983),[7] and Eco's focus on the omnipresence in films such as *Amarcord* (1973) of the reconstruction and invention of memory serves to demonstrate how the cinema will always resort to objects and actions within the external world without granting them an iconic status within the world of the film. Before the cinema can begin to narrate, it must recreate or create an illusion of reality, but this implies that the prefilmic itself is an artistic construction, and reality, far from being an entity to be transcribed, becomes a warehouse of sign-vehicles at the author's disposal. Inherent in the notion that Fellini "has lived to redeem the cinema from what is external to itself" (Umberto Eco, "Thoth, Fellini and the Pharaoh," in Peter Bondanella and Cristina Degli-Esposti (eds.), *Perspectives on Federico Fellini*. New York: G. K. Hall, 1993, p. 294), there is a recognition of the freedom film, as any creative text, potentially offers for creation and, ultimately, for interpretation. What Eco achieves through these inquiries into the cinema as a semiotic phenomenon is ultimately a model for the "cultural" world within which signifying entities and their addressees interact; a world of signs structured around codes accepted by a society in a given historical moment (Eco, *A Theory of Semiotics*, p. 61). Within such a cultural universe, whether a sign-vehicle refers to an actual phenomenon or not is less important than the cultural foundation from which it speaks to and of other signs, just like the word and phenomena /rosebud/ does, engaging in a network both of infinite expression and of the creation of meaning understood as "unlimited semiosis" (pp. 68–9).[8] A continuous translation of "words into icons, icons into ostensive signs, ostensive signs into new definitions," this process of invention and reinvention is not, Eco states, a "desperate situation," but rather, it constitutes the very condition for the development of "cultural history" (p. 71).

This macro-level understanding of culture as continuously creating and recreating itself may be said to find a micro-level counterpart in the ability illustrated above of film to engage the viewer in its connotative practices through these very codes.[9] What Eco in *The Open Work* talks of as "possibility" and of being "in movement" are, of course, not merely characteristic of the cinema, but it would unquestionably be the moving image – both a product and an aesthetic materialization of the fragmentary nature of modernity itself – that would best embody the "open" nature of modern art (Eco, *A Theory of Semiotics,* pp. 1–23). In contrast to traditional art which, in its aim to reproduce the universe understood in terms of logic and order, may offer multiple but limited possibilities for interpretation, the worlds of Kafka, Joyce and Brecht mirror the discontinuities of the Eisensteinian universe where a "general breakdown in the concept of causation" offers several possible interpretations, leaving it up to the addressee to interpret or perform the work's completion (pp. 15–19). Discontinuous both in form and ideas, contemporary art becomes for Eco an "epistemological metaphor" for this cosmic breakdown of order, as well as for the human experience of living in a world of uncertainties and lack of coherence (pp. 90).

Deconstructed narratives and formal inventiveness apt to mirror an unstable world of endless possibilities are something Eco associates with modern theatre and fiction, but less so with film which, as a quintessentially popular medium, tends to adhere more to the average cinemagoer's demand for conventional drama (Eco, *The Open Work*, pp. 94, 115). However, as Eco notes in "Cinema and Literature: The Structure of the Plot" (1962), a text contemporary to *The Open Work* and which is included in *The Definition of Art* (1968), the cinema's relationship to the audience differs from that of the novel on more than mere commercial grounds. Drawing on Luigi Chiarini's distinction between art based on "concept-words" (*parole-concetti*) and art based on images, Eco explains that whereas the written text works through linguistic signs which at first incite a complex exploration of the semantic field before evoking emotively stimulating images in the viewer, the cinema incites an inverted process of stimulation (Umberto Eco, *The Definition of Art.* Milan: Mursia, 1968, pp. 201–2). The viewer will first have an emotive, or even physiological, reaction to its immediate impact which only in the second instance is rationalized and conceptualized in the form of critical detachment to the image. Although both the novel and the cinema are "arts of action" (*arti dell'azione*) in the Aristotelian sense of the term – meaning that they develop through a structured series of events – the novel tends to narrate action through an actual or perceived past tense (A happened then B happened), whereas the cinema consists of multiple "*representations of a present*" related to each other through editing (p. 204; original italics). If the cinema will tend to deprive the audience of interpretative

alternatives, this does not exclusively depend on its reliance on plot structures and narrative conventions, but also on its ways of reaching the viewer
with a sensual and temporal form of immediacy that in the moment of
perception dislocates the position from which subtexts may be discerned
and even invented.

What specifically distinguishes cinematic language from written
language is thus a new form of temporality which Eco illustrates with
specific reference to *The Battleship Potemkin* (Eisenstein, 1926) and *Last Year
in Marienbad* (Resnais, 1960), films that both deny narrative conventions
for a visual decomposition of time. If Eisenstein's elaborate editing constructs a polemical discourse on the basis of a succession of moments in the
present that distorts the chronological order of events, Resnais reduces
the narrative to a mere pretext for a discourse that questions conventional
ideas of temporal successions. These observations on the immediacy of
filmic language shed further light on Eco's understanding of the prefilmic as a "reconstruction of interior worlds" allowing for a "voracity" in
nostalgia (Eco, "Thoth, Fellini and the Pharaoh," pp. 293–4). In Fellini's
cinema, this implies an equation of private and collective memory with
experiences of the present, whereas in Michael Curtiz's war drama
Casablanca (1942), memory is anchored to the "intertextual collage"
within which originates its self-perpetuating nature as a cult movie (Eco,
Travels in Hyperreality, p.197).[10] While Eco considers Curtiz's film to be
aesthetically inferior to the works of auteurs such as Dreyer, Eisenstein
and Antonioni, *Casablanca* has nevertheless achieved the immortality
of a classic by placing the modern religiosity of fandom around a textual tradition that both precedes and evolves from it. Contradictory and
scarcely inventive in its plot structure, *Casablanca* rests entirely on singular
elements drawn from a repertoire of stereotypical situations, and it is the
lacking "philosophy of composition" that has ensured its status as cult film
(p. 198). In order to live on after the moment of viewing, a film has to
be disconnected in its images so that the viewer may pick out singular
situations, themes, and types that may be remembered for their own sake.
Eco's notes on the peculiarities of cult films came, as Francesco Casetti
and Barbara Crespi observe, to lay the foundations for later studies of cult
cultures and fandom (Francesco Casettti and Barbara Crespi, "Cinema
and the Question of Reception," in Norma Bouchard and Veronica
Pravadelli (eds.), *Umberto Eco's Alternative*. New York: Peter Lang, p. 273).
Peter Brooker and Will Brooker, for instance, elaborate on Eco's notion of
how the "completely furnished" world of the cult film offers itself to the
fan as "a private and sectarian world" (Eco, *Travels in Hyperreality*, p. 198)[11].

By definition, a fan cannot remain solitary, since the cultic enthusiasm for a film is at once shared and exclusive. What they reject in Eco's analysis, however, is the aesthetic criteria it adopts, allegedly assuming that "the truly venerated terms are all on the other side of the cult film" (pp. 140–1).

Eco's discussion of *Casablanca* is based on an analysis of established narrative situations he refers to as "intertextual archetypes" (e.g., "the Magic Key," "the Disenchanted Lover," etc.) and which manifest themselves in the film's first twenty minutes. At the core of these archetypes stands the flashback to Rick's and Ilse's happier days in Paris – itself a topical quotation and emblem of the always-present tense of cinematic time. While its narrative function is to give visual insight into the past experiences the characters allude to in the present action ("Can I tell you a story?"; "Play it again, Sam"), its dramatization of clichés ("the Desperate Lover," "Love is Forever," etc.), as well as the film's position in relation to both French cinema of the 1930s and to films shot after *Casablanca* (David Lean's *Brief Encounter* [1945] Vincent Minelli's *Two Weeks in Another Town* [1962]), situate the characters' desperate nostalgia within a larger framework of cinematic traditions. These and other paradigmatically related archetypes presented in the film's "prelude" culminate in two "symphonic elaborations" based upon the themes of the "Gift" and "Unhappy Love" (Eco, *Travels in Hyperreality*, pp. 200, 207). Although Eco does not explicitly relate this to his earlier observations on cinematic temporality, the synchronization of diegetic and non-diegetic memory at the basis for *Casablanca*'s cult status would seem to operate on the viewer through two different stages of stimulation by which the instant impact of images in the *present* evolve into a detached position of reflection. If the immediate reception of *Casablanca* would relate to the thematic framework of memory and nostalgia and ideally encourage an emotional identification with the two protagonists, the secondary mode of reception would evolve as a reflection on the codes of textual memory held in common between film and viewer.

The temporal modes of the cult film underscore Eco's understanding of textual creation as less reliant on authorial originality than on a process of replication whereby "cinema comes from cinema" the way books have origins in other books (p. 199), a view we recognize as fundamental to *The Open Work* and that is reaffirmed with great vigor in his *Postscript to "The Name of The Rose,"* where the author positions his novel within a larger and continuous dialogue between texts and between authors and readers (p. 522). When Eco comes to analyse *Casablanca* with its very own particular sense of nostalgia, he does so precisely for the unintentional position the film assumes within this semiosis, bringing the viewer back to a time of innocence when a film could become a cult phenomenon without presenting itself as such. Intertextual references are thus not laid down for their own sake, but they result, instead, from a plot improvised on endlessly recyclable themes. In this sense, *Casablanca* shares more affinities with *Hamlet*, the complexity of which reflects an authorial desire to fuse contradictive *topoi* and not a carefully planned ambiguity, than with *Bananas* (Allen, 1971) or *Raiders of the Lost Ark* (Spielberg, 1981), films that Eco cites as examples of the self-conscious postmodern cult film. He does, however, not hold that *Casablanca* embodies the aesthetic qualities typical of a Shakespeare play or any of the greatest modern novels. *Casablanca*'s "glorious ricketiness" performs enough order in disorder to achieve the completion of a sectarian world of fandom (p. 198), but it does not evolve into a truly "open" work. Thus, although its complexity is likely to activate "an enthusiastic reception" (Casetti and Crespi, "Cinema and the Question of Reception," p. 272), the reader's interpretation will be constrained by what ultimately is a conventional drama with limited possibilities for the invention of subcodes.

To find an example of truly open cinema we must turn to the existentially defined and graphically delineated world of Antonioni, a director Eco frequently refers to and explicitly distinguishes from most of contemporary filmmakers, including the tradition of European art-house cinema to which he belongs. One of several short texts of pastiche and parody included in *Misreadings*, the theoretically unpretentious and humourously suggestive "Make Your Own Movie" (1972) explicitly separates the master of angst and alienation from Godard, Olmi, Visconti and an "Angry Young Director" who in *Salò or the 120 Days of Sodom* (1975) did anything but write with reality (Umberto Eco, *Misreadings*. Trans. William Weaver. New York: Harcourt Brace, 1993, p. 153).[12] "Make Your Own Movie" captures the essence of the aforementioned directors by listing stock-situations of their films and drawing a scenario from these lists. The pretext for Eco's essay is the wide diffusion in 1993 of the video camera which has subsequently enabled everyone to be his or her own director – all that is required to make a movie is a video camera and a scenario to follow. Inherent in this notion of the democratization of the means of cinematic reproduction, there is a wink towards Walter Benjamin's thoughts of the death of the "aura" in the age of art's technological reproducibility (pp. 103–5), as well to what Eco more ironically observes with regard to hyperreal American museums where "the absolute fake" has become more real than the original (Eco, *Travels in Hyperreality*, p. 8). In contrast to Michelangelo's unmistakably unique *Pietà* – a sign whose "token" is also its "type" and which as such

escapes the infinite replicability of sign-vehicles – these cinemas reduced
to schematic scenarios are clearly located to the range of signs which may
be "indefinitely reproduced according to their types" (Eco, *A Theory of
Semiotics*, pp. 178–9). The "types" Eco establishes as the essence of the
avant-garde directors' respective poetics are deliberately detailed in their
peculiarity, suggesting not merely that their replication potentially could
become more real than the real, but, more significantly still, that the original works leave larger room for the director's eccentricities than for the
viewer's contribution to the creation of meaning. By contrast, the rudi-
mentary and deliberately vague types Eco suggests for the scenario of a
homemade Antonioni film ("An empty lot. She walks away" [Eco, *Travels
in Hyperreality*, p. 146]), hints, beneath the irony, to a more inscrutable
uniqueness that no fake could reproduce without losing the inexhaustible
levels of meaning for which this type of auteur-oriented cinema allows.[13]

It is, however, in *The Open Work*, and, curiously enough, in relation
to the aesthetics of television, that Eco most systematically explores the
works of Antonioni.[14] The productive process typical of live television
where filming, editing and broadcasting are parallel actions, comes not
only to question conventional ideas of authorship, creative process and
result, but the improvised coherence of such television programs is also
seen to be reflected in the open forms of contemporary art. Live television
implies a series of technical choices taken when the event unfolds, and
these choices of perspectives and angles are, according to Eco, "*interpretations* and *creations* – *choices* and *compositions*" of external experiences among which the observer selects, producing their *imitations* and
inserting them within an frame of unity (Eco, *The Open Work*, p. 111; original italics). Only an "integrated intellectual" like Eco could confidently
relate a television director's work to Aristotle's concept of poetry, asserting
that they are both based on distinction and reproduction of experiences,
as well as to psychological forms of perception and cognition which search
for "order in the midst of chaotic diversity" (pp. 111–12). What makes Eco
recognize the "aesthetic potential" in live broadcasts as an attempt to iso-
late and organize experience according to "a perspective of value" is the
"*impromptu* story" that evolves from the TV director's ability to predict,
or intuit, the course of events (pp. 109–13). Ideally organic in its ultimate form, such a narrative relies on elements of chance and interpretation
which Eco sees as analogous to the lack of causality in open works, from
Shakespeare, to Woolf and Joyce, and lastly, to Antonioni, a director precisely renowned for his categorical rejection of plot structures in favour of
studies in the *temps mortes* of cinematic temporality.

Not by chance does Eco focus on the experimental films that gave Antonioni the critical reputation as the "director of alienation" (Michelangelo Antonioni, *Fare un film è per me vivere*, ed. Carlo di Carlo and Giorgio Tinazzi. Venice: Marsilio, 1995, p. 249), a definition to which Antonioni himself referred when he spoke of the quintessentially modern "illness of sentiments," pointing to the correlation that exists between his concern with emotionally troubled characters, and the dramatically empty narratives of his films (Michelangelo Antonioni, "La malattia dei sentimenti," *Bianco e nero*, 22 (1961): 70–3). When audiences seem to have accepted the universes of *L'avventura* and *La notte* where "things happen not by narrative necessity, but, at least in appearance, by chance" as more or less representative visions of the world, this is in part due to their television habits which have made them more receptive to narrative structures where one is constantly waiting for something to occur (Eco, *The Open Work*, pp. 115–16). Both formats of avant-garde cinema and live television broadcasts reflect the immediacy of life as chance, the crucial point of distinction being that in Antonioni, chance takes the form of possibilities. *L'Avventura* demonstrates a use of montage by which the author creates "a 'willed' chance" which deliberately violates all the plausible expectations the spectator may have brought to the events depicted on the silver screen. Situations of tension emerge but remain unresolved due to a "decantation of dramatic action" whereby chance events are organized into the open format of a *"field of stimuli"* imposing intellectual and moral dilemmas the spectator cannot ignore (pp. 116–17; original italics). The sense of social and spatial alienation that haunts Antonioni's characters is thus mirrored and reinforced by the film's formal structures, aiming to alienate in the sense of estranging the spectator the way a Brechtian play would. In *L'eclisse* (1964), Antonioni does not resort to traditional psychological parameters to explain the sterile love affairs of his apathetic characters; instead, their indeterminacy is reflected in that of the film's structures and comes as such to act upon the viewer in ways the logics of causality would not normally permit (pp. 135, 148–9).

For Eco, this mode of formal alienation signals the era of the open work, when art reflects the artist's dilemma of realizing that "the system of communication at his disposal is extraneous to the historical situation he wants to depict," a dilemma that may only be resolved through the inventions of a formal structure that both embody and become a model for this situation (p. 143). In reflecting a universe devoid of unifying parameters, art may also propose a new vision of the world and as such achieve the pedagogical function of creating awareness of and providing means by which to navigate the universe deprived of order. An artist's social commitment and instructive or representational intentions may, however, also be misread, if the addressee superimposes "different connotative subcodes on the ones foreseen by the author," a situation Eco illustrates with reference to Antonioni's *Chung Kuo Cina* (1973 [Eco, "On the Contribution of Film to Semiotics," 7]). Shot during the director's five-week-long visit to China in 1972, the documentary portrays the Cultural Revolution as it is reflected in the streets, or among farmers and workers in fields and factories, rather than as a dialectical formation of a free country. The intention, Antonioni explains in the preface to the film's script, is to offer the viewer an experience as rewarding as meeting the Chinese people was for him, and if this fails, he continues – convinced after years of filmmaking that "images have a meaning" – "if Antonioni's film is erroneous, the fault belongs to Antonioni and not to the faceless phantasm that is the cinema ..." (Michelangelo Antonioni, *Chung Kuo Cina*. Ed. Lorenzo Cucco. Turin: Einaudi, 1974, pp. x–xvi). At the film's release and for three decades thereafter, the Chinese who had the chance to see it could not have agreed more with him, perceiving this representation of their country as, in Renmin Ribao's uncompromising words, a reactionary and "serious anti-China event and a frenzied provocation against the Chinese people" (Renmin Ribao, *A Vicious Motive, Despicable Tricks – A Criticism of Antonioni's Anti-China Film "China."* Peking: Foreign Languages Press, 1974, p. 1). Eco, however, keen to defend one of his favourite directors and at the same time make yet another argument for the coded nature of the cinematic image, approaches the conflicting positions as a question of coding in relation to cultural differences, rather than as a failure of representation on Antonioni's part.

The aptly titled "De Interpretatione: The Difficulty of Being Marco Polo" (1977) seeks to understand why Antonioni's unintentionally controversial film came to be hated by "800 million persons" who certainly did not see it and, more importantly, despised by their political rulers who, in associating it categorically with "Soviet revisionism and American imperialism," failed to perceive of the author's "cordial participation" in the reality he in fact was invited to document (Eco, *Travels in Hyperreality*, p. 282).[15] When *Chung Kuo Cina* appeared at the Venice Film Festival, four years after its release, in the name of freedom of expression and of information–and despite mass protests from Chinese interest groups–Eco benefited from the company of a Hong Kong film critic who provided him with an alternative set of connotative codes than the ones he otherwise would have applied to Antonioni's documentary. While a Western

addressee might construe Antonioni's focus on China's non-official real-
ities as a commitment to show both the birth of justice among a recently
liberated people and the dignity of a culture so radically different from
the West, this predilection for the old presents, from a Chinese perspective, a denigratory image of the revolution and foregrounds China as
an inferior and a not-yet industrialized country. Instead of Antonioni's
"docile" imagery, Chinese viewers would typically have wanted a "strong"
representation, with a symbolic take appropriate to the revolution, rather
than the "realistic gusto" they can only decode as "resignation" (p.
285). What aesthetic principles a Chinese addressee might impose upon
Antonioni's poetic vision appears evident from Ribao's reactions to one
specific shot of the Nanking Bridge which allegedly forms a deliberate
assumption of "very bad angles in order to make it appear crooked and
tottering" (Ribao, *A Vicious Motive, Despicable Tricks*, p. 11). Eco points,
however, to the specificities of Western cinematic language which conveys
vitality through asymmetry and where framing a shot from below signifies grandeur, in opposition to the tendency within Chinese aesthetics
to privilege a frontal imagery of symmetry and distance (Eco, *Travels in
Hyperreality*, p. 286). The situation of mutual misreadings is thus just as
much an aesthetic question as it is a political one, and to solve it requires
a recognition and understanding of the codes involved both in the sta-
ging and in the interpretation of the prefilmic reality.

A testament to the interpretative possibilities of the open work at its
most extreme, *Chung Kuo Cina* provides not only a practical means of
verification for the most essential elements of Eco's theoretical stance, but
also a dramatization of his conviction that "when political debate and artistic representation involve different cultures on a worldwide scale, art and
politics are also mediated by anthropology and thus by semiotics" p. 283).

This, it becomes clear now, has been the fundamental hypothesis at
the basis of Eco's theories all along, but few of his writings allow such an
insight into what disjunctions may be at work in separating the artist's
acts of signification from the addressee's inventions of subcodes. More
crucially still is the occasion Antonioni's film offers to demonstrate what
civic function semiotic approaches to art and culture may have, ideally
creating awareness the way Barthes' *Mythologies* (1957) first did and still
does around subtle structures of meaning embedded in processes of
signification that tend to go unquestioned. In Eco's theory and critical
practice, semiotics takes the form of social commitment, revealing the
ideological implications in apparently unambiguous images, while also
teaching us to alter our perspectives and to approach genuine works of art

(and in the contemporary period, this implies open works of art) not for their potential to incite ideological conflict but for the opportunity they afford us for dialogue in a moment when all other channels of communication appear to be blocked by socio-political differences.

NOTES

1 This paper was originally presented at the conference "Film and the University" held in New York in 1976.

2 This was later incorporated into *La struttura assente* (1968, *The Absent Structure*).

3 Eco's concept of sign is based on Charles S. Peirce's theories and defined as "everything which can be taken as significantly substituting for something else" (Eco, *A Theory of Semiotics*, p. 7).

4 Eco refers specifically to Metz's essay, "Le cinéma: langue ou langage?" *Communications*, 4, (see Christian Metz, *Film Language: A Semiotics of the Cinema*. New York: Oxford University Press, 1974, a translation of *Essays sur la signification au cinema*, Vol I. Paris: Klinksieck, 1971) and Pasolini's essay, "La lingua scritta dell'azione", *Nuovi argumenti* (April–June 1966), (see Pier Paolo Pasolini, *Heretical Empiricism*, Washington: New Academic Publishing, 2005, a translation by Ben Lawton of *Empirismo Eretico* [Milan: Garzanti, 1972]).

5 Eco's major argument against Pasolini's "semiologic ingenuousness" is precisely that the object of semiology is to "eventually bring natural facts to the level of cultural phenomena, and not to bring facts of culture back to the level of natural phenomena" (Eco, *The Absent Structure*, p. 152). This and all further translations are mine, unless otherwise indicated.

6 This was orginally presented at the conference 'Film and the University' held in New York in 1976.

7 This later appeared in Peter Bondanella and Cristina Degli-Esposti (eds.), *Perspectives on Federico Fellini* (New York: G. K. Hall, 1993), pp. 293–4.

8 Quoting Peirce (*Collected Papers*), Eco defines the process of "unlimited semiosis" in this manner: "Therefore a sign is 'anything which determines something else (its *interpretant*) to refer to an object to which itself refers (its *object*) in the same way, the *interpretant* becoming in turn a sign, and so on *ad inifinitum*'" (2.300). Thus the very definition of "sign" implies a process of unlimited semiosis (Eco, *A Theory of Semiotics*, p. 69; original italics).

9 Peter Bondanella points to the dependence of Eco's theory of the open work on Peirce's concept of unlimited semiosis, a relation Eco himself was not conscious of when he first published *The Open Work* in 1962 (p. 83).

10 Eco's interest in cinema as a revisualization of the past would seem to have inspired his recent novel *The Mysterious Flame of Queen Loana* (2005), where the reconstruction of a lost memory proceeds largely by means of images.

11 See Peter Brooker and Will Brooker, "Pulpmodernism: Quentin Tarantiano's Affirmative Action." In Debora Cortmell *et al.* (eds.), *Pulping Fictions*, London: Pluto, 1996, pp. 131–51.

12 Along the line of these texts and representative of Eco at his most reader-friendly is *How to Travel With A Salmon & Other Essays* (1994), which includes acute instructions on "How to Play Indians" according to the conventions of the Western, and on "How to Recognize a Porn Movie." The latter type of film curiously tends to share Antonioni's sense for *temps mortes*, but for completely different reasons, as extensive and narratively empty travel passages serve to create the impression of a normality that is then subsequently denied by the transgression of explicitly graphic depictions of sexual acts (pp. 222–5).

13 A scenario for a Godard film, for instance, would include the following elements: "He arrives and then bang a refinery explodes. The Americans make love. Cannibals armed with bazookas fire on the railroad. She falls riddled with bullets from a rifle. At mad speed to Vincennes Cohn-Bendit catches the train and speaks. Two men kill her. He reads sayings of Mao. Montesquieu throws a bomb at Diderot. He kills himself. He peddles *Le Figaro*. The redskins arrive" (pp. 146–7).

14 This is not the only instance in which Eco draws parallels between TV and cinema: in "The Phantom of Neo-TV: The Debate on Fellini's *Ginger and Fred*," Fellini's comedy of manners is seen as a parody of what Eco calls "Neo-television" – a "complex phenomenon consisting of lots and lots of TV channels, all shot through with ads, and programs that copy one another... Each program talks about itself and addresses an audience that is part of the program ..." (Eco, *Apocalypse Postponed*, p. 110).

15 Antonioni was officially invited by the Chinese to make a documentary on the revolution, and the film is, in his view, the result of a compromise reached after three days of negotiations with Chinese officials (Antonioni, *Chung Kuo Cina*, xi–xiii), whereas the latter part saw it as something far less. *Chung Kuo Cina* was banned, and not until 2004 did it enjoy a public, and triumphant, screening in Peking (Francesco Sisci, "Anche Pechino per Antonioni," LASTAMPA. It. 3 August 2007. www.lastampa.it/_web/cmstp/tmplrubriche/giornalisti/grubrica.asp?ID_blog¼498&ID_articolo1/432&ID_sezione ¼180&sezione).

Selected bibliography on Eco

The following list of Eco's copious literary production lists all the texts discussed by the various authors included in this anthology. Eco's works have a very complex publishing history. In some cases, the available translations (the texts that most readers of this anthology will be using) are not complete versions of the Italian originals. For example, *Opera aperta: forma e indeterminazione nelle poetiche contemporanee* – literally *Open Work: Form and Intederminancy in Contemporary Poetics* – becomes rendered by two different translations, *The Open Work* and *The Aesthetics of Chaosmos: The Middle Ages of James Joyce*. *Apocalittici e integrati: comunicazioni di massa e teorie della cultura di massa* – the literal translation of which is *Apocalyptic and Integrated Intellectuals: Mass Communications and Theories of Mass Culture* – is only available in a partial English translation as *Apocalypse Postponed*. Parts of *Lector in fabula: la cooperazione interpretativa nei testi narrativi* – literally *The Reader in the Story: Interpretative Cooperation in Narrative Texts* – are translated and included in *The Role of the Reader: Explorations in the Semiotics of Texts*, but the English text also contains essays that originally appeared in the Italian edition of *Opera aperta*.

To sort out this confusing editorial problem, the present anthology follows this method: (1) the following bibliography of Eco's major works will provide complete bibliographical information for both Italian originals and available translations; (2) in the event that existing English editions are not complete or literal translations of the Italian originals, each text in this instance will list a literal English translation; (3) in those instances where authors felt obliged to cite the Italian original (an English version being lacking or incomplete), a translation by the author will be provided. Whenever possible, this system will permit a simple system of annotation, giving the English title and page number in the text proper without the necessity of a footnote.

1956

Il problema estetico in San Tommaso [*The Aesthetic Problem in Saint Thomas*]. Turin: Edizioni di filosofia. 2nd revised edn. *Il problema estetico in Tommaso d'Aquino* [*The Aesthetic Problem in Thomas of Aquinas*]. Milan: Bompiani, 1970. Translation: *The Aesthetics of Thomas Aquinas*. Translated by Hugh Bredin. Cambridge, MA: Harvard University Press, 1988.

1958

Filosofi in libertà [*Philosophers in Freedom*]. Turin: Taylor. Now included in *Il secondo diario minimo* (see 1992).

1959

"Sviluppo dell'estetica medievale" ["The Development of Medieval Aesthetics"]. In *Momenti e problemi di storia dell'estetica*, vol. 1. Milan: Marzorati. Enlarged Italian edition.
Arte e bellezza nell'estetica medievale [*Art and Beauty in Medieval Aesthetics*]. Milan: Bompiani, 1987. Partial English translation: *Art and Beauty in the Middle Ages*. Translated by Hugh Bredin. New Haven, CT: Yale University Press, 1986.

1962

Opera aperta: forma e indeterminazione nelle poetiche contemporanee [*Open Work: Form and Intederminancy in Contemporary Poetics*]. Milan: Mondadori. 2nd edn., 1967; 3rd edn., 1971; 4th edn., 1976. Translated (with omissions and revisions) into two separate books in English:

(a) *The Open Work*. Trans. Anna Cancogni. Intro. David Robey. Cambridge, MA: Harvard University Press, 1989.
(b) *The Aesthetics of Chaosmos: The Middle Ages of James Joyce*. Trans. Ellen Esrock. Note to the 1989 edn. by David Robey. Cambridge, MA: Harvard University Press, 1989.

1963

Diario minimo [*Minimal Diary*]. Milan: Mondadori, 1963. Numerous editions and printings to the present.
Partial translation: *Misreadings*. Trans. William Weaver. New York: Harcourt Brace, 1993.

1964

Apocalittici e integrati: comunicazioni di massa e teorie della cultura di massa [*Apocalyptic and Integrated Intellectuals: Mass Communications and Theories of Mass Culture*]. Milan: Bompiani. Partial translation: *Apocalypse Postponed*. Ed. Robert Lumley. Bloomington: Indiana University Press, 1994. One section translated as "A Reading of *Steve Canyon*," trans. Bruce Merry, in Shenna Wagstaff (ed.), *Comic Iconoclasm* (London: Institute of Contemporary Arts, 1988), pp. 20–5; one essay translated in *The Open Work* (see 1962a).

1965

Il caso Bond. Ed. Umberto Eco and Oresto del Buono. Translation: *The Bond Affair*. Trans. R. Downie. London: Macdonald, 1966.
Le poetiche di Joyce: dalla "Summa" al "Finnegans Wake" [*The Poetics of Joyce: From the "Summa" to "Finnegans Wake"*]. Milan: Bompiani. [Translation: see 1962]

1967

Appunti per una semiologia delle comunicazioni visive [*Notes on a Semiology of Visual Communications*]. Milan: Bompiani. [Non-commercial book intended for Eco's students expanded to become *La struttura assente* in 1968.]

1968

La definizione dell'arte [*The Definition of Art*]. Milan: Mursia.
La struttura assente [*The Absent Structure*]. Milan: Bompiani. Partial translation of one essay in *The Open Work* (see 1962a).

1969

L'industria dell cutura [*The Culture Industry*]. Ed. Umberto Eco. Milan: Bompiani.

1971

Le forme del contenuto [*The Forms of Content*]. Milan: Bompiani.

1973

Il beato di Liebana [*The Blessed Liebana*]. Milan: Ricci. Partial translation of Eco's introductory essay published as "Waiting for the Millennium" in *FMR* 2 (July 1984): 63–92.

Il costume di casa: evidenze e misteri dell'ideologia italiana [*Home Customs: Evidences and Mysteries of Italian Ideology*]. Milan: Bompiani. Partial translation of several essays in *Apocalpyse Postponed* (see 1964) and *Travels in Hyperreality* (see 1977).

"Il linguaggio politico" [*Political Language*]. In G. L. Beccaria (ed.), *I linguaggi settoriali in Italia*. Milan. Bompiani.

Il segno [*The Sign*]. Milan: Istituto Editoriale Internazionale.

1975

Trattato di semiotica generale. Milan: Bompiani. Translation: *A Theory of Semiotics*. Bloomington: Indiana University Press, 1976.

1976

Il superuomo di massa: retorica e ideologia nel romanzo popolare [*The Superman of the Masses: Rhetoric and Ideology in the Popular Novel*]. Milan: Cooperativa Scrittori. 2nd rev. edn. Milan: Bompiani, 1978. Partial translation of two essays in *The Role of the Reader* (see 1979).

A Theory of Semiotics (see 1975)

1977

Come si fa una tesi di laurea [*How to Write a Doctoral Thesis*]. Milan: Bompiani.

Dalla periferia dell'impero: cronache da un nuovo medioevo [*From the Periphery of the Empire: Chronicles from a New Middle Ages*]. Milan: Bompiani. Partial translation of several essays in *Travels in Hyperreality*. Trans. William Weaver. New York: Harcourt Brace Jovanovich, 1986. Partial translation (one essay): *Apocalypse Postponed* (see 1964).

"On the Contribution of Film to Semiotics" *Quarterly Review of Film Studies*, 21 (1977): 1–14.

1978

"Semiotics: A Discipline or an Interdisciplinary Method?" In Thomas A. Sebeok, (ed.), *Sight Sound and Sense*. Bloomington: Indiana University Press.

1979

Invermizio, Serao, Liala. Ed. Umberto Eco. Florence: La Nuova Italia.
Lector in fabula: la cooperazione interpretativa nei testi narrativi [*The Reader in the Story: Interpretative Cooperation in Narrative Texts*]. Milan: Bompiani. Partial translation (not actually a complete translation of *Lector in fabula* but, rather, a collection of major essays written between 1959 and 1979, including selections from *Opera aperta*): *The Role of the Reader: Explorations in the Semiotics of Texts*. Bloomington: Indiana University Press.

1980

Il nome della rosa. Milan: Bompiani. Translation: *The Name of the Rose*. Trans. William Weaver. New York: Harcourt Brace Jovanovich, 1983. *The Name of the Rose Including the Author's Postscript*. Trans. William Weaver. New York: Harvest Books, 1994.

1981

"Guessing: From Aristotle to Sherlock Holmes." *Versus* 30 (1981), 3–19.

1983

"A Correspondence with Umberto Eco." Stefano Rosso (ed.), *Boundary 2: A Journal of Postmodern Literature*, 12, 1 (1983): 1–13.
Raymond Queneau. *Esercizi di stile* [*Exercises in Style*]. Trans. Umberto Eco. Turin: Einaudi, 1983. (Original French edition of 1947 entitled *Exercises de style*.)
"A Guide to the Neo-Television of the 1980s." In (eds.), Zygmunt G. Baranski and Robert Lumley. *Culture and Conflict in Postwar Italy: Essays on Mass and Popular Culture*. New York: St. Martin's Press, 1990. English translation of an article in *L'Espresso* (January 30, 1983).
The Name of the Rose (see 1980)
Postille al "Il nome della rosa". Milan: Bompiani. Translation: *Postscript to "The Name of the Rose"*. Trans. William Weaver. San Diego: Harcourt Brace Jovanovich, 1984. Reprinting with the novel: *The Name of the Rose Including the Author's Postscript*. New York: Harvest Books, 1994.
Il segno dei tre. Milan: Bompiani. Translation: *The Sign of Three: Dupin, Holmes, Peirce*. Bloomington: Indiana University Press.
Sette anni di desiderio [*Seven Years of Desire*]. Milan: Bompiani. Partial translation of several essays in *Apocalypse Postponed* (see 1964) and *Travels in Hyperreality* (see 1977).

1984

"The Frames of Comic 'Freedom'." In Thomas A. Sebeok (ed.), *Carnival!*. Berlin: Mouton, pp. 1–9.
Postscript to "The Name of the Rose" (see 1983)
"The Semantics of Metaphor." In Robert E. Innis (ed.), *Semiotics: An Introductory Anthology*. Bloomington: Indiana University Press.
Semiotica e filosofia del linguaggio. Turin: Einaudi. Translation: *Semiotics and the Philosophy of Language*. Bloomington: Indiana University Press.

1985

"Innovation and Repetition: Between Modern and Post-Modern Aesthetics." *Daedalus*, 1, 14 (1985): 161–84.
"Reflections on *The Name of the Rose*." *Encounter*, 64, 4 (1985): 7–19.
Sugli specchi e altri saggi [*On Mirrors and Other Essays*]. Milan: Bompiani. Partial translation of a section in *Travels in Hyperreality* (see 1977).

1986

Art and Beauty in the Middle Ages (see 1959)
Travels in Hyperreality (see 1977)

1988

The Aesthetics of Thomas Aquinas (see 1956)
"An *Ars Oblivionalis*? Forget It!" *PMLA*, 103, 3 (1988): 154–61.
"Intentio Lectoris: The State of the Art." In Giovanna Borradori (ed.), *Recoding Metaphysics: The New Italian Philosophy*. Evanston, IL: Northwestern University Press. Revised version in *The Limits of Interpretation* (1990).
Meaning and Mental Representations. Ed. Umberto Eco, Marco Santambrogio, and Patrizia Violi. Bloomington: Indiana University Press.
"Il mio piano" [*My Plan*]. Ed. Ferdinando Adornato. *L'Espresso* (October 9, 1988): 92–111.
Il pendolo di Foucault. Milan: Bompiani. Translation: *Foucault's Pendulum*. Trans. William Weaver. New York: Harcourt Brace Jovanovich.

1989

The Aesthetics of Chaosmos: The Middle Ages of James Joyce (see 1962)
La bomba e il generale. Illustrations by Eugenio Carmi. Milan: Bompiani. Translation: *The Bomb and the General*. Trans. William Weaver. San Diego, CA: Harcourt Brace Jovanovich.

On the Medieval Theory of Signs. Ed. Umberto Eco and Costantino Marmo. Amsterdam: John Benjamins.
The Open Work (see 1962a)
"La semiosi ermetica e il 'paradigma del velame'" ["Hermetic Semiosis and the 'Paradigm of the Veil'"]. Introduction to *L'idea deforme: interpretazioni esoteriche di Dante.* Ed. Maria Pia Pozzato. Milan: Bompiani, pp. 9–37.
Tre cosmonauti. Illustrations by Eugenio Carmi. Milan: Bompiani. Translation: *The Three Astronauts.* Trans. William Weaver. San Diego, CA: Harcourt Brace Jovanovich.

1990

I limiti dell'interpretazione. Milan: Bompiani. Translation: *The Limits of Interpretation.* Bloomington: Indiana University Press.

1992

"Foreword" to Omar Calabrese, *Neo-Baroque: A Sign of the Times.* Trans. Charles Lambert. Princeton: Princeton University Press.
Interpretation and Overinterpretation. With Richard Rorty, Jonathan Culler and Christine Brooke-Rose. Ed. Stefan Collini. Cambridge: Cambridge University Press. Enlarged Italian translation: *Interpretazione e sovrainterpretazione: un dibattito con Richard Rorty, Jonathan Culler e Christine Brooke-Rose.* Ed. Stefan Collini. Milan: Bompiani, 1995.
"The Quest for a Perfect Language (Blackwell Lectures, Oxford, January 1991)." *Versus* 61–3 (1992): 9–45. *La quête d'une langue parfaite dans l'histoire de la culture européene.* Inaugural lecture (October 2, 1992) at the Collége de France for the European Chair. Paris: Collége de France. Italian translation of French lecture: *La ricerca della lingua perfetta nella cultura europea.* Milan: Gruppo Editoriale Fabbri, Bompiani, 1993. [Note: this Italian text of the lecture was distributed as an insert in *La revista dei libri,* a literary magazine associated with *The New York Review of Books,* and was never sold separately as a book. It should not be confused with the subsequent book of the same Italian title that appeared in 1993 listed below.]
"Reading My Readers." *MLN* (1992): 819–27.
Il secondo diario minimo [*The Second Miminal Diary*]. Milan: Bompiani. Partial translation: *How to Travel with a Salmon and Other Essays.* Trans. William Weaver. New York: Harcourt Brace, 1994.

1993

Misreadings (see 1963)
La ricerca della lingua perfetta nella cultura europea. Rome: Laterza. Translation: *The Search for the Perfect Language.* Trans. James Fentress. Oxford: Blackwell Publishers, 1995.

1994

Apocalypse Postponed (see 1964)
"In Memory of Giorgio Prodi: A Challenge to the Myth of Two Cultures."
Trans. Marina Johnston. In Leda Giannuzzi Jaworski (ed.), *Lo studio bolognese: campi di studio, di insegnamento, di ricerca, di divulgazione.* Stony Brook, NY: Forum Italicum, 1994, pp. 75–8.
How to Travel with a Salmon and Other Essays (see 1992)
L'isola del giorno prima. Milan: Bompiani. Translation: *The Island of the Day Before.* Trans. William Weaver. New York: Harcourt Brace Jovanovich, 1995.
The Name of the Rose Including the Author's Postscript (see 1980)
Six Walks in the Fictional Woods. Cambridge, MA: Harvard University Press. Italian translation: *Sei passeggiate nei boschi narrativi: Harvard University, Norton Lectures 1992–1993.* Milan: Bompiani.
"Thoth, Fellini and the Pharaoh." In Peter Bondanella and Cristina Degli-Esposti (eds.), *Perspectives on Federico Fellini.* New York: G. K. Hall, 1993, pp. 293–4.

1995

The Island of the Day Before (see 1994)
"La maledizione del faraone" ["The Curse of the Pharoah"]. *Sette: Corriere della sera* (supplement to the Milanese daily), nos. 32–6 (1995). Written with Giuseppe Pontiggia, Gianni Riotta, and Antonio Tabucchi.
The Search for the Perfect Language (see 1993)
Il seicento: Guida multimediale alla storia della civiltà europea diretta da Umberto Eco [*The Seventeenth Century: Multimedia Guide to the History of European Civilization Directed by Umberto Eco*]. Milan: Opera Multimedia (a CD-ROM).
"Ur-Fascism." *New York Review of Books,* 42, 11 (June 22): 12–15.

1997

Cinque scritti morali. Milan: Bompiani. Translation: *Five Moral Pieces.* Trans. Alastair McEwen. Orlando, FL: Harcourt Brace, 2001.
Kant e l'ornitorinco. Milan: Bompiani. Translation: *Kant and the Platypus: Essays on Language and Cognition.* Trans. Alastair McEwen. New York: Harcourt Brace, 2000.

1998

Serendipities: Language and Lunacy. Trans. William Weaver. New York: Columbia University Press.
Talking of Joyce. Dublin: University College Dublin Press (co-author with Liberato Santoro-Brienza and J. Mays).
Tra menzogna e ironia [*Between Lie and Irony*]. Milan: Bompiani.

1999

La bustina di Minerva [*Minerva's Matchbook*]. Milan: Bompiani.
Gérard de Nerval. *Sylvie*. Trans. Umberto Eco. Turin: Einaudi.

2000

Baudolino. Milan: Bompiani. Translation: *Baudolino*. Trans. William Weaver. Orlando, FL: Harcourt Brace.
Kant and the Platypus: Essays on Language and Cogintion (see 1997)

2001

Experiences in Translation. Toronto: University of Toronto Press. Translated by Alastair McEwen.
Five Moral Pieces (see 1997)

2003

Dire quasi la stessa cosa: esperienze di traduzione [*Saying Almost the Same Thing: Experiences in Translation*]. Milan: Bompiani.
Mouse or Rat? Translation as Negotiation. London: Weidenfeld & Nicolson.

2004

"How I Write." In Charlotte Ross and Rochelle Sibley (eds.), *Illuminating Eco: On the Boundaries of Interpretation*. Aldershot, UK: Ashgate, pp. 171–92.
"A Response by Eco." In Ross and Sibley, *Illuminating Eco*, pp. 193–9.
La misteriosa fiamma della regina Loana. Milan: Bompiani. Translation: *The Mysterious Flame of Queen Loana: An Illustrated Novel*. Trans. Geoffrey Brock. New York: Harcourt, 2005.
Storia della bellezza. Milan: Bompiani. Translation: *A History of Beauty*. Trans. Alistair McEwen. New York: Rizzoli.
Sulla letteratura. Milan: Bompiani. Translation: *On Literature*. Trans. Martin McLaughlin. New York: Harcourt.

2006

A passo di gambero: guerre calde e populismo mediatico. Milan: Bompiani. Translation: *Turning Back the Clock: Hot Wars and Media Populism*. Trans. Alistair McEwen. Harville Sacher, 2007. New York: Harcourt, 2007.
Will Eisner. *The Plot: The Secret Story of The Protocols of the Elders of Zion*. New York: Norton. Intro. Umberto Eco.

2007

La memoria vegetale e altri scritti di bibliofilia [*Vegetable Memory and Other Writings on Bibliophilia*]. Milan: Bompiani.
On Ugliness. Ed. Umberto Eco. New York: Rizzoli.
Dall'albero al laberinto: studi storici sul segno e l'interpretazione [*From the Tree to the Labyrinth: Historical Studies on the Sign and Intepretation*]. Milan: Bompiani.

FOR FURTHER READING ON UMBERTO ECO

Antonioni, Michelangelo. *Fare un film è per me vivere*. Ed. Carlo di Carlo and Giorgio Tinazzi. Venice: Marsilio, 1995.
"La malattia dei sentimenti." *Bianco e nero*, 22 (1961): 69–95.
Bauco, Luigi and Millocca, Francesco. Ed. Luciano Turrini. *Dizionario del pendolo di Foucault*. Ferrara: Gabriele Corbo, 1989.
Benjamin, Walter. *Selected Writings*. 3 vols. Ed. and Trans. Marcus Bullock *et al*. Cambridge, MA: Harvard University Press, 1996–2003.
Benvenuti, Stefano and Rizzoni, Gianni. *Il romanzo giallo: storia, autori e personaggi*. Milan: Mondadori, 1979.
Bolzoni, Lina. *The Gallery of Memory*. Trans. Jeremy Parzen. Toronto: Toronto University Press. 2001.
Bondanella, Peter. *Umberto Eco and the Open Text: Semiotics, Fiction, Popular Culture*. Cambridge: Cambridge University Press, 1997.
Bondanella, Peter and Ciccarelli, Andrea. (eds.). *The Cambridge Companion to the Italian Novel*. Cambridge: Cambridge University Press, 2003.
Bosworth, Richard. *Mussolini's Italy. Life Under the Dictatorship*. New York: Penguin Press, 2006.
Bouchard, Norma. "Umberto Eco's *L'isola del giorno prima*: Postmodern Theory and Fictional Praxis." *Italica*, 72, 2 (1995): 193–208.
Bouchard, Norma and Pravadelli Veronica. (eds.). *Umberto Eco's Alternative: The Politics of Culture and the Ambiguities of Interpretation*. New York: Peter Lang, 1998.
Brooker, Peter and Brooker, Will. "Pulpmodernism: Quentin Tarantino's Affirmative Action." *Pulping Fictions*. Ed. Debora Cartmell *et al*. London: Pluto, 1996, pp. 135–151.
Burkhardt, Armin and Rohse, Eberhard. (eds.). *Umberto Eco zwischen Literatur und Semiotik*. Braunschweig: Verlag Ars & Scientia, 1991.
Caesar, Michael. *Umberto Eco: Philosophy, Semiotics, and the Work of Fiction*. Cambridge, UK: Polity Press, 1999.
Campbell, Mary. *The Witness and the Other World: Exotic European Travel Writing, 400–1600*. Ithaca, NY: Cornell University Press, 1988.
Cannon, JoAnn. *Postmodern Italian Fiction: The Crisis of Reason in Calvino, Eco, Sciascia;, Malerba*. Rutherford, NJ: Fairleigh Dickinson University Press, 1989.

Capozzi, Rocco. "Hypertextuality and Cognitive Experiences in the Labyrinths of Words and Images." In M. Buccheri, E. Costa, and D. Holoch (eds.), *The Power of Words*. Ravenna: Longo. 2005.

"Intertextuality and Hypermedia: Towards Electronic Hyper-Intertextual Analyses." *VS (Versus. Quaderni di studi semiotici)* 77/78 (May–December 1997): 161–74.

"The Return of Umberto Eco. Baudolino *Homo Ludens*: Describing the Unknown." *Rivista di Studi Italiani*, 18, 2 (2000): 211–35.

Capozzi, Rocco (ed.), *Reading Eco: An Anthology*. Bloomington: Indiana University, 1997.

Casetti, Francesco and Crespi, Barbara. "Cinema and the Question of Reception." In Norma Bouchard and Veronica Pravadelli (eds.), *Umberto Eco's Alternative*. New York: Peter Lang, 1998, pp. 257–75.

Cipolla, Gaetano. *Labyrinth: Studies on an Archetype*. Brooklyn, NY: Legas, 1987.

Coletti, Teresa. *Naming the Rose: Eco, Medieval Signs, and Modern Theory*. Ithaca, NY: Cornell University Press, 1988.

Cotroneo, Roberto. *La diffidenza come sistema: saggio sulla narrativa di Umberto Eco*. Milan: Anabasi, 1995.

Crovi, Luca. *Tutti i colori del giallo: il giallo italiano da De Marchi a Scerbanenco a Camilleri*. Venice: Marsilio, 2002.

Danesi, Marcel. *Encyclopedic Dictionary of Semiotics, Media, and Communications*. Toronto: University of Toronto Press, 2000.

De Angelis, Augusto. *L' albergo delle tre rose*. Milan: Mondadori, 1936.

De Benedictis, Raffaele. "That History Which is Not in Umberto Eco's *Baudolino*." *Forum Italicum*, 36 (2002): 393–410.

De Carli, Lorenzo. *Internet memoria e oblio*. Milan: Bollati Boringhieri. 1997.

De Lauretis, Teresa. *Umberto Eco*. Florence: La Nuova Italia, 1981.

Della Coletta, Cristina. *Plotting the Past: Metamorphoses of Historical Narrative in Modern Italian Fiction*. West Lafayette, IN: Purdue University Press, 1996.

Farronato, Cristina. *Eco's Chaosmos: From the Middle Ages to Postmodernity*. Toronto: University of Toronto Press, 2003.

"Umberto Eco's *Baudolino* and the Language of Monsters," *Semiotica*, 144 (2003): 319–42.

Fleissner, Robert F. *A Rose by Another Name: A Survey of Literary Flora from Shakespeare to Eco*. West Cornwall, CT: Locust Hill Press, 1989.

Fontanille, J. *Figure del corpo*. Roma: Meltemi, 2004.

Fontanille, J. and Zilberberg, C.. *Tension et signification*. Hayen: Mardaga, 1998.

Francese, Joseph. *Socially Symbolic Acts: The Historicizing Fictions Of Umberto Eco, Vincenzo Consolo, And Antonio Tabucchi*. Fairleigh Dickinson University Press, 2006.

Frare, Pierantonio. "Il pendolo di Foucault o della negazione." *Vita e pensiero*, 72, 5 (1989): 373–85.

Friedman, John Block. *The Monstrous Races in Medieval Art and Thought*. Cambridge, MA: Harvard University Press, 1981.

Gane, Michael and Gane, Nicholas (eds.). *Umberto Eco*. 3 vols. Thousand Oaks, CA: Sage, 2005.

Ganeri, Margherita. *Il "caso" Eco*. Palermo: Palumbo, 1991.

Giovannoli, Renato. *Saggi su "Il nome della rosa"*. Milan: Fabbri, 1985.

Glynn, Ruth. "Presenting the Past: The Case of *Il nome della Rosa*," *The Italianist*, 17 (1997): 99–116.

Gritti, Jules. *Umberto Eco*. Paris: Éditions Universitaires, 1991.

Gumilev, L. N. *Searches for an Imaginary Kingdom: The Legend of the Kingdom of Prester John*. Trans. R. E. F. Smith. Cambridge: Cambridge University Press, 1987.

Haft, Adele J., White, Jane G., and White, Robert J. *The Key to "The Name of the Rose."* Ann Arbor, MI: University of Michigan Press, 1999.

Haycroft, Howard. *Murder for Pleasure: The Life and Times of the Detective Story*. New York: D. Appleton-Century, 1941.

Haycroft, Howard (ed.). *The Art of the Mystery Story: A Collection of Critical Essays*. New York: Biblo and Tannen, 1976 (new edition of 1946 original).

Higgins, Iain MacCleod. *Writing East: The "Travels" of Sir John Mandeville*. Philadelphia: University of Pennsylvania Press, 1997.

Holsinger, Bruce. *The Postmodern Condition: Medievalism and the Making of Theory*. Chicago: University of Chicago Press, 2005.

Hutcheon, Linda. *A Poetics of Postmodernism*. New York: Routledge, 1988.

Ickert, Klaus and Schick, Ursula. *Il segreto della rosa decifrato*. Florence: Salani Editore, 1987 (original German edition, Munich: Wilhelm Heyne Verlag, 1986).

Inge, Thomas (ed.). *Naming the Rose: Essays on Eco's "The Name of the Rose"*. Foreword by Umberto Eco. Jackson: University Press of Mississippi, 1988.

Irvin, John. *The Mystery to a Solution: Poe, Borges, and the Analytical Detective Story*. Baltimore, MD: The Johns Hopkins University Press, 1994.

Juarrero, Alicia. "The Message Whose Message It Is That There Is No Message." *MLN*, 107, 5 (1992): 892–904.

Landow, George P. *Hypertext. The Convergence of Contemporary Critical Theory and Technology*. Baltimore: Johns Hopkins University Press, 1992.

Landow, George P. and Delaney, Paul (eds.). *Hypermedia and Literary Studies*. Cambridge, MA: MIT Press, 1990.

Lukács, George. *The Historical Novel*. London: Merlin Press, 1962.

McHale, Brian. *Constructing Postmodernism*. London and New York: Routledge, 1992.

Magli, Patrizia, Manetti, Giovanni, and Violi, Patrizia (eds.). *Semiotica: storia, teoria, interpretazione: saggi intorno a Umberto Eco*. Milan: Bompiani, 1992 (with an important Eco bibliography updated to 1992).

Mandeville, John. *Mandeville's Travels*. Ed. M. C. Seymour. Oxford: Clarendon Press, 1967.

The Travels of Sir John Mandeville. Trans. and intro. C. W. R. D. Moseley. Harmondsworth, UK: Penguin, 1983.

Merivale, Patricia and Sweeney, Susan Elizabeth (eds.). *Detecting Texts: The Metaphysical Detective Story from Poe to Postmodernism*. Philadelphia: University of Pennsylvania Press, 1999.

Most, Glenn W. and Stowe, William W. (eds.). *The Poetics of Murder: Detective Fiction and Literary Theory*. San Diego, CA: Harcourt Brace Jovanovich, 1983.

Musarra, Franca *et al.* (eds.). *Eco in Fabula: Umberto Eco in the Humanities*. Florence: Franco Casati Editore, 2002.

Musca, Giosuè. "La camicia del nesso ovvero *Il pendolo di Foucault* di Umberto Eco." *Quaderni medievali* 27 (1989): 104–49.

Ng, David. "Eco and the Funnymen." *Village Voice* online (July 5, 2005), pp. 1–3. www.villagevoice.com/books/0527,ngeco,65582,10.html

Nielsen Jakob. *Hypertext and Hypermedia*. San Diego, CA: Academic Press, 1990.

Nowell, Charles E. "The Historical Prester John," *Speculum*, 28 (1953): 435–45.

Nunenberg, Geoffrey (ed.). *The Future of the Book*. Berkeley: University of California Press, 1996.

Oliva, Carlo. *Storia sociale del giallo*. Lugano: Todaro Editore, 2003.

Otter, Monica. "Functions of Fiction in Historical Writing." In Nancy Partner (ed.), *Writing Medieval History*. London: Hodder Arnold, 2005, pp. 109–30.

Panek, LeRoy Lad. *An Introduction to the Detective Story*. Bowling Green, OH: Bowling Green State University Popular Press, 1987.

Pansa, Francesca and Vinci, Anna. *Effetto Eco*. Preface by Jacques Le Goff. Arricia: Nuova Edizioni del Gallo, 1990.

Peirce, Charles S. *Collected Papers*, 8 vols. Cambridge, MA: Harvard University Press, 1931–58.

Philosophical Writings. Ed. Justus Buchler. New York: Dover, 1995.

Petitot, Jean and Fabbri, Paolo (eds.). *Nel nome del senso: intorno all'opera di Umberto Eco*. Florence: Sansoni, 2001.

Petrilli, Susan. "Modeling, Dialogue, and Globality: Biosemiotics and Semiotics of Self." *Sign Systems Studies*, 31, 1 (2003): 65–105.

Petronio, Giuseppe. *Sulle tracce del giallo*. Rome: Gamberetti Editrice, 2000.

Pischedda, Bruno. *Come leggere "Il nome della rosa"*. Milan: Mursia, 1994.

Polo, Marco. *The Travels of Marco Polo*. Intro. John Masefield. London: Dent and Sons, Ltd; New York: E. P. Dutton, 1908; rpt. 1954.

Radford, Gary. *Eco*. Belmont, CA: Wadsworth, 2002.

Raffa, Guy P. "Walking and Swimming with Umberto Eco." *MLN*, 113 (1998): 164–85.

Ribao, Remin. *A Vicious Motive, Despicable Tricks – A Criticism of Antonioni's Anti-China Film "China"*. Peking: Foreign Languages Press, 1974.

Rice, Thomas J. "Mapping Complexity in the Fiction of Umberto Eco." *Critique*, 44, 4 (2003): 349–70.

Ross, Charlotte and Sibley, Rochelle. (eds.). *Illuminating Eco: On the Boundaries of Interpretation*. Burlington, VT: Ashgate, 2004.

Ross, Sir E. Denison. "Prester John and the Empire of Ethiopia." In *Travel and Travelers of the Middle Ages*. Ed. Arthur Percival Newton. London: Routledge and Kegan Paul, 1926; rpt. 1949, pp. 174–94.

Rossi, Paolo. *Il passato, la memoria, l'oblio. Sei saggi di storia delle idee*. Bologna: Il Mulino, 1991.

Rozett, Martha Tuck. "Constructing a World: How Postmodern Historical Fiction Reimagines the Past." *CLIO*, 25 (1996): 145–50.

Sebeok, Thomas A., Petrilli, Susan, and Ponzio, Augusto (eds.). *Semiotica dell'io*. Rome: Meltemi, 2001.

Serri, Mirella. *I redenti*. Milan: Corbaccio, 2005.

Simone, R. *Il sogno di Saussure*. Bari: Laterza, 1992.

Sisci, Francesco. "Anche Pechino per Antonioni." LASTAMPA.it. August 3, 2007. www.lastampa.it/_web/cmstp/tmplrubriche/giornalisti/grubrica. asp?ID_blog=98&ID_articolo=32&ID_sezione=180&sezione=

Slessarev, Vsevolod. *Prester John: The Letter and the Legend*. Minneapolis: University of Minnesota Press, 1959.

Stam, Robert. *Film Theory. An Introduction*. Oxford: Blackwell, 2000.

Stein, Robert M. "Literary Criticism and the Evidence for History." In Nancy Partner (ed.), *Writing Medieval History*. London: Hodder Arnold, 2005, pp. 67–87.

Stephens, Walter. "Ec(h)o in fabula". *Diacritics*, 13, 2 (1983): 51–64.

Talamo, Manlio. *I segreti del pendolo: percorsi e giochi intorno a "Il pendolo di Foucault" di Umberto Eco*. Naples: Simone, 1989.

Tani, Stefano. *The Doomed Detective: The Contribution of the Detective Novel to Postmodern American and Italian Fiction*. Carbondale: Southern Illinois University Press, 1984.

Uebel, Michael. "Imperial Fetishism: Prester John among the Natives." In Jeremy Jerome Cohen (ed.), *The Postcolonial Middle Ages*. New York: Palgrave, 2001, pp. 261–82.

Vernon, Victoria V. "The Demonics of (True) Belief: Treacherous Texts, Blasphemous Interpretations and Murderous Readers." *MLN*, 107 (1992): 840–54.

Violi, Patrizia. "Individual and Communal Encyclopedias." In Norma Bouchard and Veronica Pravadelli (eds.), *Umberto Eco's Alternative: The Politics of Culture and the Ambiguities of Interpretation*. New York: Peter Lang, 1998, pp. 25–38.
"A Semiotic of Non-Ordinary Experience." *VS*, 83/84 (1999): 243–80.

Wagner, Bettina. *Die "Epistola presbiteri Johannis" Lateinisch und Deutsch*. Tübingen: Max Niemeyer Verlag, 2000.

White, Hayden. *Metahistory. The Historical Imagination in XIXth-Century Europe*. Baltimore, MD: Johns Hopkins University Press, 1973.
The Content of the Form: Narrative Discourse and Historical Representation. Baltimore, MD: Johns Hopkins University Press, 1987.

Winks, Robin W. (ed.). *Detective Fiction: A Collection of Critical Essays*. Englewood Cliffs, NJ: Prentice-Hall, 1980.

Wittkower, Rudolf. "Marvels of the East: A Study in the History of Monsters." *Journal of the Warburg and Courtauld Institutes*, 5 (1942): 159–97.

Yates, Frances. *The Art of Memory*. Chicago: The University of Chicago Press, 1966.

Index